RECLAIM THE STATE

RECLAIM THE STATE

Experiments in Popular Democracy

HILARY WAINWRIGHT

VERSO

London • New York

First published by Verso 2003
© Hilary Wainwright 2003
All rights reserved

The moral rights of the author have been asserted

Verso
UK: 6 Meard Street, London W1F 0EG
US: 180 Varick Street, New York, NY 10014–4606
www.versobooks.com

Verso is the imprint of New Left Books

ISBN 1–85984–689–0

British Library Cataloguing in Publication Data
A catalogue record is available from the British Library

Library of Congress Cataloging-in-Publication Data
A catalog record for this book is available from the Library of Congress

Typeset in Garamond by Helen Skelton, Brighton, UK
Printed in the UK by The Cromwell Press

In memory of
Ruth First, Ralph Miliband and Richard Wainwright

Where there is much desire to learn, there, of necessity will be much arguing, much writing, many opinions; for opinion is but knowledge in the making … To be still searching what we know not, by what we know; still closing truth up to truth as we find it. It is this that makes up the best harmony, not the forced and outward union of cold, and neutral, and inwardly divided minds.

John Milton, *Areopagitica*, 1664

CONTENTS

FOREWORD

WANTED:
NEW FORMS OF POLITICAL POWER

January 2003, Davos, Switzerland

Luiz Inacio 'Lula' da Silva, metal worker turned President of Brazil, stands before the annual gathering of capitalism's ruling elite and challenges them to change their ways: 'It is not possible to continue with an economic order,' he declares, 'in which some people eat up to five times a day and others go for five days without a meal.'

The theme at the Davos World Economic Forum is trust. Lula is in a strong position; he has a mandate of 62 per cent of his country's electorate behind him. The world's leading businessmen and politicians sitting before him are not so mandated. The Forum organisers have commissioned a survey to measure 'trust in institutions to operate in society's best interests'. It finds a majority with 'little or no trust' in either global corporations, large national corporations, Parliament and Congress, or the International Monetary Fund (IMF). The mood among the captains of capitalism is grim. 'The confidence of just a few short years ago is gone', reports the *Financial Times.*[1]

Lula has flown to Davos directly from southern Brazil. The night before his speech at the Swiss retreat, he was in Porto Alegre's open-air amphitheatre addressing a crowd of 100,000, gathered for the third World Social Forum. Among them were activists from the South

Africa-based Treatment Action Campaign, who had waged a successful international campaign against the multinational drug corporations (most of whose chief executives were at Davos) over their control of global 'healthcare' markets.[2] In the same way that this effective campaign for the availability of generic drugs involved the power of sustained popular action alongside the bargaining pressure of Southern governments, so Lula does not pretend that government action alone can solve the problems of inequality in Brazil – or that any governments can by themselves overcome inequality worldwide. He does not ask simply for trust therefore, he asks people for action, pressure, self-organisation. Learning from his party's municipal experiences, his government will now try to create structures through which this people's power can have direct influence on how the country is run. It could be a difficult experiment: this idea of strengthening elective democracy through institutions of direct participation is new and relatively untried.

Lula stands on the podium issuing a direct challenge to the priorities of the global elite – at the same time as this elite, especially through the IMF, is placing enormous constraints on his ability to carry out his election mandate. He and his party, the Brazilian Workers Party (*Partido dos Trabalhadores* or PT) have become symbols of a new, participatory approach to political power. But it is not just in Brazil that people are inventing their own forms of democracy in order to create the just social order that Lula demands, but cannot on his own deliver.[3]

November 2002, Florence, Italy

In a vast hall in Florence's biggest conference centre, the atmosphere at the European Social Forum (ESF) is electric. Paul Ginsborg, an English-born professor of politics at Florence University and campaigner against Berlusconi's abuse of the judiciary, is speaking about participatory democracy. Alongside him is the mayor of the coastal town of Grottammare, where they try to practice such democracy. Over 60,000 activists are here from every European country: Russia, Estonia and Ukraine as well as Spain, Germany and France. Trade union organisers are here as well as environmentalists, feminists and groups campaigning against the racism of 'fortress Europe'. People involved in trying to change traditional left political parties, like Italy's *Rifondazione Communista*, debate alongside people who prefer to concentrate their energies on creating independent social movements.

'Only solution, revolution' incanted some of the paper sellers at the gates. Others, no less radical in their long-term goals, have in mind a different vision, of reforms that pave the way for further transformation in a steady, cumulative process towards participatory democracy as the basis for both economy and state. '*Subversio dolce*' is how Paul Ginsborg describes this strategy. It does not translate well – 'sweet subversion' – but the tension in the words does hint at the aim of achieving a transform-ation more profound than a one-off reform.

Ginsborg is part of a 'Laboratory for Democracy'. This emerged from a campaign against Berlusconi's abuse of his powers over the judiciary and the media, and is inspired by a belief that representative democracy is too weak to defend pluralism and social justice. The group is part of a wider network in Italy committed to developing institutions of participatory democracy as a way of achieving immediate reforms, while simultan-eously creating a means of democratising power itself – subverting the system.

At the ESF, a major spur to such subversion throughout Europe, indeed worldwide, was the General Agreement on Trade in Services (GATS). At first sight an obscure and technical document under secret negotiation in both the European Union and the World Trade Organisation, GATS aims to force countries to open their public services to the private market. Elected members of the European Parliament, like the Green MEP Caroline Lucas, report how they have to resort to acting like spies to find out what's going on. 'I have been instructed to keep the papers in a locked safe, to refrain from copying or e-mailing them, and to shred them after reading', she says. Forums such as these allow activists and organisers to 'strategise' – they come together to plan international strategies (which in between times are fleshed out through e-mail) about how to pull down these blockages on democracy; how to alert people to what is about to hit their services; above all how to build genuinely international campaigns. Participants in Florence felt that the ESF took the possibilities of effective international pressure several leaps forward: 'The ESF was really inspiring', says Clare Joy from the World Development Movement. 'We got a sense that a strong GATS campaign was forming at the European level.'

It was not only in the conference centre that people felt it necessary to look beyond conventional politics. On the streets of Florence, the joyful, enthusiastic response to a near million-strong demonstration against the war on Iraq indicated widespread support for new ways of calling politicians more effectively to account. As the crowds wended their way down the wide Florentine avenues, singing the songs of the Italian resistance – 'Bella ciao, bella ciao, bella ciao, ciao, ciao' – and shouting the slogans of the stop the war movement, young children handed orange juice from elegant panelled windows, and elderly women threw bread from their balconies – to which the crowds joked back 'Prosciutto, prosciutto'. Sweet subversion indeed.

October 2002, Oslo, Norway

On a cold Sunday morning streams of young people from all over Norway pour into the morning debates at the Manifest 02 conference. Pål Hellesness, the imaginative ex-member of the leadership of Red Youth ('I got too old' – he's twenty-seven) describes the thinking behind Manifest 02 thus: 'The main left parties had become either very sectarian or very pragmatic. The Red Youth wanted to bury the hatchet and move in a new way with democracy, deeper than parliament.' Over 1,000 young Norwegians are attending – quite a number in a country with a population of only four million. Some are as young as fourteen.

It is not the first time such young people have come together in Oslo. In the previous July leading members of the youth organisations of Norway's two left parties united when 12,000 people demonstrated against the World Bank. 'We all agreed we needed to provide a political arena for young people to come together without being dominated by one party', explains Audun Lysbakken, at twenty-five the youngest member of the Norwegian Parliament, for the Left Socialists. 'The generation that came to left politics in the 1990s, my generation, was formed by a climate of defeat and a feeling that the left had lost the political initiative to the right. Discussion tended to be limited to single issues. Our generation is searching for a way beyond this. The protests at Gothenburg and Oslo show that large numbers of young people are thinking about the system and wanting radical alternatives.'

Manifest 02 was organised to meet that need. It was a space to discuss 'system issues' but in a very different way from the discussions on the left in the 1970s and 80s. 'The old parties were often incapable of producing results; they were sectarian and inward looking', argues Lysbakken, going on to speak of 'a confidence and optimism' in his generation. There is also a distinctive interpretation of socialism: 'We believe it is the enlargement of democracy. That's where we converge with the anti-capitalist movements; they are above all about democracy.' Hellesness agrees: 'If there's no democracy in economic affairs, it's undermined everywhere else. Through the WTO [World Trade Organisation] a small group are defining the parameters within which the rest of us live and work. People are saying "We don't want you to define our lives, we want self government".' In the thinking of these young people, democracy isn't just a vision for the future, it concerns ways of organising in the present. 'In the past, socialism has been seen either as a protest or an alternative programme; now it must be about building co-operation between different movements for social justice', says Sigrid Staurset, a twenty-two-year-old organiser of Manifest 02. 'We have to be humble and strengthen the movements without controlling them. This is how a new ideology will be built.'

Pål Hellesness gives the example of a successful campaign of direct action to save an old inner-city working-class area, Svartlamon in Trondheim, from demolition. 'The residents' organisation became a very wide alliance including environmental projects and also co-operatives to create local jobs. It won support from residents across the city. The politicians had to give in.' On a national scale there is a similarly innovative alliance, based on the six major public-sector unions and a huge array of user organisations, to defend but also improve the welfare state.

The rise of the far right Progress Party gives an extra urgency in Norway – and indeed many other parts of Europe – to efforts to go beyond conventional politics and reach out to people who are losing hope. The Progress Party won over 15 per cent of votes at the last election. But in the polls its support goes as high as 30 per cent. Meanwhile votes for the Labour party, historically Norway's party of government, have fallen to 20 per cent.

The Manifest 02 gathering was widely judged a breakthrough: 'It was obvious that a lot of young people from all sorts of different organisations and who had never previously been working together were thinking in the same direction', said Pål Hellesness. 'Now there is a lot of working out to do.'

October 2002, Ottawa, Canada

Libby Davies used to be a community organiser and 'shit stirrer', as she puts it. Then she became a councillor, and for the last five years has been an MP for downtown East Side Vancouver, the lowest income neighbourhood in Canada. 'Two hundred homeless are squatting in a building bought by the provincial government for low-cost social housing but never finished. They are moving the action from the legislature where it has come to a dead end to the realm of people power, to get things moving again. We're supporting them but they are taking more powerful action than we can. This is what we mean by the new politics, isn't it?'

She is speaking from the floor at the first conference of the New Political Initiative (NPI). Two hundred or so people, most under thirty-five, a few in their sixties and seventies, are gathered in the hall of the federal parliament's West Wing – the site where MPs and others drew up Canada's first written constitution. This time, the Canadian citizens occupying the room are preparing an initiative aimed at giving political voice and support to Canada's dense network of social movements. The way Libby thinks of her role as an MP is symbolic of the NPI's approach. 'I work with activists to help them get control of the political process', she says. She is an MP for the NDP (the National Democratic Party, Canada's social democratic or Labour party – a small third party in the Canadian parliament but one that occasionally wins control of provincial governments), but unlike many of her fellow MPs (across the world), Libby does not see herself as the route to political power but as a provider of information, publicity and any other kind of support that will enable people to achieve a stronger control over power themselves. 'I help individuals but I also connect them with each other so that they can get organised.' One way the NPI is developing this kind of relationship between social movements and electoral politics is through the idea of the 'Consulta'. Inspired by the Zapatista,[4] the Consulta is an extensive discussion with different social movements about how they see their relationship with electoral politics and what kind of political voice, if any, they want.

Canada's NPI is a novel political hybrid. In the words of one conference briefing, it is: 'Neither an opposition within the New Democratic Party, nor a party in waiting, but a network of individuals committed to the idea of a new kind of political party on the left in Canada, rooted in the popular movements and radically democratic in its practice.' The NPI is ready to live with a certain amount of uncertainty, fluidity and what conventionally might be seen as impossible tensions. Some of its leading members, like Libby, are members of the NDP, others – like another 'shit stirrer', the radical author, broadcaster and Rabble website publisher, Judy Rebick[5] – are determinedly not. It seems to express an uncertain but creative mood on the left and amongst activists for social justice, a mood abroad in Canada as elsewhere.

September 2002, Kaoshiong, Taiwan

'We feel responsible for the state of our society', says Simon Chang, leader of Taiwan's independent union of telecom workers. Speaking at the opening of a unique conference of independent unions together with environmental activists, Mr Chang conveys a sense of urgency. He goes on: 'Telecom workers have a special status in Taiwan as public servants and intellectuals.' Behind him is an impressive silk banner declaring the theme of the conference – 'Globalisation, Trade Unions and the Environment'. It reflects the international perspective of the organisers. Indeed, conversation with Chang is peppered with stories of dramatic tactics learnt from the South Korean trade unions,[6] of creating a network of South East Asian unions and of reaching workers in the modern sweat-shops of China. 'Trade unions cannot stay at home', he says.[7]

The purpose of the conference is to explore political strategies to tackle both the extreme pollution created by the careless pace of Taiwan's economic growth, and the authoritarian nature of the Taiwanese state. 'We need to create a new kind of power', says Mr Chang. The afternoon panel illustrates possible sources of that power: all the speakers are from coalitions acting on environmental issues, employment and democracy. The Meinung People's Association is a good example. It has mobilised sufficient popular support across the town of Meinung and plain of Pingdung and beyond, to hold up, for the time being, a government decision to flood the beautiful Valley of the Yellow Butterfly. It is a sophisticated campaign, part of a wider network of anti-dam campaigns across Taiwan and internationally. It has worked with sympathetic engineers to show that there are alternative approaches to the water supply, using the underground lakes in the region, as well as curbing the thirsty greed of Taiwan's industrial production.

The central organisers of this conference are two quietly determined young labour researchers, Hua Mei and Yu Bin. They were both active in the democracy movement against the Kuomintang dictatorship in the 1980s. There has been long debate in Taiwan among democracy movement activists about whether or not to focus their efforts on reforming established political parties, in this case the Democratic People's Party (DPP). Hua Mei decided against it but has learnt a lot from observing the mainstream political process from her base in the trade union and feminist movements. 'Here was a party led by people from the elite in Taiwanese society, winning the support of many of the ordinary people. It gained central power very quickly. But people are very easily betrayed.' To illustrate this Hua Mei points to the DPP's commitment, in opposition, to stop building new nuclear power stations – just one of the many toxic ingredients of Taiwan's 'economic miracle'. 'And then, in government, it gives the go-ahead to the building of the fourth such station by the northern coast in Taipei county', she says.

The conclusion she drew was that social movements must be stronger intellectually and they must link with each other. 'This became my priority', explains Hua Mei. At one point many labour movement activists thought the way forward was to create a new 'genuinely left-wing party'. This failed, however, as a result of various leading politicians acting in a duplicitous way. Now another generation of activists believe that stronger, more democratic social and trade union movements are the answer to the political system's lack of democracy: 'We cut off any emotional connection to the DPP', says Hua Mei, although some activists still go to work in the DPP government, without joining the party. Once there they strike strategic bargains, providing ideas and know-how for out-of-touch DPP politicians in return for being given autonomy and resources to support social movements. Hence at the conference top table sat Ding Yung-Yen, an old comrade of the others and now Secretary of the Labour Bureau. He had arranged the funding of the conference. The 'new power' of which Simon Chang talked clearly keeps pragmatic relations with the old.

Five meetings, held in three different continents in the space of just five months in 2002–03 – all of them searching for new forms of political power. If this search is taking place in Brazil, Italy, Norway, Canada and Taiwan, where else is it occurring? Certainly the activists gathering in Porto Alegre, Florence, Oslo, Ottawa and Kaoshiong feel themselves to be part of a wider, international, process. These and many other tentative but determined moves into new political territory are responses to the abject failures of mainstream left parties to fulfil their promise. Founded to champion equality, solidarity and democracy, the historic parties of labour have ended up acquiescing in and – in the case of British New Labour – aiding and abetting the political power of private business. This process has been part of a wider crisis within democratic institutions. Throughout the 1980s and 90s, the deceivingly faceless forces of the financial markets and multinational corporations gained a dominance that has in many parts of the world all but sabotaged the fragile machinery of democracy.

While elected governments have failed to challenge the anti-democratic pressures from corporations, new and diverse movements have taken responsibility for democracy upon themselves and raised the global alarm about decisions taken in secret without any respect for popular control, local, national or international. The networks which have grown up to stalk the elites of the new corporate order have success-fully called into question the moral legitimacy of the drive to impose the rule of the market. But for this moral victory to be anything more than symbolic, and temporary, there needs to be a more material follow-through, asserting democratic power in the neighbourhoods, cities, regions, nations and continents where corporations make their profits: there needs to be a movement for democracy in everyday life. If the private economic forces that have undermined the power of the vote are to be successfully challenged, a next task for movements for democracy and social justice must be to tie them down and limit their room for manoeuvre. That requires pressure: working alternatives and bargaining power exerted at many levels of sustained democratic organisation. From my experience working with *Red Pepper*, a UK magazine of resistance and green left alternatives, it is clear that working for democracy locally and connecting up globally are inseparable.

The anti-capitalist protests and forums at a global level, from Seattle through to the World Social Forums in Brazil, have seriously dented whatever was the legitimacy of 'free market' globalisation. The leading players in the global market-place are just beginning to work out their response. The discussion of 'trust' at Davos, between representatives of the most mistrusted organisations in the world, is one sign of that. Also at Davos these organisations discussed what they should do to rebuild trust. One solution lay, they concluded, in 'partnerships' through which corporations could draw on 'the knowledge and legitimacy of NGOs'. They also promised 'new financing mechanisms' such as the Global Fund to fight AIDS. This fund will enhance 'access to drugs still too expensive for most AIDS patients' – a totally self-serving proposal since many of the companies backing it are the same companies that have been blocking generic drugs and hence ensuring that the only alternatives available are their own, and at a high price. The corporate elite are clearly moving in on social justice but they are doing so on their terms, their charity, their voluntary self-regulation; indeed anything, so long as it does not involve democratically determined laws and regulations.

By contrast, the search in this book is one not for more apolitical, and anti-democratic, palliatives. It is a search for stronger forms of democratic politics by which people can realise the radical changes that many are working for in their everyday lives. How can the loss of legitimacy of the old order be turned into an opportunity for establishing new forms of democratic power, locally and internationally? To answer this question, we need to know more about how people are currently reinventing democracy. What working principles are they developing? What difficulties do they encounter? How might lessons be learnt from local and particular experiences? The purpose of this book is to explore such questions. It is intended as a practical contribution to the development of these new democratic and egalitarian forms of power.

When old institutions fail, people invent. A bit like the experiments through which new scientific discoveries are made, the organisational innovations that people make through trial and error are a vital motor of social progress. All of us working for democratic, egalitarian social change are, in that sense, like practical scientists engaged in this process of invention but also observing what can be learnt from the successes and mistakes of the experiences of others. For this reason I decided to go on an exploratory journey to observe for myself the ways in which people were reinventing democracy against the odds. Such detailed attention to the creativity of practice is one of the most fruitful sources of new theory. It is also a logical method if we see the basis of democracy as being each individual's creativity and the possibility of forms of social co-operation which enable that creativity to be realised for the benefit of all.

In the next section I argue that we need to return to this foundation. I show how narrow democracy has become and I argue for a plural and social theory of knowledge to guide the emergence of an open and participatory remaking of politics. I then map out my journey, describe what I observed and finally consider where the experiments I witnessed might lead.

A 'MASS OF SENSE':
KNOWLEDGE, POWER AND DEMOCRACY

In this search for more vigorous forms of democracy through which to struggle for social justice, it helps to have a compass by which to check our sense of direction. The most reliable that I could find, which uses as its pointer the assumption of the creative potential and value of every human being, is the following statement of Tom Paine in *The Rights of Man*:

> It appears to general observation, that revolutions create genius and talent; but those events do no more than bring them forward. There is existing in man, a mass of sense lying in a dormant state, and which unless something excites it to action, will descend with him, in that condition, to the grave. As it is to the advantage of society that the whole of its facilities should be employed, the construction of government ought to be such as to bring forward, by quiet and regular operation, all that capacity which never fails to appear in revolution.[1]

It is this last sentence which gives substance to the idea of democracy – literally 'the power of the people'. It also provides a standard by which to judge would-be democratic institutions, for if such institutions do not in fact draw on the capacity of every member of society, then the people do not in practice have control, and society is poorer as a result.

Tom Paine's argument about the capacities of the people was part of his case against monarchy and for democracy based on a representative system. He painted a hopeful picture of representative democracy:

> ... the representative system diffuses such a body of knowledge throughout a nation, on the subject of government, as to explode ignorance and preclude imposition ... There is no place for mystery; nowhere for it to begin. Those who are not in the representation, know as much of the nature of business as those who are ... In the representative system, the reason for everything must publicly appear. Every man is a proprietor in government, and considers it a necessary part of his business to understand ... and above all, he does not adopt the slavish custom of following what in other governments are called LEADERS.[2]

How is it that people in some of the oldest democracies feel so little sense of ownership, or in Paine's language 'proprietorship', of government?[3] How is it that their right to vote, a defining political right of a democracy, appears to so many to be hardly worth exercising? How, in particular, did the social democratic parties of Europe, founded to control the interests of private business, become so vulnerable to the encroachment of private business on their very tool of democratic control – the state? How did the neo-liberal ideology championed by Britain's Margaret Thatcher manage to have such a long lasting influence? What lessons can be learnt from what went wrong in the past, for today's process of recreating democracy?

From representative to elite democracy, and the radical challenge

When representative democracies were finally established first in the US and then – cloaked in the mantle of monarchy – in the UK, neither of them lived up to Paine's radical vision. The federal constitution of the US, with all its checks and balances, seemed more concerned to protect the new propertied classes than to make every man 'a proprietor in government'.[4] Democracy broke through in the UK and throughout

Europe over a hundred years later in the early twentieth century, quickened both by movements for the franchise such as (to use examples from the UK) the Chartists and Suffragettes, and by the sacrifices of the soldiers in the First World War which could not convincingly be justified in terms simply of patriotic duty – sacrifice without representation. But in both continents this democratic breakthrough of the propertyless masses was followed throughout the first half of the twentieth century by persistent efforts from those in the seats of established power – administrative, financial, juridical and political – to narrow the scope of democracy, and blunt its consequences for the way that societies were governed.[5] This was no doubt a result of alarm at the growing organisations of the industrial working class, and then a misplaced reaction to the shock of fascism and the fear of Soviet communism. It was effectively a continuation in modern form of the nineteenth-century fear of the mob, or 'swinish multitude'.

By the 1950s democracy had been reduced, in the complacent words of the influential US political scientist, Seymour M. Lipset, to 'the formation of a political elite in the competitive struggle for the votes of a mainly passive electorate'. He added that 'the belief that a very high level of participation is always good for democracy is not valid', as if that was the end of the matter.[6] Joseph Schumpeter made a similar point in what became the textbook of 'elite democracy', *Capitalism, Socialism and Democracy*: the voters, he said, 'must understand that, once they have elected an individual, political action is his business not theirs'.[7] Competition between elites with popular participation kept to a minimum: that was the state in which democracy was frozen by the political culture of the Cold War.

While public participation declined, the power of private business grew. The later years of the Cold War were also the early years of the stealthy growth of multinational corporations, for this was the period – the 1960s and 70s especially – when international competition was leading to the mergers, acquisition and foreign investment that produced

3

the corporations that now overshadow elected governments.[8] The weak form of representative democracy just described could not keep pace with the growth of private corporate power, and neither did it reign it in; instead it became complicit in the growth of this unaccountable force and, like the host body of a parasite, weakened itself in this process. It also failed to provide an adequate means by which the people could control the public sector. This failure of elected governments to exercise democratic control even over their own public services undermined the bargaining position of formally democratic state institutions over the private sector.

In the US and Western Europe, the first real pressure for a more thorough-going democracy began with the restlessness of a new generation brought up on a commitment to democracy and against the background of a real war fought to defend it. They expected the reward for the sacrifices of earlier generations to mean more than an occasional choice between barely distinguishable middle-aged men with overgrown egos. The challenge began with the students in the late 1960s rebelling against both the authoritarianism of higher education and the imperialism of the US war against the Vietnamese. A radical momentum developed through the 1970s with the feminist movement, radical grassroots trade unionism, militant community anti-racist organising, and movements around gay and disability rights, and it shook up established social democratic parties and parts of government. These diverse movements (I don't want imply that they were all saying the same thing or that their relationships with each other were always harmonious) provided, in their different ways, a basis for reinvigorating democracy at a very timely moment.

Messy and inchoate as they were, not consistently or coherently democratic themselves, the new movements nevertheless embodied a deep conviction in, and pressure for, thorough-going democracy. With their emphasis on participatory democracy they were reminiscent of Paine's ideals. These movements showed the potential capacity (and desire) of people for self-government, and they suggested the benefit to society of this capacity being fully employed. The mood of that time has been well documented, as have its political rebellions.[9] What is not so well known or absorbed into the political bloodstream are the ideas which emerged from this dissent, ideas which envisaged radically different state institutions, involving new, more vigorous forms of democracy and more responsive forms of social administration.

Initiatives coming from the feminist movement illustrate this argument particularly well. The women's movement posed a fundamental challenge to the way the welfare state was organised. Women depended on state institutions in so many different ways, especially as mothers. They needed public resources, but in their experience the way that these resources were managed was not responsive to their needs. Not only did the women's movement assert women's rights in personal relationships but it sought to transform, there and then, any public relationships dependent on the subordination of women – including women's relationships with and within the state. Sometimes the impetus for trying to reform the state was a need unmet by public policy: this was how centres for battered women and rape crisis centres, for example, came into being. Many of these ended up being funded by the local state or even incorporated into it. In the process such projects demonstrated ways of managing public resources and dealing with 'the public' that were co-operative and internally egalitarian.

Take a story from the city of Bologna. In the late 1960s, a group of working-class women influenced by the women's movement started a childcare service which then won the support of the radical local council. 'It was based on a large-scale popular movement', one of the women told the writer Brendan Martin. 'Women needed a service for their children. The local administration had no money to develop facilities, so the women got organised.'[10] That first pre-school, now called La Villetta, has since been supplemented by thirty others, all run in accordance with the organisational and pedagogical principles that inspired the first. Serving a total city population of 130,000, this is a high quantity of service by international standards, but it is the quality of the childcare and the nature of the municipal support which underpins it, that really defines the success of the project. In an age when the private sector is so often said to hold the keys to high standards in public services, here is a true story of the opposite: the municipality's continuous commitment to improvement has set an international benchmark, while its methods of administration draw on the insights and practices of a social movement. Final responsibility for the service lies with the elected city council, but its practical management is based on a form of participation involving both staff and parents. This participation pools insights and know-how unavailable to the conventional hierarchical state administration.

The radical movements of the 1970s also included trade unionists in manufacturing, who pressed for a widening of democracy in a direction which would influence the organisation of industry. In Western Europe especially, throughout the 1960s and early 70s, radical trade unionists had considerable bargaining power on the factory and office floors of would-be corporate giants and they often pushed the negotiating agenda beyond wages and conditions to issues affecting the environment, the nature of the product, the design of new technologies. Their collective self-confidence soon spread to those who worked for the state and for a brief moment groups of trade union activists held out the vision of a democratic form of social ownership in which workers and local communities would have some real influence.

Whether through an opening up of local government, innovative plans for user involvement in the health service, or proposals for worker participation in publicly or socially owned companies, this new thinking about the state – an approach summarised by the phrase ' in and against the state'[11] – combined a commitment to the public provision of services with a desire to reform radically the way that public services were managed. Implicitly, this practice built on the social democratic principle that there are certain needs – for example, health, education, aspects of housing and transport – which are a 'public good' and a social right, and whose provision should not be left to the workings of the market. In order for the state to provide these public goods it needs revenue: so public provision implies a commitment to redistribution through the tax system or through cross-subsidies within public services. But the new thinking in the 1970s went further – it insisted that the delivery and management of public services should directly involve the frontline staff and people whose needs they were meeting. State institutions carried out the redistribution which gained the revenue, but that should not mean that state managers should be the only people determining how these resources would be administered. This approach was argued for, and in small ways enacted, in different parts of Europe and the US. Many of these innovative ways of providing a service were eventually broken, however, by the inert weight of traditional local government structures or by pressures from hostile national governments.

The most ambitious and high-profile European experiment in participatory democratic government influenced by these earlier movements was the Greater London Council (GLC) between 1981 and 1986. When Ken Livingstone's Labour administration gained office it found the GLC to be a classic piece of cumbersome, bureaucratised, public-sector machinery, host no doubt to many forms of corruption, but founded on the principles of redistributive taxation. It employed many skilled people motivated by a powerful ethic of public service. The radical left created shrewd alliances with these officials and shook up traditional forms of administration, giving autonomy to frontline staff, breaking down conventional hierarchies and challenging the rule of straight, male, white, able-bodied workers in senior council employment. They delegated council resources to democratic community and voluntary groups, involving them in decision-making rather than merely 'consulting them'. They used economic powers of local government to stimulate co-operative and social enterprises. The underlying belief was in the transformation of the state by making day-to-day relationships between workers and users, and between workers and managers, more democratic, open and responsive. They did not seek simply to 'take hold of the reins of state' and steer it in a benevolent direction, as traditional reformers had done. For this brief period the GLC was a state institution with a budget larger than some nation states, which challenged Prime Minister Thatcher and offered an attractive alternative to Labour's traditional way of governing, the unpopularity of which she depended on.

As Norman Tebbit, Mrs Thatcher's right-hand man put it: 'The GLC represents modern socialism. We must kill it.'[12] The subsequent authoritarianism with which the right imposed the so-called 'free' market then blocked all attempts at alternative, democratic reforms of the public sector.

Political responses: social democracy and neo-liberalism

Elites across the world reacted with alarm to the lack of deference of the 1968 generation, their confident sense of the rights of the people and their pressure to open up what had become the cosy institutions of government. The Trilateral Commission through which US, Japanese and European political and economic leaders discussed issues of common concern declared in the early 1970s that 'expectations were becoming dangerously high for the stability of democracy'.[13] But it was not just conservative elites who felt threatened by these challenges to established authority.

The leadership of social democratic parties, like the Labour Party in Britain, the Social Democratic Parties in Germany and Sweden and the Socialist Parties of France and Italy lacked the political faculties to comprehend this new democratic groundswell. It was as if they were deaf to any voices but their own. The combination of Cold War polarities and an elite model of government led them to tend to see the new radicals as a mob, or communism in hippy disguise. In fact these movements could have kickstarted a radical modernisation process of economic reorganisation as well as the state and political parties. This applies not only to the reform of the public sector but also to the transformation of the private sector. A successful widening of democracy to build strong forms of industrial democracy on the basis of the strength and radicalism of shop-floor trade unions at this time could have constructed a decisive barrier to the later erosion of democracy by the tides of the corporate-driven market. The result of the traditional parties of the left[14] finally rebuffing these pressures (often after prolonged internal struggles with their youth organisations)[15] was that they were doomed to enter into a hopeless project of propping up a tired social democracy. 'Tiredness' was not a simply a generational matter but a result of promoting a political vision that remained hinged to unreformed, unresponsive, state administrations. The conservative response to these radical democratic pressures contributed to the vulnerability of these social democratic parties by the 1980s to both the ideological appeal of the 'free market' against 'the nanny state' and the apparent dynamism of the big private corporations as an elixir of efficiency.

This raises a deeper question about the understandings of political agency that underpinned how the institutions of these mass parties of the left operated. These parties effectively have (or had) in their membership and electoral support a significant proportion of society, including well-organised groups such as the trade union and co-operative movements. In other words, they had in their ranks a huge capacity and energy for democratic self-government and yet their institutions did not provide the means of expressing or exerting this capacity to achieve the parties' goals of redistribution, democratic public ownership and provision of services. In country after country, these parties, although elected to control concentrations of private wealth and power, have ended up being controlled by the centres of unaccountable economic power.[16] The history is a familiar one, but the usual explanations are inadequate and the political remedies usually proffered do not rethink radically enough issues of political power and organisation.

Nye Bevan, the Welsh leader of the left of the British Labour party throughout the 1950s, and one of the most passionate advocates of parliamentary democracy as a means to socialism, noted as early as 1944 the process by which social democratic governments succumb to the pressures of private business. After observing government and parliament from the inside, he made the following remark at the Labour Party Conference of that year:

> In practice, it is impossible for the modern state to maintain an independent control over the decisions of big business. When the state extends its control over big business, big business moves in to control the state. The political decisions of the state become so important a part of the business transactions of the corporations that it is a law of their survival that most decisions should suit the needs of profit-making.[17]

These are not the words of a cynic. Before entering parliament Bevan had been a miner, then a miners' union official and then an organiser of workers' education. In 1935, he had written enthusiastically about his mission as an MP, extending his struggle against the mine owners and other capitalists by political means: parliament for Bevan was 'a sword at the heart of private property'.[18]

There are many explanations of how the parliamentary sword was blunted, or the grip of those who wielded it weakened. Complacency attendant on the achievement of office saps the ambition to use it. Using elected office actually to carry through a radical change causes conflict and uncertainty, with all the accompanying risk to political careers and party stability. Systems of patronage can tame the potential combatant. Other explanations go deeper into the nature of the state:[19] state institutions are not socially neutral; their higher echelons are staffed predominantly (though not invariably) by people trained to protect the existing order against radical challenge, and well connected to do so. Their priorities are determined by entrenched relationships with financial, industrial and military interests.

Another, related, explanation focuses on the considerable bargaining power which big business can deploy, a power which has grown massively since the days of Nye Bevan. In its armoury big business holds the threat of investment strikes and well-resourced lobbies like the business round table in South Africa or the Confederation of British Industry (CBI) and European round table in Britain and Europe.

All these explanations contain important truths. But there remains a gap in our understanding: documenting the pressures to compromise does not fully explain why the parties on the whole complied. We are still left with the unanswered question of why these social democratic parties have so rarely organised to challenge these pressures; why they have so rarely reinforced the sword of parliament with the spear of democratic organisation amongst their supporters outside parliament. In many instances resisting unaccountable private vested interests would, after all, be defending parliamentary democracy as well as championing the needs of those that these parties claim to represent. And we are talking about parties that are not without resources and connections: those with mass working-class organisations formally behind them, whose activists are potentially a major force for change.

To fully understand and learn from their weaknesses we need to focus on how party leaderships understood the capacities and role of their membership and the wider support of the organised labour movement. These understandings, entrenched in party institutions, flowed from their view of political agency and how social change is to be achieved. The presumption behind conventional social democratic thinking was that the state under the control of the party was the prime agency of social change, the engineer of social justice. Moreover, the predominant conception was of the state as an agency for change operating *on* society, effectively from above, like an engineer fixes a machine. The role of the labour movement, the mass supporters, was to get the social engineers into place so that they could deploy the instruments of state. Implementation of policy was seen as a technical matter, best left to the experts.

Much left-wing thinking in the social democratic tradition was in terms of the metaphor of the machine: 'the machinery of state'. The aim was to take control of a single lever, steering wheel, or other single mechanism that, in the right hands, could bring about the desired change. Insofar as this process involves working with social organisations other than the party, the latter are little more than pistons to be set in motion by the pull on the central lever. Mechanical metaphors assume that those steering the state can know the laws of society, identify the variables, take action, and predict and measure the consequences. The language of machinery fitted an understanding of change as coming primarily from state action, of which the majority of people were simply passive recipients. As a consequence party leaderships tended to treat the mass base of their parties simply as a source of electoral or financial support, sometimes taken-for-granted, not as a distinct source of potential power to pursue shared goals.

A revealing example of an (eventually thwarted) attempt to pursue an alternative approach, treating trade unionists as active partners able to bring complementary power and knowledge to the problem of achieving party policy in the face of powerful and ruthless private corporations, comes from the diaries of British Labour politician Tony Benn. In 1974, as minister for industry, Benn was given responsibility for renationalising the aircraft manufacturing industry, and had to consider whether this should include the components industry, the leading company of which was Lucas Aerospace. Officials presumed he might want to talk to Lucas's management, but instead he wanted first to talk to the unions. The civil servants were asked to contact the Confederation of Engineering and Shipbuilding Unions, the body which at that time brought together national officials of the engineering unions. And Benn wanted to go further than the full-time officials, he wanted to talk to the 'lay' representatives too – engineers, designers, labourers. He did not just want information, he wanted to explore different possibilities. This involved understanding the situation independent of the perspective of those who presently held power. In other words, he needed the insights, the know-how, the connections and the potential power of those who worked on the inside of the industry. When he asked his civil servants to arrange this meeting of shop-floor representatives, 'all hell broke loose', he reports.[20] His strategy of working with shop-floor leaders in the shipbuilding and aerospace industries so as to build up the inside knowledge and power without which the government could not transform those industries was deeply unsettling, not only to businessmen and most civil servants but also to most of his fellow members of the cabinet.

In countries like Germany, Denmark and Sweden, more or less proportional electoral systems enabled 'the participatory left' (a short-hand for the new left influenced by the social movements of the late 1960s and early 1970s onwards) to become an electoral challenge to social democracy, the one kind of challenge which can hurt and therefore have an influence. Sometimes that has been through Green Parties (most notably Germany), sometimes radically transformed Communist Parties in coalition with other forces on the radical left (Denmark, Sweden and Spain), at other times splits from social democratic or Communist parties (Norway and to some degree Italy). Where such radical electoral challenges have had some success (most notably Northern Europe), there is a stronger continuity between the participatory left of the late 1960s, 70s and 80s and the new movements for social justice that have mobilised since the late 1990s against corporate globalisation. Moreover, in these countries the democratic experiments of this left have been more able to withstand the onslaught of neo-liberalism.

In Britain and the US however, the participatory left had only short-lived local opportunities, if any, for political expression. Here, the movements that produced and nourished this new left were swept aside by the ruthlessness with which the Thatcher and Reagan governments exploited the West's Cold War triumph to push through their programme of privatisation, deregulation and anti-labour legislation.

Through US domination of the international economic institutions, most notably the International Monetary Fund, this attack on all forms of state regulation and provision, and all constraints on the private accumulation of capital, became a global process. It was a brute exercise of power particularly in the South[21] and in the East. In the latter case the US, through the IMF, closed off all alternative directions for the ex-Soviet dominated societies, 'killing' in Norman Tebbit's terms, any immediate chance of democratic forms of socialism. In a sense the neo-liberal right continued to feed off the polarities of the Cold War: perpetrating the idea that the only alternative to the authoritarian state was the unregulated market. The post-Communist, anti-state mood of the time enabled this radical right to cover its brutality with the deceptive glove of 'free-market' ideology. The market's 'invisible hand' was held up against the authoritarianism of the state – ironically by politicians like Thatcher and Reagan as they perpetrated a new form of international state-supported authoritarianism. Although the revolt against the 'all-knowing state' of the command economies was in some part a product of democratic civic movements – in Czechoslovakia and East Germany for example – it was the ideology of the free market which flourished in the immediate aftermath of these peaceful revolutions. This rhetoric of freedom gave a moral camouflage to what was an exercise of US state power in the interests of the leading corporations of the West.[22]

The underlying issue: the politics of knowledge

Nearly two decades after the fall of the Soviet bloc and the triumph of capitalism, in a world in which the gap between rich and poor has widened, and the numbers dying from malnutrition and suffering from the inadequate provision of the infrastructure of daily life – water, sanitation and housing – have escalated, it cannot be said that rampant capitalism has morally vindicated its triumph. But neither does a return to either the Soviet attempt at a command economy or the social democratic politics of the post-war West offer convincing solutions to the persistent problems of inequality and the erosion of democracy. One of the purposes of this book is to explore how all over the world people are experimenting with new solutions, often in the course of resistance to the dehumanising consequences of a market unleashed. The stories of these experiments in the following chapters will speak for themselves, but to understand and generalise the significance of these experiences we need some theoretical tools. To sharpen mine I want to explore how the dominant political traditions consider the nature and significance of human creativity for political organisations, including state institutions. I want to consider several questions, such as: what kinds of human creativity count as a source of relevant knowledge or know-how for economic and social organisation? How far can this knowledge or know-how be socially organised? How far is such knowledge necessarily individual and how far is it social? Whose knowledge counts in public decision-making and organisation? How is knowledge shared or kept exclusive? What is the relation of knowledge and creativity to power and organisation? Even this brief list of questions illustrates the fundamental importance of a conscious theory of the politics of knowledge, in its broadest sense, for rebuilding democratic politics.

Interestingly, the political right's re-legitimising of the ideology of the free market drew explicitly and systematically on a theory of human creativity and knowledge – specifically in the sphere of economics. Similarly, social democracy's flawed understanding of political agency is influenced by too one-sided a theory of knowledge and social creativity. Moreover, the participatory left's ability to provide insights for a genuine third way rests on a distinctive theory of knowledge implicit in their practice. Understanding the approaches of the first two helps to demonstrate the importance of the latter. I will start with the neo-liberal right because they have been the most explicit and systematic in their politics of knowledge.

Neo-liberalism: the tacit knowledge of the entrepreneur

Neo-liberalism owes its ability to reinvent itself ideologically to the foundations laid by Friedrich von Hayek. The central stone in these foundations was his critique of the 'all-knowing state' in the name of practical, everyday knowledge. It is a flawed theory, as I will briefly demonstrate, but it has had a remarkable resilience, perhaps because the challenges of the social democratic left to neo-liberal economics did not dig up its philosophical foundations with sufficient thoroughness. Hayek's arguments linger on, even if his name is no longer common currency: too many leading politicians in parties historically of the left defer to 'the private market' as if it has special moral qualities – qualities that arise from intellectual foundations laid by Hayek. Many of these erstwhile left, now neo-liberal believers in the market, began their political lives as fervent believers in the social-engineering state.

In his essay, 'The Use of Knowledge in Society', Hayek made a powerful attack (as the social movements also did from a completely different stance), on the dominant positivistic view that what counted as valid knowledge was codifiable – able to be formally stated, preferably in the form of a scientific law or a statistical generalisation – and provided the basis for certainty and predictability.[23] Against this, Hayek argues that much economic knowledge is unavoidably tacit, and hence uncodifiable, and also fallible, ephemeral and incomplete. He points to the 'existence of a body of very important but unorganised knowledge which cannot possibly be called scientific in the sense of knowledge of general rules: the knowledge of particular circumstances of time and place'.[24] In fact, there are things 'we know but cannot tell', and this tacit knowledge can be essential to economic success; much of the knowledge used by entrepreneurs to make their way in the market is ephemeral and particular. Such knowledge can never be centralised or codified, or known by a single brain. Not only is such knowledge non-codifiable, it is also inherently insufficient for predictions concerning the future. Uncertainty is therefore a feature of our knowledge both of the present and of the future.

This argument provides a powerful basis for the neo-liberal critique of the social-engineering state, given the latter's tendency to presume to be all-knowing, at least over the areas for which it is responsible. The state, argues Hayek, cannot second-guess or substitute for the day-to-day economic decisions of the entrepreneur: if it tries to do so the outcome will be economically disastrous and likely to lead to political dictatorship.

Hayek further argues that because of the fallible, incomplete character of knowledge, we enter the world as if socially blindfolded. The nature of human knowledge is such that we cannot know, or even approximate, the social consequences of our actions. Therefore there can be no direct link between social purpose and social outcome, he argues. The social structures that we create, we create unintentionally. That's why, in Hayek's thinking, social order is the 'haphazard outcome of our individual activity'. In Hayek's view, the free market is one example of such a haphazard outcome, refined through the evolutionary process of trial and error. The role of the state, according to Hayek, is not to interfere in this 'spontaneous order' – for example, to remedy the roughness of its justice – for such well-intentioned remedies will invariably have unintended consequences disturbing to the evolutionary process. Rather, the role of the state is to protect this spontaneous order from human interference, whether on the part of politicians or of particularistic interests such as trade unions. (Hayek is not so stern, however, about the particularistic power of large corporations which can presumably be equally damaging to the precarious mechanisms of the free market.) There is no space in his argument for purposeful civic initiatives.

For Hayek, *accident* is the main mechanism of social evolution. If that is so, processes of trial and error whereby feedback loops could, through democratic debate and argument, refine the effectiveness of human actions, are impossible. Democracy and social choice thus become marginal and even redundant. In this view, social evolution differs little from natural evolution. The only difference is that the state, which Hayek suggests be led by wise men over forty years old, elected only every fifteen years and therefore not susceptible to any particularistic pressures, can discover the trends of this spontaneous evolution and make society conscious of them in order to safeguard them. Hayek's argument thus leads him (and many latter-day neo-liberals with him, even though they do not share his bizarre prescriptions for the state), in spite of his libertarian claims and his pretensions to be the philosopher of freedom, to favour order and tradition over human agency and creativity

What leads him to this contradiction is his implicit assumption that practical knowledge is exclusively an individual attribute, not a social structure. While he did not explicitly argue this, he just assumed it – it is vital to his conclusion.

If knowledge is understood as a social structure, however, as socially produced and, in effect, socially distributed, then his theoretical case for the free market crumbles. If knowledge is a social product, it can be socially transformed by people who take action – co-operating, sharing, combining different kinds of knowledge – to overcome the limits on the knowledge that they individually possess. This view of knowledge as a social product opens up the possibility of people gauging, through exchange with others, the possible consequences of their intended actions and therefore being able purposefully to influence social relations. It removes Hayek's blindfold, at least partially. It follows from this that a social structure, or any given social order, is no longer the haphazard outcome of individual activity, but the consequence of human intention in circumstances that humans only partially comprehend. This brings purposeful human agency and democracy back into evolution. In summary, a recognition that knowledge can be both tacit and non-codifiable, *and* social, means that conscious social evolution is possible. It consists of people's attempts rationally, though never perfectly so, to construct collective projects that are then grist to the mill of trial and error.[25]

A crucial step in this refutation of Hayek is a recognition of the political importance of tacit and practical knowledge. As we shall see, the understandings of the *social* character of this practical knowledge arising from recent social movements – the women's movement, radical trade unionism and the environmental movement for example – can do justice to a theory of knowledge that recognises its practical and tacit character without conceding to neo-liberalism's dogmatic individualism in a way that the methodology of social democratic politics cannot.[26]

Social democracy: the scientific basis of the engineering state

The social democratic view of the state as, effectively, neutral machinery to be steered in the right direction by a party leadership elected into the driving seat was underpinned by definite and, in hindsight, highly restrictive, assumptions about the nature of knowledge and expertise. The general assumption was that the knowledge relevant to bringing about social change was scientific and statistical – capable of being codified and made available to the trained mind of the state official, expert academic adviser or professional politician. All other forms of knowledge – as expressed, for example, in the daily lives of ordinary people and in the media of popular culture – are either eclectic, 'common-sense' versions of scientific knowledge (or what in the past was accepted as scientific knowledge), or superstition, speculation, emotion, or some other form of belief that, whatever else it may be, does not count as knowledge relevant to public policy. The crucial assumption here is that all that counts as valid knowledge at any one time can be codified. It can therefore be centralised and, in effect, appropriated and distributed by a single institution, the state. Beatrice Webb, one of the architects of the British welfare state, summed up the conventional orthodoxy on knowledge when she said 'we have little faith in the "average sensual man". We do not believe that he can do much more than describe his grievances, we do not think he can prescribe his remedies'.[27] Such positivistic understandings of knowledge have been long questioned in Western philosophical circles, but in the relatively stable, not to say sclerotic, circumstances of the Cold War, there was a considerable lag before such questioning could uproot the institutional foundations that positivism gave to public policy. It's an approach which still persists even beneath the many efforts to 'consult the people'. For increasingly state bodies do search out people's opinions, and try to tap into local information, with surveys and consultations of various kinds. Opinions are gauged through 'drop-ins', information is gleaned through questionnaires. Such consultation exercises have all too often, however, been concerned primarily to win assent rather than genuinely to develop new understandings. At best, they have asked citizens to indicate preferences between options drawn up by experts, thus strengthening the legitimacy of the final decisions which have been made on the basis of conventional expertise.

There have of course been important traditions on the left which emphasised co-operation, mutualism and direct collective action as necessary partners of the state in a more plural vision of the process of social transformation. Such libertarian traditions implicitly recognised the importance of skills and capacities which were practical and tacit, difficult to codify or centralise, but nevertheless vital to the achievement of a socialist society, or simply a move in that direction.[28] These traditions have been firmly pushed to one side, however, in favour of an emphasis on the state's monopoly over the instruments and expertise of social reform.

Assumptions about who has valid knowledge and who can bring about change have had inevitable consequences for relationships between party leaders and their members and supporters. They further explain the passive role, noted earlier, that party members and voters are given in the social democratic scenario of social change. If leaders and civil servants are seen as the knowing agents of change, members are the supporting cast. They can have opinions, debate passionately within the party, pass resolutions critical of the leadership, even support an alternative leadership, but the idea that they could in themselves be a mine of new knowledge, precisely the knowledge which could bring about social transformation, is unthinkable. Evidence of this is in the way in which the research and policy departments of these parties have been pulled towards the centre, becoming part of the leadership apparatus. Only exceptionally do they engage in any collaborative work with members and supporters beyond an expert elite. Trade unionists are not seen as skilled people (however informal their skill) who produce goods and deliver services, know the inside workings of essential activities, and have potential power over how and whether the work is carried out. These assumptions about what is valid knowledge mean that party members and supporters are overlooked as sources of irreplaceable wisdom about their localities and workplaces, the environment, the needs of children, parents, the elderly or of people facing different kinds of discrimination and indignity – as well as wider analytical and historical knowledge. They are simply seen as foot soldiers for the party's electoral battles.

But in reality, government unavoidably does depend on practical uncodified knowledge from somewhere; it relies daily on inside information about the workings of industry, services, communities. And this knowledge cannot be second-guessed or deduced from scientific laws, it has to come directly from people with practical experience. In the absence of a conscious acknowledgment of the importance of such knowledge for achieving social change or a strategy for gathering it through people with a common interest in such change, *social democratic governments have ended up unconsciously relying on the practical knowledge of those who manage the status quo.* An understanding is needed of the car industry, for example: the solution is to bring in some consultants close to the industry and some leading business people. The trade unions may be consulted as a formality, but only on a limited agenda of wages and conditions. Yet the knowledge of those trade unionists is potentially a vital source of power. An understanding of the party's mass base as an essential source of potentially transformative knowledge in itself would have led to a very different relationship between social democracy and big business, and a more dynamic basis from which to administer public services.

These are some of the underlying reasons why social democratic parties end up in the arms of those who manage the system that these parties were elected to transform. As a result, people no longer get, even vaguely, what they thought they had voted for. Just as the radical right promised freedom and delivered new forms of authoritarianism, social democratic parties have promised social justice but allowed growing inequality. What might be called the politics of knowledge does not of course provide a full toolkit for overcoming this, but it does illuminate how parties of the left were blinded to the massive force for change which existed beneath their very eyes.

The participatory left: the democratisation of knowledge

In their practice the participatory left began to make use of these wasted resources for change. Their rejection of the idea that the state was a neutral means to policy ends, and their scrutiny of all the hierarchies, divisions and forms of subordination hidden behind this 'neutrality', led to many examples of the release of the practical knowledge of workers in, and users of, public services. This occurred through participation in the actual running of the services and sometimes through campaigning for alternatives to cuts, closures or privatisation. The social movements of the late 1960s onwards exemplified in their practice a new approach to the organisation of knowledge. The importance of this when mapping out the evolving new forms of democratic power is illustrated by the examples of Bologna and the GLC. The generation that engaged in these activities was the first that could take the welfare state for granted – or so they thought. They built on their parents' achievement of basic social rights and went on to press for democratic control over public resources and the quality of social relationships within welfare state institutions. One of their most important challenges concerned knowledge. In their practice, and sometimes their theory, the feminist, student, radical trade union and community movements – and the politicians who supported them – overturned assumptions about knowledge that underpinned both the institutions of Western parliamentary states and the social democratic parties that attempted to drive the state machinery towards social justice. These movements questioned the definition of what counts as knowledge, the narrowness of the sources of knowledge considered relevant to public policy, the restricted categories of people whose knowledge was valued and the processes by which knowledge is arrived at.

The 'in and against the state' social movements were built on sharing the practical, everyday knowledge of their members. That was their lifeblood. This knowledge was by its nature fragmentary, rooted in intuitions, emotions as well as ideas, in the things people do rather than only those they write down. It could not always immediately be turned into 'policies' or 'demands', but had to be discussed and pieced together first. The very organisation of these movements demonstrated how knowledge could be shared. Their horizontal networks provided means of sharing knowledge for a common purpose. This pool of practical expertise could then be supplemented by other kinds of knowledge – theoretical, historical, statistical. Looking back, what had been invented by the first phase of the participatory left was an open, networking approach to knowledge which more recently has been qualitatively developed with the – sometimes double-edged – help of the Internet.

Many of the initial forms of organisation in the women's movement, for instance, were about women sharing and reflecting on each others' experiences in order to get to the roots of 'the problem that had no name' but which so many felt they shared. Much of what women talked about at this time had never previously been considered 'knowledge', and yet it led to an explosion of criticism of existing public services and economic policies. Such criticism was almost invariably backed up with not only alternative policies on paper but also practical experiments in implementing at least some elements of these alternatives. Such self-consciousness produced an emphasis on taking action in the here and now; in Bologna, for example, it became a basis for a deepening of democratic control of state resources.

In this way, the early women's movement as a whole did assert an innovative model which rated non-codified knowledge as potentially of public benefit.[29] The same is true of developments at the base of the trade-union movement, at a time when shop-floor organisation had strong bargaining power. Groups of skilled workers developed detailed plans for converting armaments factories to socially useful production. They drew on a rich seam of primarily tacit knowledge to produce designs and prototypes that no state planner could have conceived. The best-known was the alternative corporate plan developed by the workers at Lucas Aerospace.[30]

These are examples of knowledge that was at the time uncodified and, in the case of tacit skills, inherently uncodifiable; knowledge that is nevertheless vital to an economy, a society, and a political system able efficiently to meet people's changing needs. These movements asserted a knowledge and an awareness of needs over which state institutions in their ignorance trample. They challenged the conventionally narrow mentality of science and its applicability to social policy. This combined rebellion and creation of alternatives is a feature too of today's global movements for social justice. One reason for the growth and impact of these movements is that through them people become knowing creative agents of change. The whole process by which these movements develop, like those of the late 1960s and 70s, depends on a mutual valuing of people's active energies and creativity. It is a political methodology which the old social democratic parties, with their conceptions of knowledge and political agency, could not even have contemplated. The new movements also illustrate and develop Paine's continuously timely remark – what they are so consciously utilising is the 'mass of sense' that otherwise continues to lie dormant.

Knowledge, power and democracy: foundations for a genuine third way

It is now well established that the rigid hierarchies to be found in many state organisations are inefficient. One reason why this is so is that hierarchies tend to suppress the insights and knowledge of those at the middle and the bottom. This hierarchical system accords with the conventional model of representative democracy which assumes that the democratic element in state decision-making comes only from the elected members – ministers or senior councillors. The logic of policy implementation is pyramidal with the minister at the apex, the civil service in the middle and the populace at the bottom – the receiving end. The presumption has been that values and policy formulation could be sharply distinguished from their implementation, which was assumed to be a value-free, machine-like process. In a parliamentary democracy, this has meant that the politicians elected by the people decide on the policies; then the experts elaborate the details and supervise their implementation. These neutral civil servants, it was assumed, possessed all the knowledge necessary for the elaboration and implementation of policy.

The fact that these traditional command structures have a democratic legitimacy at the top of the hierarchy – the elected politician – is probably one reason they have persisted longer in parts of the public sector than elsewhere. Furthermore, expert-based bodies of knowledge are held to be neutral, somehow cut off from the conflicts and vested interests swirling around in the rest of society. Once one recognises the ways that state institutions depend on practical knowledge from relationships with outside bodies with all the accompanying vested interests – for good or ill – such neutrality becomes unconvincing. So too does the idea that democratic control over state institutions, at any level, can be achieved simply through politicians elected every few years, often with only irregular contacts with their constituents. The chapters in this book explore through practical experiences, the new forms of democracy, the reinforcements that electoral politics need for democratic power to regain the initiative.

My argument is that the views of knowledge developed in practice, if not in theory, by the democratic social movements of the late 1960s onwards have an unrealised relevance today. They provide some otherwise neglected tools to provide an alternative to the social-engineering state other than that presented by neo-liberalism; tools for democratising public institutions rather than privatising them. These are by no means the only important resources for the creation of a participatory left, however. One of the hopeful features of the new global movements, with their exchange of ideas alongside the coordination of campaigns, is the discovery of how similar ideas are being arrived at through very different experiences and traditions, producing an important spur to further clarification and development. The chapter on participatory politics in Brazil, for example, illustrates the powerful influence of the educational philosophy and methods of Paulo Freire, which in their understanding of human creativity and the conditions for its development provide essential foundations for participatory democracy.

Understandings of knowledge, and of people's capacity and ways of organising this and ensuring its full expression, lie at the foundation of different economic, social and political arrangements. This is the reason I have dwelt on the different understandings of knowledge that lie behind social democracy and free-market capitalism on the one hand and the approach of recent democratic social movements on the other.

I would argue that a recognition of both the importance of practical knowledge (as against the assumptions of traditional social engineering) and the social, sharable nature of knowledge (as against the assumptions of neo-liberalism) provides a vital foundation stone for a genuine 'third way'. The occasionally resuscitated Third Way associated with Tony Blair and Bill Clinton (one is never quite sure whether to refer to it in the past tense) certainly involves abandoning the old social democratic traditions of social engineering, but unfortunately it also involves giving up on social transformation – though it pursues a path of meagre social amelioration. The result is a deceptive hybrid. The language is reminiscent of the radical left: Tony Blair's speeches used to be peppered with references to 'empowerment' and 'the new politics'. But much of what is called empowerment is 'giving independence' to what were public-sector organisations – hospitals, schools, housing – and encouraging them to be self-governing with business sponsorship and borrowing on the financial market. All too often these organisations are left floating off into a sea of corporate sharks who pick and choose what they fund according to commercial self-interest. 'The community' is usually represented on the board of such institutions, but their role is limited by the commercial priorities of the sources of – mainly private – funding. There was much wrong with the old social democratic state, but sufficiently strong state institutions of many different forms are needed to achieve the equality of resources and standards to which people have a right. Moreover, without basic conditions of equality people's 'mass of sense' will not be realised. It will not even be expressed. People will be submerged into the 'culture of silence' which Freire describes as the product of poverty and the powerlessness and hopelessness that often goes with it.[31] On the basis of redistributive state institutions, all sorts of decentralisation, devolution and participation are then possible within a policy framework set by elected politicians, rather than unaccountable bankers. Otherwise the entities empowered are not people but those corporations, normally private, who have the resources to move in where the state has moved out. 'Empowerment' without strong regulative and redistributive action by the state ends up as empowerment of private business, and effective privatisation of what were once public goods.

One of the weaknesses of this new variant of neo-liberalism under which we presently live is that it does not have a distinct or coherent understanding of knowledge. On the one hand its approach to politics – the management of political parties, the running of government – reproduces the social engineers' desire for predictability and centralised control, along with the assumption that knowledge of the political world can be scientific and that predictability and central control is possible. On the other hand its approach to the private market, in Hayekian fashion, almost romanticises the tacit know-how of the business person, and ascribes to the market itself almost magical powers of coordination and efficiency.

An understanding of the practical and social character of knowledge does not of itself imply any particular set of strategies or political institutions. But if it is combined with the goal of democracy defined by Tom Paine – 'the construction of government ought to be such as to bring forward, by quiet and regular operation, all that capacity which never fails to appear in revolution' – it does point to a methodology for developing and creating them. It points to the likelihood that the creativity and innovation necessary for social transformation will come first from practice. Therefore the priority for work on new democratic institutions must be to investigate practical experiments to develop such institutions and then to reflect on this critically, together with those involved, and finally to generalise lessons learned. In this way the development of a genuine third way is going to be a vast collective enterprise in which every individual desiring democratic change has both a creative and a critical role to play.

It is a collective enterprise which is of course already underway. As I set off to understand the ways in which people are organising to gain democratic control over the decisions shaping their lives, I had several groups of questions in mind. The first focuses on the connection between resisting unaccountable power and creating democratic alternatives. Under what conditions does 'the mass of sense' which comes forward in moments of intense resistance, become the basis of lasting institutions?

The second group concerns balancing the need for centralised power to redistribute wealth and constrain private interests with the need for people to have access to real power over resources in their localities. What kind of institutions strengthen popular control without also strengthening parochialism? How far is it possible to distinguish between genuine open-ended experiments in the sharing of power between state institutions and processes of popular participation on the one hand and top-down support for participation by official bodies on the other?

The final questions relate to electoral democracy, which has proved too weak to provide a sufficient basis for popular control over state institutions, let alone looming private economic interests. What are the practical problems of creating popular power beyond the ballot box? How can stronger forms of democracy be created in the face of the increasingly lawless power of both global corporations and the global superpower?

THE JOURNEY:
RECLAIMING DEMOCRACY

I decided to make the first of my destinations a place where I could witness the nearest thing to a working example of participatory democracy that I could find. I wanted to explore some of the conditions which made it possible and the principles by which it worked. Ideally, I wanted an example that had developed and bedded down over a significant period of time. Preferably, it would also have creators who were self-conscious of the significance of what they were doing and were themselves exploring the wider political relevance of their innovations. I chose Porto Alegre and the Brazilian Workers Party (PT), a party which originated in a popular struggle against a decade-long dictatorship. This history shaped the party's distinctive vision of democracy: the PT combines respect for the rule of law and liberal democratic rights with a belief – partly inspired by the methods of organisation of the trade union, rural and urban movements which formed its base – in the need for direct forms of popular participation. The PT aspires to bring the state apparatus fully under democratic control and, at the same time – indeed as one consequence of this – to exert effective bargaining power in dealings with the market. It is also a party unusually free of the Cold War dichotomies of market-versus-state, public-versus-private. Whereas elsewhere Cold War thinking has entered deep into the intellectual unconscious, creating mental blocks about new possibilities, the long experience of the popular resistance in Brazil has created innovative traditions of democratic thinking. For example, while the PT is highly critical of the institutions of the Brazilian state, with all their corruption and bureaucracy, its alternative is not to turn to the private sector but to the creativity and energy of those who suffer from this inefficiency, whether as public-sector workers or as citizens, and work with them as a driving force for democratic change and social efficiency. Its approach to economic production, similarly beyond the choices of the Cold War, is to encourage co-operatives and other forms of democratic common ownership and use public and democratic pressures to establish a strong bargaining relationship with the private sector. 'The Berlin Wall didn't fall on us', was how Marco Aurelio Garcia, history professor and now Lula's closest advisor on foreign policy, put it.[1] He was arguing that the party felt none of the guilt or shame about the Soviet experience that has led many parties on the left to be timorous about challenging the inequalities of the capitalist market and unimaginative about presenting alternatives based on reforming the state.

Most important, the PT has spurned the conventional political assumption that the winning of office in itself conveys a monopoly of power. Though subject to many conflicting pressures, it has demonstrated in its government of cities a distinctive approach to electoral success that is at the same time radical and modest. In the words of the PT's Celso Daniel, its aim is to 'share power with the movements to which we owe our success'. In practice, this 'sharing power' has meant opening up the previously closed black box of the municipal budget to a popularly based decision-making process known as the Participatory Budget (PB). The result, after fifteen years of trial and error, is a systematic, rule-governed form of popular participation.

The attraction of Porto Alegre was of a working experiment in the sharing of power, the combining of participative with representative democracy. But a question raised by the experiments in participatory democracy in this and other Brazilian cities remained with me for the rest of my journey: does the local have any special importance in the present, global, struggle for democracy and social justice? Since the purpose of this book is to contribute to the search for effective forms of democratic political power to overcome the injustice wrought by a market dominated by transnational corporations, I could have focused more on the growing web of international networks of dissent: the 'Our World is Not for Sale' campaign against global privatisation, for example, or the 'Labour Behind the Label' campaign against sweatshop labour (see Resource). Instead, I felt myself drawn to local initiatives for social justice, the nodes rather than the web itself. After all, to be effective, international networks and campaigns need to be rooted in people's everyday lives, including those who do not have the resources to be internationally mobile, either physically or electronically. Potentially, especially if wider connections are made, the local is a bargaining base. Multinational companies have to invest somewhere. The cheap labour and the skilled labour they depend on have to live somewhere. Governments need the support of citizens who vote specifically on the basis of where they live. This notion of transforming the ways that the powerful depend on the consent of the people into sources of bargaining power for democratic control is a recurring theme in this book.

The issue of the wider connections – of local trade-union organisations to a national or international campaign, of local women's or student groups to a national movement, of local campaigns to democratise municipal government to a national political party committed to open participatory politics – is crucial to the possibility of developing this bargaining power. In the 1970s in the UK, for example, through the national and international shop stewards 'combine committees', different, geographically disparate factories owned by the same company were linked to one another; in this way trade unionists gained the strategic intelligence, collective self-confidence and wider support to wield the bargaining power they had locally. These trade unionists had a strong sense of local identity and tradition, and this was a vital motivating factor, but their identity also came from their national and international sense of solidarity. Similarly, the local successes of the PT and the popular urban movements in Porto Alegre would not have been possible without the political traditions and institutions of the PT as a national party, and the trade union and landless movements as national and international movements. It is not a question of 'local good, global bad'.

Political movements based solely on local loyalties and identities, lacking any connection to other localities, and gaining strength only from their particularity, risk either being very short-lived or profoundly reactionary. At the same time, national and international organisations that fail to provide a framework through which local initiatives can develop and have wider impact, becoming a deeper source of strength for these organisations, are doomed to remain on the surface of political change.

Moreover, it is in local contexts that political parties or alliances sympathetic to participatory forms of democracy are more likely to have gained office, or at least social movements are more likely to have made a lasting political impact. So it is possible through local experiences to explore in an empirical way the relationships between popular participation and electoral politics, relationships which could provide important insights for what is achievable nationally or internationally.

I wanted to observe localities where people were consciously trying to create change in difficult circumstances. It was not success stories I was after, so much as observing people creating some leverage, while the wider trends went against them, over the globally influenced pressures shaping their lives. The process of gaining bargaining power takes time, and understanding that process required getting to know the people contributing to this creativity, becoming close enough to them to observe their work, even participating in it. For me this meant carrying out my research over a few years in the course of my daily life.

I chose three sites in Britain of genuine but contradictory participatory politics in the making. I visited an effectively abandoned estate in the south-eastern town of Luton; the old northern industrial city of Newcastle, trying officially to rebrand itself as the modern city of culture; and the historic industrial area of my home town, Manchester, recently transformed into the site of the Commonwealth Games. Each place bore the marks of a recent economic showdown. In Luton, the fortress-like building that used to be the Vauxhall motor plant now stands almost empty while former car workers commute around the south east in search of livelihoods; in Newcastle the streets of the riverside's industrial communities are presently targets for the bulldozer; in East Manchester, the boarded-up houses and factories are only now, after decades of neglect, receiving serious attention. In each place, however, there is a thriving city centre. An hour's bus ride from the Marsh Farm Estate in Luton, where young people say there 'are no sources of buzz', are well-equipped commercial leisure centres. The bus from Newcastle station drives past the Centre for Life, the £60 million 'interactive life sciences' visitor centre, complete with motion simulator (though now rumoured to be going bankrupt), to Scotswood where the city council cannot afford to rebuild schools and community facilities. Similarly, Manchester city centre offers numerous bars, restaurants and health clubs effectively barred to most East Mancunians, 52 per cent of whom are on housing or other benefits.

To explore with due sobriety the hope that local efforts can recreate democracy, it was necessary to visit places chosen not because they were exceptional but because they were ordinary, and Luton, Newcastle and East Manchester represented a familiar spectrum of relationships within the global economy and the state. This spectrum reflects the uneasy hybridity of the UK's political economy: as international economic pressures encouraged by the government push it towards the American model of minimal state regulation, some local authorities aspire to European standards of social democracy (though many continental social democracies themselves face pressures to privatise and deregulate). All three councils, Luton, Newcastle and Manchester, are run by the Labour

Party. In all three, local people are reacting to the failures of conventional politics by trying to create, in their own daily lives, more effective means of democratic control.

By the 1990s in Newcastle Tynesiders had become fatalistic about the power of multinational corporations to close their factories down without regard for the communities that depended on them; it was the realisation that public services were being threatened by private takeovers – and this under a Labour government – that prompted action. Council unions and community groups had been through twenty years of struggling, bargaining and campaigning to keep council services out of private hands, and had been successful. They applied the lessons of these years to the new, more ambiguous, disguised forms of privatisation under New Labour, and in the process developed strategies for rethinking the public sector. This Geordie struggle is an example of how explosions going on in the British crucible have implications for all those across the world who would challenge private companies trying to move in on public services.

In Luton and East Manchester the kick-start that led local people to overcome divisions and demoralisation was, paradoxically, government money. But it was government money granted on unusual conditions. In 1998 Tony Blair stood on the steps of the Aylesbury community centre in south London, in one of the most deprived estates in the whole of the UK, and announced that thirty-nine of England's poorest estates would receive £50 million each for a ten-year programme of regeneration. What's more, a condition of the funding was that local decisions be 'community led'. He was outlining the government's New Deal for Communities (NDC). Like many of New Labour's innovations, the NDC programme drew on US experiences under President Clinton. The NDC draws in part on US ideas of developing 'community capacity' to solve social problems within the community. The NDC and a wider programme of Neighbourhood Renewal, introduced four years later and aimed at a further eighty-eight deprived areas, is part of a determined move away from universal social provision towards selective, targeted policies for the socially excluded. This selective support for 'community-led' regeneration is a way of addressing the problems of Margaret Thatcher's worst victims without tackling Britain's grossly unequal distribution of resources. Such redistribution would need progressive taxation and increased social security and unemployment benefits. It would also involve a serious redistribution of power and resources to elected local government. What is distinctive about New Labour's version of neo-liberalism is that it combined continued deregulation and privatisation with an almost apolitical form of remedial action for those the market leaves behind. This action relied heavily on the notion of community, understood as having very little to do with political democracy.[2]

At this point we encounter a recurring issue in this book's discussion of participatory democracy: the tension between participation as a way of building the capacity of communities to help themselves, and participation as a means of strengthening people's control over state resources and institutions. This tension can become acute when community participation is sponsored by the government, or some part of the state. Official talk of community participation has always been ambiguous – state bodies have long realised it is good tactics to draw potential dissenters into their own orbit and grant them status and the semblance of power. But New Labour's approach to community, following models from the US, can be in direct conflict with the aim of gaining greater democratic control over state institutions.

On the one hand, the post-Thatcher economic consensus around low public spending, privatisation and deregulation tends to centralise government control over money, thus weakening the autonomy of local and regional government and closing down possible channels which could conduct pressure for increased public spending. This tendency was most visible under Mrs Thatcher and in the US, Ronald Reagan, though in more disguised and nuanced forms it continued under Tony Blair and Bill Clinton. On the other hand, in the face of the failure of the promised 'trickle down' of market-led prosperity, policies were needed to address the continued poverty and social exclusion of significant and often geographically concentrated sections of the population. This is where 'the community' came in: a *pot-pourri* of new left community politics and conservative communitarianism produced policies aimed at mobilising the capacities of poor neighbourhoods to solve their problems themselves – especially crime, poor environment and 'community disintegration'. There is much of use in such community-oriented social policy if it is combined with well-resourced, responsive public services, but too often such 'capacity building' has been steadily substituted for state-provided services, and accompanied by various forms of privatisation. A former Labour minister for local government in Britain, Alan Whitehead, described a common attitude amongst his colleagues: 'There was a view that communities are good things: they could tell you what was needed and administrators would go and carry it out without the intermediate layers of political democracy. Appeals to community were sometimes used to bypass local government.'[3] Although public services are in need of reform, their foundations of redistribution and democratic accountability are irreplaceable. Community self-help, on its own, leaves untouched the wider inequalities that often lie behind a locality's problems. All too often it becomes self-exploitation.

In reality 'community empowerment' cannot be kept separate from wider, more potentially controversial issues of 'democracy' and 'politics'. Certainly, people in the NDC neighbourhoods that I visited understood 'community led' as an invitation to have a real say over the future of their neighbourhood. They saw the opportunity to participate as a long-overdue right which they were quick to claim, not a gift for which they should be grateful. Three years after Blair's Aylesbury Estate declaration, the citizens of that neighbourhood voted overwhelmingly against a government-backed proposal to transfer council houses to a housing association. Instead they wanted to spend their money on refurbishing council houses and giving tenants more control over the management of the houses. This strong sense of stewardship, combined with a confidence in the democratic right to be in the lead, is producing a driving force for democracy which goes beyond the neighbourhood boundaries paternalistically set by the government. At times, far from limiting themselves to self-help, the new-style community activists in Luton and East Manchester have ended up pressing for policies which, if followed through, would recreate the welfare state on a more democratic basis. Moreover, in both places some of those actively involved in these processes have begun to reach out not only to people working in similar circumstances across the country but also to people trying to create more effective means of democratic control over city governments worldwide.

I feared that the focus of so much of my detailed research on Britain would limit its relevance, but as I discussed Britain with people in different countries, I found an intense curiosity. There was a strong sense, even into the twenty-first century, that what was hitting Britain – forms of privatisation, deregulation and anti-trade union legislation – was heading their way. The introduction of these policies goes back to Mrs Thatcher and what became known as 'neo-liberalism' because of its return to the neanderthal days of pre-welfare state political economy. She was the most coherent and explicit champion of the political and economic order that is shaping the first decades of the post-Cold War world. Thatcher provided the ideological drive and 'vision', while the US provided the global economic and, in the background, military clout to drive the follow-through. Owing to a convergence of circumstances, including the implosion of the Soviet Union, Thatcher and her soulmate Ronald Reagan were able to go a significant way towards clearing the political obstacles to this vision, notably destroying anything but the limited formalities of representative democracy.

The aim of Thatcher and her neo-liberal friends was to destroy any part of the state susceptible to the pressures of the people or organised on the basis of non-market principles: for example, the principle of universal provision of public goods. Hence any part of the state that could not be controlled absolutely from the centre was in her sights. The claim was to be getting government off the backs of the people, but the practice was to destroy all those mechanisms (flawed as they admittedly were) – from trade unions through to local government – that were able to put pressure on the central state, influence spending or regulate the private market in any way. In reality the aim was to get the people off the back of government, out of the public sphere and to push expectant citizens back into the privacy of the market and the family. The goal was effectively a state free of the people, except for periodic elections to choose who managed it, elections in which fewer and fewer people would participate – an almost accurate picture of the US today.

Working with people who had been on the sharp end of this attempt to remove them from the political process throws much into relief. A significant amount of what I observed, often in spite of the intentions of New Labour, was people inventing new ways of getting back onto the back of government, controlling its resources, 'occupying its rhetoric', in words commonly used in the Marsh Farm NDC. Observing the dismal legacy of Mrs Thatcher's onslaught on taken-for-granted institutions which had gone some way to guaranteeing the security and wellbeing of many people's everyday life, brought home how many state activities in parliamentary democracies were democratic gains against narrow vested interests. As such they needed to be defended, improved and, above all, brought under stronger democratic control.

Many on the left (myself included) have tended to highlight the ways in which the welfare state and state-owned industries have been distorted by their coexistence with capitalism. Consequently we have downplayed the fact that they represented a successful exercise in the power of the vote constraining the pressures of the private market. There is no doubt that these democratic gains were distorted both by the commercial pressures of capitalism and by the undue weight of the military – both in terms of public spending and its attendant secretive centralising culture – imposed by the logic of the Cold War. Public services also contained all sorts of weakness stemming from the top-down nature of public provision, and the assumption, however well-meaning, that only the experts know what the people need. In their defence, we should remember that such hierarchical structures and inherent paternalism were common to most large institutions at the time they were conceived. But certainly, now that most of the elements of the distinctively public (i.e. responsive to the needs of the people) features of the state are being destroyed, it is clearer than ever that the Chartists and Suffragettes' achievement of the suffrage had made possible state activities that genuinely reflected the needs of the people. The vote may be a clumsy, and insufficiently sensitive or direct, means of making public services responsive to the needs of those who use them, but its universality makes it a necessary – but not sufficient – safeguard of the principle of public service: that 'public goods' should be provided to meet social needs which the private market would not reach.

Such redistribution, in addition, was not only about taxation to 'externally' fund public services; it was also about the constant cross-subsidy from the wealth-generating part of a service to those parts that met social needs; from the main line on the rail network to the outlying stations; from the city-centre branch of the telecom or postal service to its rural offices. It is this very redistributive element of public services which makes possible their distinctive form of efficiency, defined by their ability to meet the needs of the public. 'The public' itself also has a wide span. It reaches from the chronically sick to the occasionally sick; from the difficult children to the responsive ones; from the remoter places to the city centres; from the poor postal districts to the wealthy ones. To meet the needs of such a public, state provision is fundamental. Put bluntly, the market provides nothing for those who lack the cash to spend in it. As services like railways are sold off to the private sector and run for a profit; as public services lose their universal and democratic character; as many previously public-service jobs become private-sector jobs without the sense of a useful contribution which motivated many to work for the public sector; and as the vote is emptied of its content because government loses its social purpose and power, anger is growing. As the impact of all these shifts towards the market accumulate, it becomes clearer and clearer that recreating democracy must also be about reclaiming, inventing and reinventing those state institutions – including international ones – that are necessary, though not sufficient, to achieving redistribution, the provision of public goods and social and environmental regulation. But it must be about doing so in a way which involves far stronger, more direct control by the people.[4]

PORTO ALEGRE:
PUBLIC POWER BEYOND THE STATE

It's six in the morning in Rio de Janeiro and even the Atlantic waves are sleepy. I'm working here on my way to Porto Alegre. Rio is one of the most beautiful cities in the world, but scarred by an equally extreme global record in poverty and pollution. The natural beauty of the landscape – lakes, forests, dramatic rocks, stunning views of the bay – keeps pushing its way through ugly and environmentally careless state and corporate constructions. The contrast between natural beauty and social and political squalor is characteristic of Brazil: in Rio as elsewhere, a wide coalition of people helps both nature and the poor to break through.

Hours after my arrival, my friends Jose Ricardo and Neide whisk me to an 'embracing of the lake' (*abraço à lagoa*) a 20,000-strong protest against the pollution of an inner-city lake. It was organised through *Viva Rio*, which aims to stop pollution, corruption and poverty from killing the convivial life of the city. Environmentalism in Brazil seems to be inseparable from action for social justice. The talk amongst the protesters is of police corruption – a brave local minister of security has just been sacked for speaking openly on the subject. Election campaigns for the city's mayor are underway and flags of the then opposition *Partido dos Trabalhadores* (PT, the Workers Party) mix with the banners of social movements and of groups of fishermen whose livelihoods are threatened. Dead fish float on the lake's edges, giving it an ominous silver frame. People believe that the election of a PT mayor will lead to action on the demands of *Viva Rio*, but they also know they will need to keep up their campaign beyond elections.

Nowhere evokes Brazilian conviviality and its contradictions more than Copacabana, where the British Council has booked me a suitably down-market hotel. The excitement of looking out on to a sunny beach or watching the aspiring Ronaldos on the makeshift football pitches along the beach does not last long. Copacabana too is polluted, socially and environmentally. No one swims, unless they're tourists. On the hills behind the Copacabana Palace Hotel, past haunt of Gina Lollobrigida, Elizabeth Taylor and Princess Diana, can clearly be seen the corrugated iron roofs of the *favelas* – the slums that surround Rio and every other Brazilian city.

Fifty-two million Brazilians out of a total population of 170 million, that is 34 per cent of the population, struggle in poverty. Meanwhile, the income of the richest 1 per cent of Brazilians adds up to 13.7 per cent of the national income – the same percentage shared by the poorest 50 per cent of the people. In 1994 the country elected as its president an academic with a record of struggling for social justice, Fernando Henrique Cardoso. Once elected, Cardoso continued (when the occasion demanded) to speak the language of social democracy, meanwhile following the neo-liberal Washington formula and opening up Brazil to trade and financial flows, privatisation of state enterprises, and high interest rates. The result, here as globally, is that the gap between rich and poor has grown. The widely respected newspaper *Folha de São Paulo* reports: 'Inequality increased in Brazil between 1992 and 1998, and the proportion of wages to national revenue, which was 44% of GDP in 1993, fell to 36% of GDP by the decade's end.'[1] Cardoso has been the man in the South with whom Tony Blair conducts his Third Way business.

The alternative – tackling inequality through the participatory budget

The PT has another way, however. Since its foundation in 1981, it has taken up the demands of the poor – for land, for decent housing, for a basic income, against pollution, for public health and education – and made them the basis of a programme for the majority of society. The PT is not a conventional parliamentary party. Its policy has always been that it will use the knowledge of the community and share with that community whatever power it gains through electoral success. That success, it believes, will also need to be followed up with more radical, participatory forms of democracy if the state is ever to redress the inequality of Brazilian society.

It is impossible to understand the participatory methods of the PT without recognising the contribution made by Paulo Freire's ideas on education.[2] Pedro Pondial, an ex-Catholic priest from Santo André, describes his influence: 'Freire's philosophy of education is about people becoming aware of their power together to create something new as they overcome what is oppressive. That's the foundation of our participatory politics.' A PT supporter until he died in 1997, Freire saw education as a transformative tool that could create experiences of a truly equal and democratic nature, which people would then be inspired to reproduce. He had observed the way we imitate traditional relationships of power and reproduce them when we ourselves gain any kind of power. The goal of his education was to break this pattern and so obstruct the reproduction of established power. His emphasis on cultural as well as political and economic transformation is echoed in the PT's participative methods of government. The PT does not simply seek to get into office and drive the machinery of state towards the poor. Rather, it aims to open up the state machinery in the municipalities and involve all citizens – the poor especially – in deciding how it should work, a collaborative process that is both personally and socially transformative. This is just what was put into action in Porto Alegre, 700 miles south of Rio, in 1989, when the PT's charismatic Gaucho bank clerk candidate, Olívio Dutra, became mayor.

Throughout the twenty-one years of military rule (1964–85) in Brazil, Porto Alegre, capital city of the southern state of Rio Grande do Sul, was a centre of resistance. The city's neighbourhood associations (*associações de bairro*), now at the root of the administration's main innovation, the *orçamento participativo* (participatory budget, PB), provided refuge for persecuted dissidents, and later became an important source of support for the PT. Even before the election of Dutra, these neighbourhood associations and other urban movements in the city were demanding the democratisation of local government, the ending of corruption and the opening up of budget decision-making. In some ways, Porto Alegre, a busy industrial, financial and service centre in a relatively wealthy region, is not a typical Brazilian city (in so far as there is such a thing in this incredibly diverse country) for it has always had an unusually high literacy rate, even before the reforms of the 1990s (in 1991 it was 96 per cent, well above the Brazilian average of 81 per cent). But it has not bucked the Brazilian trend of extreme social inequality: in 1981 one-third of the city (total population 1.2 million[3]) lived in slum areas. At the same time, fifteen families owned almost all the urban land available for development. And, as throughout Brazil, corruption was endemic to municipal politics and administration.

The Porto Alegre PT believed that the only chance of achieving change was to open up the secretive municipal institutions – particularly their finances – to a process of popular participation. So when the PT gained control of the municipal government, it invited citizens to participate in the decisions made about the city's new investments. It was this that was called the participatory budget. It is a form of co-decision-making or shared power: through a process of meetings delegates are elected and citizens decide on the priorities for the municipal investment budget and argue for the relative importance of investment in projects of public works, services and the social economy. This principle of popular participation has spread more widely through the city's administration. 'Participation is addictive', says Betânia Alfonsi, a young urban planner who used to be in the local leadership of the PT and now works with movements in the *favelas*.

The particular combination in Porto Alegre of well-organised urban movements, strong democratic traditions and a history of left-of-centre governments provided good conditions in which to test the PT's still-undefined ideas of participation. Even before 1989, there was pressure from neighbourhood movements in the city for greater democracy in finances. In 1985, 300 delegates attended the founding congress of the city-wide UAMPA (Union of Residents' Associations) where they drew up a draft proposal for opening up the budgetary process. The submission of this proposal took urban grassroots organisations beyond purely parochial concerns and laid the basis for city-wide popular participation. In addition, it helped to create the atmosphere in which, on winning office, Dutra could discuss with the popular movements of the city how his government should manage the municipality's financial difficulties. In doing so his administration broke with the previous tradition by which deals were made among the elected political elite. From the start, the PB allowed the ordinary people of Porto Alegre to become a powerful force influencing the decisions of the municipal legislature – in which no single party had a majority.

It would at first seem that conditions in Porto Alegre were uniquely favourable to the emergence of the PB, but similar ideas had also taken root in the completely different conditions of Santo André, part of the industrial belt around the city of São Paulo and birthplace of the PT. One of the largest car manufacturing centres in the world until the 1990s, the grassroots democracy of the CUT, the leading left-wing trade union confederation, provided fertile ground for ideas of popular participation in financial decision-making. For João Avamileno, the city's vice mayor and founder member of the union, the idea of basing the municipal budget on popular participation followed logically from the way decisions were taken over CUT's budget: 'The workers in each union, through their local and regional assemblies, would discuss and decide their priorities for the whole organisation. These participatory methods are essential.'

The connection between opening up the black hole of state finance and stimulating the growth of a popular democratic power was partially anticipated in the new thinking of the PT, but it was not a fully developed part of its programme. From the mid-1980s, as the party started standing in elections, it began to debate how to use political office to achieve the radical transformation for which it was working through social movements. Celso Daniel, PT mayor of Santo André, was part of those debates. He explained to me the thinking that led to the PB: 'We believed in taking the principles of democracy from social movements, including the trade union movement, with us when we gained office. That meant we had to share political power, the management of the city, with the community.' Finance is power, Daniel believed, so opening the budget was the best test of the sharing of power.

Daniel believed that these principles, so far applied only at municipal and provincial state government level, have implications for the federal government. This has gained a new relevance with Lula's stunning victory in the 2002 presidential elections.[4] 'It's very important to try to build a regionalised central budget, because the difference between regions is huge, so if the president of Brazil becomes committed to the participatory budget process at the central level, this could be very important for the construction of a new kind of federalism in Brazil.' He explained how the present federal system in Brazil is 'very tied to the old oligarchies, the old elites'. Daniel, a close Lula adviser, would undoubtedly have held a key position in the PT government. In January 2002, however, he was murdered – one of several PT mayors killed probably by members of drugs mafias threatened by the new open method of government. His death is an extreme reminder that people with powerful vested interests, whether local and global, are not going to sit back and let 'ordinary' people encroach on their power.

I was curious to explore the principles on which the PB worked and whether these had a wider international relevance, and so from Rio I headed to Porto Alegre. It has become an international city not by prostrating itself at the feet of predatory corporations in the hope of inward investment, but, ironically, because it has become internationally renowned for 'good government'. For political, cultural and economic reasons, it nurtures this reputation. The *Rough Guide to Brazil* advised me where to stay and the city hall's glossy but thorough guide to the workings of the PB and a growing international literature on the Porto Alegre participatory experiment gave me a clear idea of the institutions and processes of the participatory budget.[5]

The process of the participatory budget

The mechanisms of the PB, though complex and original, are clear. Indeed, transparency is one of its principles. There is an annual public assembly at which the regional delegates and budget councillors are elected and the thematic priorities for the following year are chosen. This 'unique round' is preceded by many meetings at which the municipal government is called to account for the past year and people begin the debates about priorities and criteria for the election of delegates.

The main role of the delegates elected at the plenaries is to sound people out on issues such as road building, schools, health provision, sewage, economic development including co-operatives, and leisure and sports facilities, in preparation for preparing the region's priorities. They meet with local groups throughout the year to iron out problems, monitor progress, and encourage ideas for next year's budget. The delegates then gather together at the delegates' forum, where they work out budget priorities for their region by combining two objective criteria (population size and statistically measured need, e.g. the proportion of residents to each health centre or children to each school, the amount of pavements unpaved and so on) with one subjective criterion (the priority given to different issues by the community). They apply a weighting system so that quantitative weights can be given to different areas of investment. The same criteria are applied across the city. This weighting system, sometimes known as the 'budget matrix', plays a crucial role in creating awareness of the needs of both the different regions and of the city as a whole.

The delegates also keep in regular touch with the region's two representatives on the budget council (*Conselho do Orçamento Participativo*, COP), through the delegates' forum and in other day-to-day ways. The COP is a powerful body that negotiates the final investment priorities for the city on the basis of input from the regions and the thematic groups. In addition, it considers some projects proposed by the government itself. Through an open process of negotiation and reporting back, the COP draws up the overall budget and puts it to the mayor and municipal council for final agreement. The COP representatives are accountable to the regional delegates and could in theory be recalled by a specially convened plenary, though this has yet to happen. This notion of recall, or '*retorno*', is an important one, demonstrating the accountability of representatives on the powerful budget council, the apex of the whole process.

This then was the process in theory, but how did it work in practice? Fortunately for me, both sides of the participatory budget were happy for researchers to observe the process and were very helpful in making this possible. I visited Porto Alegre in 1998, not long after Peter Mandelson, former UK cabinet minister and close to Prime Minister Tony Blair, had toured Brazil trying to reflect some of New Labour's electoral glory on to President Cardoso and castigating the PT as 'old-fashioned'. But the presumptuous behaviour of a fellow countryman was not held against me. When I arrived, a polite young man met me at the city's compact and efficient airport and took me to a municipal car emblazoned with the slogan 'Porto Alegre, the city where participation makes democracy'. I had expected to have to hunt down the participatory budget: in fact it had come to greet me.

GAPLAN – the budget planning office

We drove first to meet the man at the head of the government's side of the participatory process, the *Gabinete de Planejamento* – the budget planning committee or GAPLAN. Imagining a grey-suited official, I was surprised by the friendly, young man, suit-less and tie-less, who greeted me. This was André Passos, a thirty-year-old economist and a PT member since the age of fifteen, now chief of the budget planning department in GAPLAN. His office was full of posters announcing political meetings and seminars. Part of his job is to explain the conclusions of his technical work to the citizen participants, so his political commitment to the PB is important. Later in the week I was to observe him reporting back to a 600-strong plenary, answering tough questions and fielding persistent criticisms at a typically argumentative meeting of the COP.

Legally, André Passos is employed by the mayor, but his job involves him working in two directions. At certain points in the budgetary cycle he explains and persuades on behalf of the government to the people; at others he scrutinises, on behalf of the people, the activities of the government. He coordinates the 'technical criteria' for the budget, that is the legal, physical and financial constraints that it must work within. Passos works as a servant of the public. He is powerful but not personally so; his power derives from both the mandate of the mayor and the authority of the participatory process. His work reveals how the PB influences the day-to-day operations of local government and how it has opened up a state bureaucracy that is normally hidden, helping to repel what are often corrupt pressures on council departments from private interests.

There are, of course, serious constraints on the scope of the PB. If you consider general, countrywide taxation, 57–59 per cent goes to the federal government, 27–28 per cent to the state government to be spent on health and education, and 14 per cent remains with the municipal government. Some additional taxes are also collected by the municipality and can be changed by municipal laws. Up to Lula's election, the trend was towards the municipality increasing its responsibilities (especially concerning new social services), but concentrating revenue from taxation with the federal government – a nifty device which helps central government pay the external and internal debt and leaves the social problems in the hands of increasingly constrained municipalities. In 1989, nearly 90 per cent of Porto Alegre's municipal budget went on salaries, with few funds – less than 10 per cent – left for new investments, even in basics like sewage, pavements, new schools or health centres. In 2002, 15 per cent of the budget has been spent on new investments.

Passos stresses the future importance of Porto Alegre City Council being permitted to increase its revenue through municipal enterprises. He points to an information technology company which was originally created to provide for public departments and which now offers its services more widely. The increased revenue goes back into the company and will enable it to invest in optical fibre technology, which will be a future source of further revenue. The city's water company is also municipally owned, and most of Porto Alegre's buses are built by a highly successful company owned by the city council and managed – on strong foundations of industrial democracy – by a highly respected young woman. There is also a growing network of municipally owned but co-operatively run recycling projects – all this at time when elsewhere in the world governments and corporations try to persuade us that 'modernisation' means privatisation.

Here then, in André Passos' offices, is a new local government institution. It has centralised power over all municipal government departments but its job is to ensure that they respond to the priorities set 'from below'. It was reminiscent, to me, of the 'programme office' at the Greater London Council under Ken Livingstone. This also was an innovation: its job was to monitor and ensure that all GLC departments carried out the manifesto on which the leadership of the council was elected. GAPLAN's role is far more active than this, however, and more creative: it is not simply following up the electoral mandate of one day's voting, but servicing a year-long process of democratic participation.

CRC – coordinating relations with the community

Our next stop was the offices of the *Coordenação de Relações com as Comunidades* (Coordination Committee for Relations with the Community, CRC). Assis Brasil, the CRC's jovial and universally flirtatious head, invited us to talk with him and some of the regional PB coordinators.

There are twenty coordinators, one for each of the sixteen regions of the city and four working on particular themes: women, youth, black people and older people. Some had been priests (the influence of radical Catholicism is pervasive amongst the PT and its supporters); some, women especially, had trained to join a religious order as a way of gaining education and getting out of the *favelas*, but had left before taking their final vows; others had been active in the neighbourhood movements; several had been active in the landless movement before coming to the city; and a few were intellectuals, teachers and academics.

In the first fifteen years of the PT's administration, the CRC played a crucial role in organising the PB. The CRC coordinators' most important role is working with the PB delegates elected by the regional plenaries. In practice, they help the PB delegates through the three tasks that are the responsibility of the delegates and the community. First, there are the discussions with technical people from the city hall about the practicalities of different improvements; second, there are neighbourhood meetings to develop proposals and hear people's views on them; and third, there is the drawing up of a hierarchy of priorities to put to their region's second plenary and from there to the budgetary council. Even though local government does not co-manage this part of the process, the coordinators have the responsibility of making sure that people have access to technical information and of helping groups communicate with each other, so that delegates, having to choose between competing priorities, can understand the needs of the region as a whole. In one region, Restinga, nearly fifty community meetings were held during this vital intermediary period before their priorities were agreed. 'Coordinators vary', said Luciano Brunet, who works closely with Brasil and who had been a student movement activist in the 1970s, resisting the dictatorship. 'Their role depends a lot on how strong and confident the local organisations are. Some coordinators encourage the community to be really innovative.' At one stage, there were complaints of coordinators becoming too involved and undermining the independence of the local organisations. 'Because of this,' explains Brunet, 'there's an unwritten rule that regional coordinators do not live in the region where they work or, if they do, they are not personally involved in the local organisations.'

The more Luciano Brunet explained the inner realities of the CRC and the work of the coordinators, the more it seemed that, while GAPLAN is the technical engine room of the PB, the CRC is its social and political fuel injection system. The work of the PB coordinators is crucial to the development of people's power to control the local state. They have to be extremely skilled, exerting authority with government departments, and at the same time teaching ordinary people to develop their own power and capacity to organise.

People's plenaries – accountability and vision

I was able to see co-management in action at a plenary on my second evening in Porto Alegre. It was the opening meeting of the 2001 budgetary process in the Northern zone. The first round of plenary meetings is held in each of the sixteen regions of the city. They take place in March, and focus on accounting for the previous year's spending and raising issues for the delegates to work on for the next year's budget. That evening the meeting was in the vast hall of a local secondary school. Isabella (a longtime PT supporter and my translator during my trip[6]), and I were dropped off behind a fleet of minibuses provided by the CRC's budget coordinators for those with no transport. As people entered the meeting, they registered: name, address and the name of their association, even if it was only an informal street organisation. This registration is important for several reasons, one of which is that it counts the number of people at the meeting, which is the basis on which participants elect their delegates. When the plenaries were first held, a very simple method was used: 1 delegate per 5 people at the meeting, then 1 per 10, then 1 per 20, as involvement in PB meetings grew (1,000 in 1990, 3,700 in 1991, 10,000 in 1993, 20,000 in 1997, and around 40,000 in 2002). But in 1997 the COP changed the rules to make sure that all areas of the city were represented, even those where people were not very active. Now meetings with an attendance of up to 100 choose 1 delegate for every 10 people; those with an attendance of 851–1,000 choose one 1 for every 70; and those with more than 1,000 choose 1 for every 80.

Registration took time, and while people waited, a troupe of actors put on a kind of street theatre, focusing on local problems. To an outsider, the people streaming in seemed to be a cross-section of the whole of the community: white-haired matrons; eager school students; Rasta men; the anxious poor, often black; glamorous young women; confident-looking middle-aged men. But the coordinators said that some neighbourhoods were much better represented than others and that this was another reason for the registration: it enabled them to identify areas, or groups of people, that were not well represented and find out why. Around 600 people had come to this meeting, out of a community of 3,000, and the majority were women.

It is the participants themselves who give the PB life. During meetings there is an opportunity not only to protest and let off steam, but also to explore needs and propose solutions. A statistical survey of the participation of different social groups by CIDADE, an independent research organisation, shows that a large majority of the participants are unskilled workers with only a primary level of education. Women are generally well represented: over the last four years there have been more women than men at the plenaries, and more women than men have been elected. This is impressive for a region that is renowned throughout Brazil for its *machismo*. And, in a city that until recently excluded black people from the main supermarkets and from factory jobs, it is particularly noteworthy that at least one-quarter of the delegates to the COP are black or indigenous people. PB meetings have become a focal point for people previously excluded from the political process.

The people crowding into the meeting that night saw it as an opportunity to vent their feelings to government representatives, as well as to win over their neighbours in support of their chosen causes. A local tradition of public story-telling makes for a hall full of vivid narrators of tales of municipal failings, and two groups were particularly vociferous. In the previous year's budget, sanitation had been a high priority but, complained speaker after speaker, the problems of dirty water and open sewage remained, even though a lot of money had been spent on the area. People from one neighbourhood complained about a stream that had become the local sewer, saying that they wanted it closed over so it could not be used in this way. Government officials at the meeting said that, for environmental reasons, the stream should remain a stream but they promised to clean it. Another vocal group were from a local school. They had come to a budget plenary for the first time and used it simply to shout out their complaints. The mayor at the time, Raoul Pont, responded, urging them to elect a delegate, turn their complaints into proposals and negotiate for funds through the PB.

On the platform at the front of the hall sat a mixture of people, some from the municipality's executive departments, some from the community. Alongside the mayor was André Passos, next to him Luciano Brunet from the CRC, and from the community there were the current delegates to the COP from this region, as well as two *vereadores* – elected members of the municipal legislative assembly for the area. The chair asked for an indication of how many were attending their first PB meeting. Over 300 hands went up. This is quite common; new people are constantly engaging with the process. Despite a hostile local media, recent surveys show that over 85 per cent of Porto Alegrans know about and support the PB. They find out about it through their neighbours and friends, through leaflets and through delegates. The PB itself has become a form of media.

Later in my visit I discussed these plenaries with Eduardo Utzig who, as a social researcher and a former senior government official, has a comprehensive and reflective understanding of the process. He said that the PB's influence has grown. 'The people notice if works are late and the delegates put pressure on the government. "Why is there a delay?" they ask. And, if the problem isn't solved, they mobilise the community and bring them into the city hall.' Utzig certainly felt he had been under constant direct popular pressure when he was in government, and he thought this made him more efficient. He said that the pressure does not come in a form that officials can easily control, for there is no single formal procedure. It can be direct to government departments, or to the mayor, or through the budget council or the regional PB coordinators.

The rules and criteria for the PB are precise and treated with great seriousness by government and community alike. Rules for the budgeting process are written up as a handbook, *Procedures of the Participatory Budget*, which is annually revised, reflecting the continuing process of refinement and adaptation. All those attending a plenary meeting have a copy. Thus the PB is a self-reproducing and self-regulating process, with formalised mechanisms for learning, monitoring and adapting.

COP – the budget council

Finally, all that remained to be visited was the COP itself. In many modern societies important government meetings are closed, or at least surrounded by so much red tape that they might as well be closed. But in the *petista* (as PT members are often called) version of Brazilian culture, it seems everything is open. So, along with at least two other international visitors, Isabella and I sat in on a COP meeting. There were about twenty city delegates there – a full attendance would be over forty delegates – with only two members of the government. Though the majority of people who attend the open plenaries are women, the majority of the twenty or so COP delegates attending this meeting were men. Two were black, most were mixed race, and there was one deaf man and his signer.

At the desk in front sat André Passos, Assis Brasil and two community representatives, one of whom took the chair.

By April, preparation of the budget proposal and the investment plan is complete. Proposals are submitted to the municipal assembly in December and agreed by the mayor the following February. So the meeting we attended in June dealt with concerns outside the main priorities. Discussion focused on a sports hall in one neighbourhood, some cultural activity in another. There were some complaints and some questions. Even though the agenda was not as important as at some meetings, it was a rumbustious affair, with André and Assis, as government representatives, being put on the spot mercilessly.

Betânia Alfonsi, who has a long experience of the PB, said she had been impressed by the COP meetings. 'I was surprised. I felt these people are doing far more for the city than we do in our departments.' And they are doing it unpaid. Even though COP meetings take place for two hours a week, all year round (except February), and twice a week from September until December, delegates receive no payment. 'The whole system of the participatory budget runs off militancy', explains Valerio Lopes, the president of the financial committee of UAMPA, the city's network of neighbourhood associations. 'The only people who receive payment are the municipal workers related to the process. The delegates have to take care of all their expenses, including bus tickets or petrol.'

Porto Alegre's overall budget for 2001 was R$600 million (about US$230 million), of which R$90 million was available for new investments to be decided through the PB, then ratified by the mayor and finally proposed to the municipal legislature (*Câmara de Vereadores*). At this point André Passos and his colleagues can introduce into the discussion government proposals that target the whole city, but which haven't been through the PB system. One popular city congress proposal was the re-development of the closed market into an attractive multi-use public centre. Such proposals do not automatically get accepted now, although they used to in the early days. 'People didn't have the information the government had and they weren't able to discuss on equal terms', commented researcher Sérgio Baerlie, a long-time observer of the process. He drew an important conclusion: 'Sometimes it's not enough to have the opportunity to decide, if you don't have the instruments – such as the information and consciousness – to debate on equal terms.' Delegates debate on more equal terms now than they did at first: 'People don't simply accept the budget proposals brought by the government', says Baerlie. 'They start comparing with previous years. They have the documents to do so. They have learnt. They start questioning why something else got more money than the top priority of the participatory process. Increasingly, the government has to justify itself.' Being on the COP is a steep learning curve and, in order for the expertise and confidence gained from the experience to be shared as widely as possible, seats on the council are rotated. No one can be a member, or a substitute, for more than two consecutive years, though someone can stand again after two years off.

The job of a delegate can be an uncomfortable one. Delegates at both the regional and the city level are regularly under pressure from their electors. Listen to Jussara Bechstein-Silva (hybrid German-Brazilian names are common in a city which was host to large migrations from Europe in the late nineteenth century, especially from Germany and Italy), who represents the central region on the COP. She is a forceful charismatic leader in Vila Planetário, fighting for the squatted land to be legalised and its present residents to remain in the centre of the city. She found it hard being a COP representative: 'You have to answer to the local inhabitants who are asking: "Why is it so delayed? Why is it failing?" And you have to answer to the council, too. You are pressured on both sides.' But she felt supported: 'The mayor, Olívio Dutra, came one night in the pouring rain and told us to be hopeful because the construction would be completed. And we had a lot of support from our lawyer' – a woman who worked in the planning department, part of whose job was to provide technical support for the community.

The intensive period between September and December is when the detailed investment plan is drawn up, listing the works and activities chosen for that year. The municipal chamber has never rejected the COP's budget or made any damaging amendments. The investment plan is published annually as a vital reference document, which all regional and thematic delegates refer to as they supervise the departments carrying out the work. The government uses the plan when it is called to account by any organ of the participatory budget.

The missing links

There are problems, however. As Betânia Alfonsi describes: 'the budgetary process is not enough. The COP is very powerful but it only deals with investments. You cannot plan a city just on the basis of individual investments. We have to complement it by democratising and strengthening urban planning. If not, you can get a gulf between city planning and specific investments. An example of this lack of coordination was the expansion of the sewage network, which now covers more than 80 per cent of the city. This work was not accompanied by an investment in water treatment, which has resulted in a considerable increase of untreated sewage flowing into the city's main water source, Lake Guaíba.'

There are two related issues here. One is that planning and policy have not caught up with the dynamic reality of the participatory budget. The planning department used to be the centre of power in the old administration, one centralised super-department responsible for infrastructure and planning. The PT administration broke this up in order to carry out their democratic reforms and resentment has lingered on, with key professional staff in the depleted planning department on what is essentially a long-term 'go slow'. The other issue is that government departments are fragmented and uncoordinated. There is pressure from the PB plenaries in some regions for the government to set up regular dialogue between departments.

In Porto Alegre, the process of improving the efficiency of government would not be familiar to anyone working today in local government in the UK – the setting of tougher targets at the top and the tightening of the control structure in the hope that those below deliver. In the city of participatory democracy, this is turned on its head, for it has become almost axiomatic to connect efficiency with democracy. 'We have to democratise urban planning, and we have to do so in a comprehensive way', says Alfonsi. The council's leadership is aware of this problem and has encouraged the urban planning department to embark on a major new initiative in participation. How will the new participatory structure for urban planning link to the PB? 'I'm not sure. I don't think the council leadership know either.' There are signs in some areas, however, that this participatory planning is already feeding directly into the budget process, even becoming the basis on which delegates choose priorities.

The integration of urban planning and other policy areas with the PB, and the development of a stronger, participatory approach to policy other than new investments, have become urgent priorities. As discussed earlier, the federal government in Brazil under President Cardoso opened the national economy to the full, unrestrained impact of global deregulation, with the concomitant pressures to privatise and run down the state's social capacities. As a result it has strengthened central control over public spending and has cut the funds going back to the cities whose citizens pay the taxes. Funds going to local authorities were reduced from 17 per cent of the revenue received in 1990 to 14 per cent in 1999. Further cuts have been made since. Whether or not Lula's government will be able to reverse this trend – which, given its belief in the importance of local democracy, it would like to – will depend in good part on the International Monetary Fund. Soon after Lula's election, the IMF told the new government that it had to run a primary fiscal surplus (that is, before interest payments on its debt) of 3.75 per cent of GDP or it will be denied the funds it needs to pay foreign creditors. This is a heavy pressure on the spending that the government needs to make to fulfil its electoral promises. Under the present global economic order a 62 per cent popular vote is not, it seems, sufficient to be allowed to govern.[7]

Porto Alegre cannot put up a Chinese wall, however good its policies on job creation, health, education, infrastructure and social security. It is at the frontline of a global economic and political war. Almost every reflex in the city's strengthened body politic has moved in the opposite direction to the neo-liberalism of the federal state and indeed of most governments across the world. While many governments have willingly reduced their capacity to meet the needs of their poor by, for example, cutting public spending and lowering taxes on the rich, through the PB the popular administration of Porto Alegre has expanded its ability to fulfil its citizens' social rights. It has increased its revenue through redistributive taxation, and set up a decision-making process and invest-ment plan deliberately responsive to the needs of the poor. The imple-mentation of the PB alone, however, cannot adequately protect against federal policies that destroy the economic ground on which the PT's commitment to social justice stands. There is a danger that the popular administration itself could become unintentionally complicit in imposing on local communities the burden of clearing up the unregu-lated market's social mess.

Essentially, the logic goes like this. Poor communities face greater and greater social problems. Their needs intensify. In the meantime, the municipal council's budget to help meet these needs is cut. Its capacity for providing high-quality free services, such as childcare, health, education and housing, is reduced. Local communities put forward projects for solving these problems themselves. The PB agrees with these grassroots solutions, for they fit the basic budget criteria. But what is not discussed is the quality of the service, the level of pay, how the project connects with services provided directly by the municipality, whether the need could be met in better ways, or how a project will be supervised to ensure that it is providing high-quality services.

Sérgio Baerlie illustrates this problem with the example of community daycare centres. 'The money that the municipal government needs to run by itself just one daycare centre is enough to fund several, perhaps more than ten, daycare centres run by community associations, where labour costs are much lower. The result is that today Porto Alegre has 118 daycare centres run by community associations with funds from city hall.' Baerlie suggests there is a danger here of unintentionally accepting a neo-liberal transference of social policy from the state to the community and, in the process, undermining the principle of the provision of free public services as a universal social right.[8]

Baerlie has other concerns too: 'While agreements between city hall and community organisations are public and are processed on the basis of suggestions from the people, a significant number of management issues tend to be left out of public discussion. For example, how can it be guaranteed that the professionals who are hired are not relatives of the leader of the community organisation? How do we approach the fact that parents often still have to pay for the service? In that case, what is a fair price? Why must some parents pay and others not, since in the few municipal daycare centres no monthly fee is charged? In other words, how can it be ensured that public money is managed in a transparent fashion and with the agreement of parents and the community?' He is stressing that it is not enough to seek to democratise the state but that social institutions outside the state must also democratise themselves, and this applies to the kinds of independent projects that are funded through the PB. 'No one would suggest ending agreements such as the community daycare initiative, yet without a democratic transformation of their management, there is no challenge to the neo-liberal "common sense".' The other danger is that, as private corporations increasingly involve themselves, not without self-interest, in the funding of different aspects of the 'social economy' from childcare to recycling, community organisations will lose autonomy, becoming less able to stand up for the rights and needs of their populations. They will in effect become minnows keeping the water clean for the big fish.

There is a growing feeling amongst politically minded government officials, NGO researchers and PB delegates that policy and strategy, as distinct from simply the priorities for the investment plan, need to be integrated into the process. There is active support in the regions of the cityfor popular processes of urban planning and economic development, as well as pressure on city hall departments to integrate their policy. Part of the answer seems to be to extend the participatory process of decision-making beyond the biannual city congresses, which are more consultative than decision-making, into policy development. Debates and changes are underway. Aspects of the popular administration are unusually self-reflexive for a public body, but then they are unusual public bodies. The COP is most evidently able to learn from its failings and change. There is also an openness to criticism at the heart of the government, in contrast to the defensiveness so often to be found in many political authorities. The mayor's office, for example, organised a seminar so that international researchers could share their criticisms.

The party seeks a new direction

Traditionally, the party in charge of the council, in this case the PT, would lead the formation of policy and strategy for the city, choosing a direction and developing a clear vision. But in Porto Alegre, the PB presents a problem born of success: the process of participatory budgeting has proved unpredictable. In contrast to the conventional model of a party controlling, or perceiving itself to control, a state apparatus, the PB has unleashed a more potent, more broadly based, means of controlling at least a central part of the state. Instead of the leading party taking the role of conscious political brain, the PB encourages and involves many political 'brains', many self-conscious agents of social change. This implicitly challenges the nature – though not the fact – of the PT's leadership, in so far as the PT is responsible for the municipal government on the basis of conventional electoral politics. The party has thus moved on to ground on which few political leaders have trod.

PT's ability to respond creatively is shaped by its history. Its containment, since its inception, of different ideological tendencies on the left has meant that disputes between tendencies have always played a central role in the life of the party. It has a strong belief in democracy but this can be at the expense of a responsiveness to the new problems and policy arising out of the party's, or rather the government's and the community's, immediate experience. It is a tension between democracy meaning internal party norms and rules for debating ideological differences, and democracy meaning an openness and reflectivity on the innovations and problems of practice.

Participatory budgeting appears to have changed perceptions of the PT itself in Porto Alegre: its popular support has escalated. One measure of this is the choice of a PT mayor in four consecutive elections, with a growing percentage of the vote. Another is the fact that, whereas in 1986 only 6.4 per cent of the Porto Alegre population identified with the PT, research in August–September 1996 showed 46 per cent as making this identification. The growth in PT membership in the city was also impressive: in 1990 the PT in Porto Alegre had 8,817 members; by May 2001 it had 24,033.

At the same time as the party grew in this phenomenal way, many of the most active, experienced members became part of the local government – there are around 600 politically appointed positions in Porto Alegre's local administration (this is the normal system in local authorities in Brazil). Consequently, when the PT came to office about 10 per cent of the local membership moved into government. This creation of a cadre of full-time policy thinkers and doers always runs the risk of creating a two-tier party. It was exacerbated by a battle between the two tendencies victorious in the competition for the mayoral team in the early years of the PT's government: the radical Catholics, supporting mayor Olívio Dutra; and the Maoists (now mellowed into Gramscians) supporting deputy mayor Tarso Genro. This left the Trotskyist-inclined tendency marginalised in government, even though it is very strong in the party. This process led early in the life of the PT government to what Luciano Brunet, the experienced *petista* who worked for the CRC described as 'a rupture between party and government, which weakened the party'. 'At times it seemed as if people in government didn't care what the party thought.'

This rift is still felt. There is a growing gulf between government *petistas* and the party outside. Inside, there are intense debates but, says Brunet, 'the ordinary party members can become like spectators'. The weakness of the links between party and government except at election time has been reinforced, Brunet feels, by changes which make the PT like any other traditional social democratic party, with elections for delegates to conference and leading positions only once every three years. Luciano Brunet and others believe the PT should be moving in another direction, to become more pluralistic, more closely connected with the NGOs and campaigns that many *petistas* are anyway part of. 'If you want to have a participatory democracy, you need a party which reflects it', concludes Brunet. In his view, if the PT is a conscious brain, it needs to adapt to the fact that in creating a source of democratic power beyond the state, it has dismantled its monopoly of radical brainpower.

The power to deliver

The success of the participatory budget in driving Porto Alegre's municipal administration to spend the bulk of its investment budget on making the poor neighbourhoods fit to live in is clear. Most statistics indicate progress significantly ahead of other cities: 9,000 families, who twelve years ago lived in shacks, now have regularised brick housing; nearly the whole population (99 per cent) have treated water; the sewerage system serves 86 per cent of the city, compared with 46 per cent in 1989; the number of school students going on to university doubled from 1989 to 1995; over fifty schools have been built in the past ten years and truancy has fallen from 9 per cent to less than 1 per cent. A detailed analysis of the municipal budget after 1989 shows that the lower the average income of the PB region, the higher the volume of public investment per head. The report concludes that the participatory budget has functioned as 'a powerful instrument of the redistribution of wealth'.[9]

There are also examples of the participatory budget strengthening the hand of the municipality to gain social benefits for the city from private investors. In the early 1990s, for example, the French company Carrefour wanted to build one of its supermarkets in the North Central Region of Porto Alegre. This region has many small businesses, especially shops, and these small entrepreneurs were extremely angry. They reacted by organising a lively public meeting and decided to take their concerns to the PB plenary. 'We wanted to set up a committee to negotiate for compensation for the small businesses in the area, as a condition of the new supermarket', said one of the activists. 'The participatory budget was the obvious channel for this proposal.'

The outcome was unprecedented. Carrefour had never before had to make real concessions to gain entry into a new market place. While normally its supermarkets let space inside for around twenty local shops, the Porto Alegre committee won agreement for forty at affordable rents. The company also agreed to employ young people, as they are suffering most from high unemployment in the region, and to help fund training schemes. The government had in the past successfully bargained for infrastructural improvements from transnationals like McDonalds, but it had never before obtained social improvements; it seems likely that the small entrepreneurs gained confidence, moral clout and political backing through discussing their demands and winning the support of the PB.

One of the arguments against participatory democracy is that it tends to be short lived, consisting in explosive moments of popular activity which demonstrate people's creativity but not how such creativity could be the basis of a sustainable system of government. In cities such as Porto Alegre and Santa André, however, the PB has led to the creation of lasting institutions, allowing citizens significantly greater power than they could achieve through conventional forms of democracy. Popular participation in the PB institutions grows year by year, and this extension of democracy has also brought material benefits to the city, including a redistribution of wealth, which middle-class voters recognise as benefiting the city as a whole.

But participatory democracy in these Brazilian cities is not only about structures, it is also about sustaining a culture through which people gain the confidence and sense of solidarity to feel able to participate. Like any experiment in democracy, Brazil's PT-governed cities are vulnerable – the murder of Celso Daniel is a tragic reminder of that. But the aim is the creation of positive alternatives. The co-operation and mutual respect that have grown up between PT mayors and local PB institutions rest on a wider political culture within the PT and the social movements which influence it, that assumes people have the potential for co-operative self-government. This is not a naïve belief that such potential simply has to be harnessed for participatory democracy to be born. On the contrary, the PT municipal governments have put considerable resources into popular education in the belief that elected politicians are but one route to democratic control and that the people have a right and capacity to participate directly in the affairs of state.

Conclusion: a new backbone for democracy

In one sense, the civic power which has grown up around the participatory budget depends on the state institutions being willing to share power. There would not be the sustained levels of participation, the popular basis for this civic power, if there were not significant public, i.e. state, resources at stake. But the new source of power that develops once this condition is in place has a life and dynamic of its own, which Porto Alegre's municipality respects and supports. The rules and meetings of the participatory budget institutionalise its independence and protect it against unilateral action by the state.

The transparency and publicly negotiated character of the rules for the PB ensure that it is widely respected and supported. More than twelve years since its inception, it is perceived to have a legitimacy distinct from, but not opposed to, the electoral institutions of the mayor and the municipal assembly. The government cannot change PB rules by its own authority – everything has to be negotiated in a process that, until the last legal moment of agreeing the budget, is heavily weighted towards the popular participants. The PB is an extension of democracy, not a competing structure. It effectively makes the mayor's electoral mandate a daily living pressure on the state apparatus.

Conventionally, elected representatives delegate detailed investment decisions to unelected administrators: the PB in this respect adds to the democratic legitimacy of the government of the city. Added to this moral power is the detailed knowledge and know-how that comes from the participants within the community, so that municipal councillors and the mayor are no longer dependent only on technical staff but have democratic allies with inside local knowledge who can challenge the administration if it is inefficient or corrupt. This combination of demo-cratic legitimacy and practical knowledge is proving desirable in other areas of the administration, too. Participatory decision-making has turned out to be a more socially efficient way of running things, deliv-ering, by all accounts, a better city in which to live.

The democratic legitimacy and valuing of practical knowledge inherent in participatory processes also have the power to strengthen civic power versus the private sector. In cases like Carrefour, the process was able to call the corporation's bluff precisely because the legitimacy and longevity of liberal capitalism is rooted in a proclaimed respect for democracy. Big companies rarely claim overtly that, because they have got the money, they can do what they like. The problem is, democracy rarely puts capitalism to the test; it is more often than not on its knees. In a relatively thriving commercial city like Porto Alegre, it need not be. As a desirable location for investment, it has considerable bargaining power.

It is not easy, nor quick, to construct the kind of participatory democracy practised in Porto Alegre. In 1998 the PT won the elections for the government of the state of Rio Grande do Sul. The new government began to extend the PB across the state but faced resistance in many rural areas still dominated by reactionary landowners and unable to get the system running as effectively as it had hoped. These and other factors (including bickering between different *petista* factions and accusations of public money being spent on party activities) meant that the PT lost the state government elections in Rio Grande do Sul in October 2002. On the other hand the principles of participatory budgeting are being strengthened across Brazil through Olívio Dutro becoming the minister for cities in Lula's government. His first move as minister was to arrange assemblies on a participatory budget in cities across the country to find local priorities for the spending of his ministry's budget. The constraints imposed by the IMF, however, will mean he cannot necessarily deliver, but the process will build up a democratic counter-pressure on the government to withstand the IMF's demands. Just as the participatory process that Dutra opened up when he became mayor of Porto Alegre stimulated popular pressure on the municipal government to end corruption and to stand up to the demands of multinational investors.

EAST MANCHESTER:
NO NEIGHBOURHOOD IS AN ISLAND

In 1998 Britain's Labour government announced the New Deal for Communities (NDC). Thirty-nine neighbourhoods across England were to receive around £50 million each over ten years on condition that the regeneration this money would fund, was 'community led'. Too much has been imposed from above,' said Tony Blair, 'when experience shows that success depends on the communities themselves having the power and taking responsibility to make things better.' Manchester Council lobbied successfully to get the government to make the neglected old industrial neighbourhoods of East Manchester – Beswick, Openshaw and Clayton, also the site of the 2002 Commonwealth Games – a 'pathfinder' area for the NDC programme.[1] In this way, in the autumn of 1999 there happened to be to be an experiment in participative government virtually on my doorstep. At least, such was the promise of the New Deal for Communities.

'Beacons for a Brighter Future'

So it was with curiosity in mind and a tape recorder in hand that I boarded the 53 bus at Rusholme's colourful 'curry mile' to get to Beswick's run-down shopping precinct. Until the late 1970s, the 53 had effectively been the works bus for thousands of chemical and engineering workers heading for Manchester's one-time industrial east, now home to 11,000 people. I retained little fragments of information about the area – there was once a pit near the site of the Commonwealth Games; the canals that ran through the area had been the life-blood of Britain's industrial revolution. I remembered a Manchester United supporter once proudly describing to me the humble origins of his glamorous team – 'lads playing football on a piece of scabby land in Clayton'. Not to be outdone, a Manchester City supporter told me that his team also started life in East Manchester, playing on a piece of land in the middle of Beswick locally known as Donkey Common. But to me, like many of the Mancunians drawn initially to the city by the university, East Manchester was unknown territory.

The bus dropped me outside a building site on the corner of the Ashton Old Road and Alan Turing Way – a wide road built mainly with Manchester's Olympic bid in mind, and which almost destroyed the local market. Most of the area is now intersected by similarly perilous arterial roads that slice ruthlessly through what used to be strongly connected neighbourhoods. With some trepidation I walked down this dual carriageway, past boarded-up houses, across Bosworth Street into Grey Mare Lane, home of a grim, eight-story police station, and then into the precinct where most of the shops had become council offices of one sort or another. I pressed the bell for the NDC: here I was, a seven-minute drive from the centre of the city that had been my home for ten years, and yet I felt a complete stranger.

The flip side of Margaret Thatcher's market-led prosperity was the creation of inner-city areas like East Manchester, where problems now run too deep for the under-funded city councils that have to manage them. Rusting signs left over from the 1970s proclaim 'East Manchester Improvement Area'. More often than not the surrounding buildings are boarded up. Statistics reinforce first impressions: over 30 per cent of all houses are empty; up to 30 per cent of the residents – depending on how the figures are collected – are unemployed; over 52 per cent of households receive income support and housing benefit. The local NDC has been optimistically named 'Beacons for a Brighter Future'. There is something of a tradition to NDCs giving themselves evangelical titles – in Barton Hill, Bristol, they not only call themselves 'Heart of the Community', but their shop-front is covered with voluptuous red hearts. In Beswick the entrance was austere. Waiting by the entryphone, I announced myself tentatively and walked upstairs to pick up the literature which would give me at least the official steer. The women running the reception office were friendly; a box of Quality Street was out to share. The photos on the wall showed residents and staff madly celebrating the announcement of the success of the £50 million bid. Rather rashly, this included a picture of council leader Richard Leese and residents posing with a giant £50 million cheque. 'Immediate money', it seemed to say – just what people would like to think. In fact, NDC money never comes in advance of spending, all projects are subject to a rigorous (many would say unnecessarily pedantic) process of appraisal and even then money is only released in tranches as targets are met. Still, it was interesting to see someone daring to raise people's expectations in Tony Blair's puritanical new Britain.

That night I pondered the NDC's 200-page delivery plan, drawn up in order to secure the funding by council officers after consultation with community representatives. The document hinted at a variety of communities, geographically, socially and ethnically, and I wondered how I could find them. Who were they? What did they do? And what did they make of this new hybrid (part-council, part-government, part-residents' associations, part-'voluntary sector') – the New Deal for Communities?

To get my bearings I began to visit local haunts. Savori's chip shop; the Caribbean takeaway in the precinct; Stan Pargiter's bus taking chatty pensioners to Thursday bingo; the queue for hot dogs at East Feast, the annual summer carnival organised by the East Manchester Community Forum (EMCF); Oggi's café in the Venture Centre (home to a multitude of campaigns and services run by local volunteers). I even donned helmet and tracksuit to go go-carting with the Higher Openshaw Youth Club.

Organising traditions

A local councillor had told me that this was a population of 'no hopers', meaning that those who stayed did so because they could not get out, financially or otherwise. There may be some truth in this, but many people stayed from positive choice, because of their deep roots in the area. These roots included labour movement traditions, embedded in East Manchester's industrial past, and traditions of community activism. Community organising in these villages has been divided, dispersed and under-resourced, but it has survived nevertheless.

Take Irene Barron. She got involved in the NDC after she and her neighbours turned a derelict piece of land (and base of the burgling fraternity) into a community garden. 'Someone said why not go to see the NDC for a grant. "The what?" I asked. I'd never heard of it. But I went down and talked to Tracey [the NDC's residents' liaison officer] and that led to going to the residents' forum and generally speaking my mind.' From where does she get her forthright approach to the authorities and her belief in the co-operative values of grassroots organising? 'My dad was a great socialist. He really believed that power should be with the people. "These people in the council," he used to say, "they're your servants, you must always make that clear to them."' Trade union histories popped up throughout my interviews: Veronica Powell, the quiet but shrewd resident who chaired the NDC board unopposed for its first three years, is an active member of the Transport and General Workers Union. Jeff Burns, taxi driver by day and martial arts teacher and volunteer youth organiser by night, was a trade unionist in engineering. Roy Staniforth, the most assiduous and methodical of tenant organisers, had been a shop steward. Elaine Wright, a forceful community organiser who also works as an administrator in the NDC office, had in the 1970s been a shop steward in the equal pay strike at Lawrence Scotts, a local – long closed – engineering factory. Bill Booth, leading representative of those who nurture the neat cluster of allotments by the side of Philips Park, had been a trade unionist since he went to sea in the 1950s. And so on. At times it felt as if the demanding processes of the NDC, requiring a good deal of bargaining and alertness to democratic procedure, were awakening skills and values which had lain dormant for decades.

Barbara Taylor, a driving spirit amongst the residents, is a sharp negotiator, not because of trade union traditions but because she lives and breathes the immediate needs of Newcombe Close and its inhabitants. Like a lioness defending her den, she weighs up every new development, every stranger, human or policy, by what they will mean for her patch. She is eager though to make wider connections and to see her neighbourhood in a wider context, if that will lead to change. There are also traditions of community organising established in earlier fights with the council. Sandra Webb first did battle in the late 1980s over the building of the Velodrome in Clayton, part of the preparation for Manchester's Olympic bid. Sandra lives in Bank Street, next door to the Velodrome. She and her neighbours suffered the noise and dust of the construction of the concrete edifice but were never invited to go inside. Their children were never encouraged to use its exciting facilities. Their complaints to the council were brushed aside, she says. In those days the community had no power and were, it seems given no respect. The experience has influenced her stance towards anything that emanates from the council. 'Accept nothing; doubt everything' has effectively become her motto.

Then there are the variety of organisations that make up what is rather misleadingly labelled 'the voluntary sector' (it covers a wide range of organisations, some with paid staff and others totally dependent on volunteers, some locally rooted, some connected to national or city-wide organisations). There is the EMCF, which brings together local groups of every possible kind across the whole of East Manchester in order to provide a means of organising mutual support, information exchange, joint campaigns, a much-used Playbus and East Feast. The EMCF also initiated what has become a widely valued training project in organising and management skills which now has an ever-expanding – subject to funds – life of its own. Similarly independent is another EMCF-initiated project, the Manchester Youth Volunteer Project, which has developed an acute sense of the power of young people as a force for change. The thriving Credit Union, with its welcoming 'open door' office in the Beswick precinct, is a focal point for people wanting financial advice and support, whether they are members or not. It has also been an important source of training in the values and practicalities of co-operative, mutual ways of organising. There is the long-established Settlement,[2] which provides a base for a range of community activities, from an educational playschool to pensioners' bingo. A more recent addition to the local voluntary sector is the Joint Openshaw Group (JOG), backed by a community-oriented housing association, which provides imaginative courses and recreational activities for young people. There is also a variety of projects meeting specific needs: Having a Voice, a group organising around mental health; a community IT project; a community farm. There is a growing network of people working on different aspects of recycling, most notably the community recycling company Emerge and Fairfield Composting.[3] The latter is driven by an indomitable young granny, Val Rawlinson, who has long been trying to set up a social enterprise around composting and horticulture and who persistently challenges the authorities on all things environmental. The origins of this network go back to an effective local campaign against an incinerator in the early 1990s. Finally (and as in many neglected neighbourhoods), a number of churches with high-energy clergy and low-number congregations are also a source of support for community initiatives in the area. The non-conformist United Reform Church, for example, a sort of spiritual version of libertarian socialism, explicitly aims to help people find in themselves the strength and self-confidence to resist injustice.

As is common in old industrial areas in England, this is a predominantly white area. The old census reports that 6 per cent of the population are 'non-white'.[4] There are scattered families of Afro-Caribbeans and
even fewer Asians. A group of Chinese people settled in Beswick in the
early 1990s, mainly to work at the nearby Chinese Cash and Carry. In the
1980s a number of Somali families – many fleeing war – came to the area,
but most left around 1997. Fatima, who arrived in 1965 to be with her
Mancunian husband, tells the story: 'Their houses were attacked and they
were attacked in the street; mainly by youth but parents must have
known. The police told them they must move. They said there was
nothing they could do. I think that was wrong.' As if to prove her point
Fatima has been working with the Beswick and Bradford Community
Project to document the racism the Somalis faced and also to build on the
positive support they received to overcome racism in the area. Anti-racist
work in the area has received reinforcement from among the growing
number of asylum seekers who the government has dispersed to this area.
Some bring with them traditions of political organising. Denis Turner, a
mining engineer from Sierra Leone, had, for example, stood for parliament there on a platform of multi-party democracy, but he and his wife
had faced constant attacks from the rebels. When he came to Britain
he ended up living two minutes' walk from the Venture Centre, and eager
to reach out to other people in the same predicament as him he got
in touch with the East Manchester Black and Ethnic Minorities
Group (EMBLEM). EMBLEM was initiated through the EMCF to
ensure that the voices of black people and ethnic minorities had an
impact on the regeneration process. The end result of Denis's work with
voluntary groups in the area is a regular drop-in and support centre for
asylum seekers.

These then were some of the traditions likely to shape the community
side of what it meant for regeneration to be 'community led'. Old local
traditions of democratic organisation are surviving against the odds: new
ones are being brought in by events thousands of miles away.

A picture of power

The wider context

The NDC is part of the council's strategy for regenerating the whole of East Manchester. The council planned the 2002 Commonwealth Games to be a catalyst to one of most ambitious regeneration projects in the whole country, co-ordinated by a company called New East Manchester Limited (NEM). Formed a few months after the 'community-led' idea of the NDC appeared on the horizon, NEM was initially a very much more conventional outfit than the NDC. Both it and the sports-led strategy it was formed to lead were the brainchild of city council chief executive, Howard Bernstein. Bernstein's ambition for the company was that it would update for the Commonwealth Games the strategy originally formulated for the Manchester Olympic bid, and use lessons learned from reconstructing the city centre after the devastation of the IRA bomb to regenerate the neglected estates of East Manchester. The rather crucial difference was that thousands of people live in East Manchester; the city centre was a bomb site plus patches of complete dereliction.

NEM's remit is most of East Manchester, from Ancoats near the city centre to the city boundaries with Tameside – just up the Ashton Old Road, beyond Openshaw.[5] NEM was originally created as a partnership of public and private players to redevelop acres of potentially profitable land within easy access of the city centre. 'The community' was not thought of as an active partner. In the early stages – 1998–99 – it was more or less assumed that whatever brought prosperity to the area would benefit its residents. It was not long, however, before the ethics of the NDC had at least a formal influence and three community representatives became NEM directors. Now the NEM and the NDC closely co-operate and many staff are employed by both. They even share a new pagoda-style building on Grey Mare Lane, opposite the Beswick precinct.

The council's initial approach to East Manchester left little room for residents. The focal points of the plans were: Sportcity, a complex of national sporting facilities; Asda – the biggest Asda Walmart in Europe; and a new high-value housing project by the Ashton Canal and Philips Park. In Beswick, the NEM planned to attract private developers to build family housing within a mixed price range and to commission some new social housing. Council housing in the area was to be taken over by a large new housing company, though there were also to be one or two smaller stock transfers to housing associations. What was there left, then, for the community to determine? How to get crime rates down, how to clean up the area, and possibly how to have an influence over some health and education programmes seemed to be what was on offer.

Local residents, however, had several potential sources of leverage. Most lay in weaknesses in the council position – historically, council services had failed to meet the needs of local people. The NDC management knew that in order to achieve improvements in service provision, not only money was needed but also residents' input and commitment.

Because the council's reputation as a provider of services was nil and worse, council personnel had little authority beyond what they could salvage through good personal relationships with residents. Leading politicians and senior officers knew that as any regeneration package could be undermined by a disaffected or disintegrating community, so could the good image of Manchester which the council hoped to promote through the Commonwealth Games. The commitment of most of the NDC staff to improved public services made them allies of the residents, supporting them in dealings with council officials, public agencies and the private sector. Some of the officials involved, in both the NDC and the council, had experience of the regeneration of Hulme in South Manchester,[6] where they had to work at building relationships with people who had good reason to be deeply sceptical of every sort of official. Certainly, more than the normal council processes of consultation would seem to be required here – 'We've seen it all before' could have been a banner across Alan Turing Way greeting the new, mostly ex-council, NDC staff on their way to the office.

Money and mechanisms

£50 million plus another £30 million from the Social Regeneration Budget sounds a lot of money in an area where people have seen the quality of their lives steadily decline over recent years through lack of resources.[7] 'When we came here in 1976, there were good shops, a swimming pool, youth clubs, it was a great place to live', said Beswick resident Sheila Rhodes. 'Now it's a different story.' Now the shops are mostly demolished or boarded up; there is no leisure centre or swimming pool; community centres are under-resourced; there is only one decent youth centre; local businesses have closed; transport is poor. As people moved out, unscrupulous and unregulated private landlords moved in, careless of the condition of the houses and the support that their tenants might need and content to sit back and receive their rent through housing benefit. Neither the council nor the expanding housing associations provided good, alternative models of housing management. A vicious spiral of decline set in. Public agencies from the police through to social services had given up, so it seemed to local people, and were treating the area and its residents with contempt.

The result is that the pride which people felt in their neighbourhood was shot through with constant anxiety. 'I just want to be able to leave the house without being frightened about what I'll be returning to', was how Christine Connaughton, a council tenant in Openshaw, described her bottom-line hope for the NDC. In this context, the additional money can do little more than provide basic facilities and be used as leverage to make the services which already exist responsive to the needs of the residents. It hardly compensates for the millions of pounds effectively taken out of the area in factory closures and cuts in services in the years since the Conservative Party's election victory in 1979. Moreover, fully £20 million of the NDC £50 million is to be spent on housing – going some of the way to making good the poor maintenance that is, in part, the legacy of the Conservative's ruthless starvation of council housing. Council housing makes up over 50 per cent of housing in the NDC area.[8]

National NDC guidelines stress 'community leadership' as opposed to the ritual 'community involvement', though officials in the government's regional offices whose job it is to supervise the NDCs in their region[9] frankly admit they have little idea what this means. At a minimum it has meant either a majority of community representatives on the NDC board or that they are the largest subgroup. On the thirteen-strong East Manchester NDC board for example, made up of representatives from the community, public agencies, the 'voluntary sector' and private business, the six community representatives form the largest subgroup. One of them, Veronica Powell, is in the chair.

Since an important theme in this book is the connections between local experiments in participatory democracy and the political process, it is worth noting the lack of direct involvement in the East Manchester NDC of the local elected councillors. In most NDCs, local councillors are present on the board or at least observe, but in East Manchester residents had had enough of party politicians. 'They think they've got power and influence but we want to speak for ourselves. They can come if they are residents and then they must come as ordinary residents', said Powell. The low election turnouts in these wards shows that this reflects a widespread disillusion with party politics. Turnout at the local elections in 1998 in the two wards that cover these urban villages was less than 15 per cent, though in one ward at least it has risen significantly since.[10] As residents have grown in confidence they work well with councillors on equal terms.

In many NDCs, though not East Manchester, community representatives on the board are directly elected by a vote of every adult citizen. In some of these other cities NDC neighbourhood elections have commanded high turnouts – double, sometimes treble the turnout in local council elections.[11] In Manchester, the community representatives on the NDC board are elected by residents' associations and are accountable to the Residents' Forum, an umbrella group of residents' associations formed to prepare for the NDC. As I write, however, residents and NDC staff are reconsidering the nature of elections for the board, a sign of how the process of community involvement has developed a certain momentum of its own: 'It's got to be opened up. I don't think the present voting system is truly accountable', says Irene Barron, chair of a residents' association in Clayton. (At the time of writing, each association has two votes for candidates who must be supported by a majority of their own association.) Some residents favour every resident having a vote, with a requirement that candidates are members of local residents' groups. Other ideas have been suggested. It is a continuing debate.

The formal way in which the majority of residents' representatives participate in the NDC is through monthly meetings of the Residents' Forum where people can have their collective say about the way the regeneration money is being spent. Residents may brief their representatives or make demands and complaints to the NDC's seemingly unbossy boss, Sean McGonigle, who originally chaired and now sits in on all the meetings.

The Voluntary Sector Consortium is the other organisation involving local people which has a (single) representative on the NDC board. This consortium was created specifically to bring together the diverse range of voluntary groups to form a group that could be a coherent 'partner' within the NDC. The NDC has given support to the consortium, and in return its work has been nourished by these organisations. But there has also been a tension between 'the voluntary sector' – often rather artificially bundled into one camp – and the residents' forum – again rather misleadingly assumed to be homogenous.

There are a number of factors which have produced mutually reinforcing suspicions and distance. First, the NDC was organised originally through the city council's housing department. The department had also worked with and funded local residents' associations which were formed primarily around issues of housing management. These associations were the council's main point of liaison with 'the community', and they became the NDC's main channel of communication with the same.

Second, voluntary organisations in East Manchester, as across the country, bore the marks of having to compete for funds which were becoming increasingly scarce. As a result, differences in goals and values have become sources of division and mutual wariness, and it has sometimes been difficult for the voluntary sector to develop a united and concerted strategy towards the NDC. Third, the voluntary groups are sometimes seen as 'outsiders' and residents question the legitimacy of their role in the decision-making process. The reality varied: like those in the NDC and other public agencies, some staff live as well as work locally, while some live further away. Some, like EMBLEM, are locally managed and staffed, others are managed as city-wide organisations with an East Manchester base. There is also the inevitable, and healthy, controversy about who reaches 'the community' best.

More generally, there existed in the early years of the NDC a protectiveness of established relationships which is only now beginning to open up as a result of working together on the ground. Discussion is underway at least informally about how to open up the main processes of participation to at least the local community groups. 'It would improve the NDC's ability to reach out. At present it does not connect with people like me; I always have to go and find out what is going on', said Val Blake from EMBLEM.

Long-established voluntary organisations are concerned that the NDC, with all its money (relatively speaking) and thirty-seven staff, unintentionally takes things over. The NDC has had to become aware that it may sometimes be treading on the toes of existing community projects. Voluntary groups have complained of situations where the NDC helps to fund an established activity and then has too much say in shaping and determining its future, weakening the independence and long-term survival of the project. 'The NDC is only here for ten years after all. We've got to negotiate with them a method by which they can support us which strengthens our independence and self-reliance. At present the system can be quite disempowering, even though it aims to be the reverse', says Sue Bowen, co-ordinator of the EMCF, in her usual direct manner. This presents a dilemma: while the NDC is committed to community leadership, centrally held government purse strings mean it must meet 'outcome' targets. The government urges speedy delivery; its centrally decided timetable does not take account of the messy, chaotic phases that a genuinely democratic process often inevitably goes through. Short-term outcomes are often valued above processes that could lead to longer term success and stability. This can lead to a reluctance to take risks, and to enable people to arrive at new solutions through trial and error – a necessary part of participatory democracy. In Manchester this tendency was reinforced by the imminence of the Commonwealth Games. The date of the games, July 2002, acted as an unspoken deadline during much of the NDC's first three years.

The messiness of a democratic process is rarely visible in the formal structures, but is more so in practical decisions like how a vital service should be managed, in whose interest, or which projects should get funding and on what conditions. Final decisions on how to make the NDC's £50 million and the council's mainstream spending responsive to local needs are formally agreed at the NDC board, but preparatory work should be done through the 'task groups' that focus on specific themes.

Participation in these open task groups is intended to be another way for local people to exert some influence over spending decisions. The double job of a task group is to initiate projects and monitor spending. Groups exist for crime, housing and neighbourhood management, education and training, youth, social issues, environment and business development. My interviews with residents revealed varying experiences of these groups. Housing and crime have become issues over which the public agencies in the area, particularly the police and the council's housing department, are vigorously called to account by the task groups. Some of the others, however, soon became too dominated by public agencies or large NGOs: 'We didn't feel welcome' is a remark repeated by several residents about the environment group, for instance. As people's confidence has grown, however, so has a determination to make the public agencies pay attention to their ideas. Some of the most effective forms of residents' involvement – well beyond the residents' associations – has been through specific projects with teenage parents, for example, or with drug users, or with young offenders, or old people.[12] This work is providing a lot of new knowledge about people's needs. 'We need to find ways in which this work can influence the main decision-making structures; a lot of ideas are coming from this kind of work', says one of the NDC officers involved.

People power: successes and frustrations

A night out at Donaheys

After several months of sitting on the sidelines of the monthly cycle of meetings, I had got to know the main players and started to feel at home. I even found myself invited to play Anne Robinson in an NDC version of the TV programme *The Weakest Link* planned for the end-of-year celebrations in February 2001. In the rambling surroundings of Donaheys night club, the evening proved to be an interesting symbol of the shifting power structures within the community.

The evening event followed a day conference of the voluntary sector, the NDC, residents and people from local public agencies, held to review the first two years' work. The hope for the conference was that as well as being an exchange of information, it could ease tensions among some of the 'partners' – 'partnerships' being officialese for what in reality are complicated and unequal relationships. After the conference, there was a mood of relief – a sense of so far, so good. There were still eight years to make sure that this regeneration would not be the patch-up job of the past and would be sustainable after the money had been spent. Now, it was time to relax. The style of the evening was more voluntary sector than council – organised primarily by Tracey Annette, the NDC's residents' liaison officer, and Sue Bowen from the EMCF, children from the Medlock Valley School made the podiums, a friend of a friend provided the music, Inspector Jones drew up the quiz questions – all for free. Away from the procedure-dominated style of the city council, NDC staff are freer to improvise a more responsive, flexible method of working. 'We all muck in', said Cath Moran, the NDC office manager.

Among the first contenders to face humiliation were two priests. Tim Presswood, a collarless Baptist clergyman, strongly influenced by liberation theology and valued member of the NDC board, was the first to fall victim to the ruthless voting tactics of his co-participants in the game that night. Father Tim, the respected local priest at St Bridget's Catholic Church and chairman of the Education Action Zone, was the second. Other contestants to fail included Sean McGonigle and Steve Mycio, the deputy chief executive of Manchester City Council. Between them they presented a perfect model of senior public officials: relaxed, humorous, customer friendly but nevertheless in control. (Steve Mycio, who has a handwritten note in his office which reads 'Are we meeting the needs of the people of Manchester?', brought an interesting background to the job: as a militant young shop steward of the National Union of Public Employees he had superglued shut the doors of the housing offices during a strike, a sure way of ensuring that the pickets were successful.)

The final round was between Sandra Black and Sheila Rhodes. Sheila Rhodes is a woman of great determination who had chosen to live in Beswick in the late 1970s when it was considered 'posh', but who has watched the neighbourhood decline for some time now. At first, the council brushed aside the residents' demands – for prompt repairs, for painting, security – but: 'We stuck around and with persistent mythering we eventually got a housing officer who treated us with respect.' How tenants accustomed to this informal and highly localised power cope with becoming formally powerful over a wider area of policy, is an important part of the East Manchester story.

Sandra Black is from a very different background, though is equally determined. Originally from Belfast, she describes herself – quite inacc-urately – as inarticulate because she left school at fourteen, and at first did not speak out much at residents' forums. When she's unhappy with what the authorities are doing, however, her inhibitions disappear: 'There are few grey areas for me: I see things as black and white and I'm not easy to talk round.' Now retired, she has time to fight for her community. Both of these women were well known to the audience, part of a network of middle-aged women who take a determined pride in the area and have a fighting self-confidence that with money, political support and a genuinely equal partnership with local people, East Manchester can be transformed. In another era they might have been councillors, but they could never toe the line in the way of present-day politicians.

As the evening wore on, the audience instinctively chose to break the rules to support these two women: they positively willed the women to win. Any difficult question and a murmured answer would float magically up from the floor. Sandra or Sheila would look innocently at the ceiling and then come out with the accurate information, to loud cheers. By the time we arrived at the final round the questions hardly mattered, the people had won.

Who benefits from success?

Is this victory really symbolic of real 'people power' in the East Manchester villages of Openshaw, Clayton and Beswick? The type of power in which the NDC is dealing (as are all the participatory structures discussed in this book) is power over resources – money, land and buildings. In Manchester, as in many 'successful' cities across the Western world, power over such resources determines who benefits from the unevenly distributed prosperity which capitalism can bring. There's no doubt that Manchester City Council has led a near miracle in inner-city regeneration, if the city is understood as a unit; its growth is probably second only to London. But like any modern city, Manchester is divided into deeply different parts – the divisions faithfully reproducing the concentrations of money in different parts of the city. Those people in twenty-seven of Manchester's thirty-three electoral wards – 80 per cent of the population – live in 10 per cent of the most deprived wards in England. The city's boundaries were tightly drawn in the Conservative Party's reorganisation of local government so that the council's tax base includes none of the 'gin-and-jaguar' suburbia from which some redistribution would be in order.

The problem faced by Manchester Council when it won the money to start the NDC in the east of the city was that all their efforts at economic development did little more than reproduce the inequalities of the rest of the capitalist economy. Many new jobs were being created, but they were going to skilled and already employed people changing jobs and coming in from outside the city: the level of unemployment in poorer localities remained stubbornly unchanged.[13] The state of housing shows a similar picture: there are many new homes in the centre of Manchester, but only for those who can afford to buy. While parts of suburbia transport themselves to the lofts, duplexes and condominiums of the city centre, none of this wealth trickles down to the thousands of city residents half a mile away who cannot afford such 'lifestyle'.

Can a single neighbourhood achieve a different kind of distribution from the rest of the city, through resident participation in the management of funds dispensed, and closely monitored, by central government? How far do efforts to achieve popular participation come up against obstacles that require change in city-wide, national or even international institutions? Can shifts in power towards local people over local management of public resources act as a pressure for a wider redistribution of wealth and power? And is the wider political system sufficiently democratic for that local pressure to work its way through to the real centres of power? All of these are questions raised by the new policies of regeneration. The experiences of other cities has not been hopeful.[14]

Consultation, old-style

The idea of a shift in power towards local people was not part of Howard Bernstein's original vision for regenerating East Manchester. The trickle-down of economic benefit and an improvement in the quality of life certainly was; his assumption was that this would happen through the council striking good bargains with the developers, after which the residents would be asked for their opinions on the developers' plans.

In its early days, before the NDC had really got underway, NEM had contracted a traditional property consultant, Grimleys, to prepare 'the masterplan' for East Manchester.[15] Grimleys in turn subcontracted the publicity for the consultation with local residents to another private company. It was at one of these subcontracted events that I had my first taste of consultation in East Manchester.

Late one Thursday afternoon in Autumn 1999, I approached the beleaguered-looking Openshaw Community Centre, expecting a crowded room in which I could be a fly on the wall. To my dismay, I walked into an almost empty room. In one corner was a brash display board sporting photos of council leader Richard Leese and residents drinking champagne against the background of the EMCF playbus. It seemed out of place in an environment where, as yet, there was so little to celebrate. Two staff from Grimleys were patiently listening to two tenants anxious about what would happen to their street. My hopes of eavesdropping surreptitiously were declining rapidly. Alun Francis, the NDC's youth officer, was registering names – three so far. I owned up to why I was there. Another tenant wandered in, angry that she'd only got the leaflet that day. Then came an anxious-looking woman, friendly but tweedy, who turned out to be the then chief executive of NEM. Evidently the subcontracted consultancy firm had bungled delivery of the leaflet inviting people to come and she was, albeit politely, fuming.

This may have been a bad day, but the nature of the NEM's consultation was revealing. It was far distant from anything that could conceivably be called 'community led', and from the complicated dynamics which were beginning to develop in the NDC's relationship with local people. It was a 'Please come and look at the plan in your local community hall, and we'll answer your queries'-type consultation, whose hallmark is precisely an absence of relationships approaching anything like equality. An egalitarian approach would involve a deliberative process: debate, and joint decision-making. Even run efficiently, these 'drop-in' or questionnaire consultations, on their own, echo the benevolent social engineering of Beatrice Webb which presumed that most people can only complain and have no ability to contribute to the solution. All consultations need do is register particular individual problems or needs. No other relationship is established, and problems thus gathered may or may not be acted upon.

Grimleys' final 'plan' ran to twelve volumes, but none of them showed much understanding of the needs and demands of local residents. A subgroup of NDC and NEM staff and board members eventually rewrote the plan drawing on their working relationship with local residents. The alternative masterplan became a 'draft framework' with as much room in it as possible for future resident involvement in the local detail. The rewrite of the plan left open to democratic pressures what would otherwise have been tied up by the private sector. The NDC's approach to involving the community is experimental rather than coherent. 'We're on a learning curve' is a constant and refreshing refrain coming from officials. What that learning means in reality remains to be seen.

Questions of accountability

The first sign of learning was over the appointment of staff. It was an indication of a deeper issue of staff accountability; who has power over the management of the NDC. Resident representatives felt very strongly that the NDC staff should be responsible to the board, not to the council. National NDC rules imply that all spending is managed by an independent board, and that a well-established body, normally the local city council, acts simply as guarantor of its financial probity. In Manchester the NDC board was not a distinct legal entity. It was administratively independent of the council, but the full implications of this were yet to be worked out in practice. Lines of accountability were blurred because many staff were seconded from the council, or had half their salary paid by the council. Meanwhile resident board members, who had responsibility for ensuring the NDC met local needs, grew frustrated with having no authority to make things happen. The matter came to a head over the selection of the leader of the important 'neighbourhood nuisance' team. This took place without any resident involvement. The man who had been the acting team leader for some months had built up strong trust and respect among the residents. He wasn't given the job.

I sat in on the January 2001 meeting of the board. Things were visibly tense. Gone was the relaxed atmosphere that normally exudes from informal repartee between Sean McGonigle and resident reps. Elaine Wright, the residents' spokeswoman on this occasion, sternly introduced a statement which asked 'If the NDC is resident-led, should we not be informed of what's going on?' 'Absence of information,' it said, 'leads to mistrust and a feeling of discontentment.' To prove their point, the residents listed a series of grievances. They referred back to a previous promise that they would be invited onto interview panels as observers for any important jobs. They raised the issue of secondments – from the council – and how widely they were advertised. Their lack of trust on these employment issues had come to such a point, they said, that they feared NDC posts were being taken over by the council's housing department. Indeed, legally, the leader of the neighbourhood nuisance team was employed by the housing department. Their statement concluded with the demand that 'In future all positions in the NDC have a Residents Representative on the interview panel.'

In the discussion that followed Steve Mycio put the council's point of view: 'The NDC isn't the council, it can have its own procedures.' This opened up the wider issue of local employment, how to make sure that local people had access to the growing number of public-service jobs in the area. Six months later, it was agreed that two residents would be involved in all stages of employing new staff – from composing the job description to sitting on the final interviewing panel. Other public agencies employing staff in the area have been asked to consider similar commitments. The system is not fully working, however. Some appointments or secondments happen in a hurry and there is only a small core of residents on the board who have enough time to do this detailed employment work.

This first serious conflict between the residents and NDC management illustrated a distinctive feature of the NDC's dynamic. The council and ex-council officers who originally began the NDC did not automatically share their power from the beginning. This was not a neighbourhood version of Porto Alegre. But they did generally give way, or at least negotiate some change, within the council's overall policy framework, when the residents pushed on issues over which the NDC had power.

The question of staff accountability also raised the issues of how far representatives of a particular neighbourhood can have the final say, and how staff who need to be accountable to local people also manage their wider statutory or democratic obligations to the city as a whole. These concerns arose most intensely over the issue of housing allocation and who should be housed in the empty houses in the area. What would happen when residents of Beswick or Clayton got suspicious of the policies of the council's housing department for accommodating homeless people, fearing that they would get an 'anti-social' family living nearby? Up until now the solution has been a fairly disastrous combination of the council imposing a good, egalitarian housing allocation policy without either explanation or adequate back-up services and, on the other hand, tenants' leaders trying to find solutions by making informal arrangements with housing officers to get the tenants they want. The opening up of these resulting tensions has led, at least in theory, to open negotiations of housing criteria, based on the wider housing obligations of the council and involving all the relevant services, not just housing. The transfer of the housing stock to the new housing company Eastlands, however, will also transfer the problem to the council/resident board of the new company.

On this issue as on many others, the term 'community led' can be misleading. There is a significant difference between issues where decisions about a local service only affect local residents and therefore can be taken at a community or neighbourhood level, and those where wider groups of people are affected. On the latter, it does not mean that community participation – and a real sharing of power – is inappropriate. Rather it means that forms of participation become more complex, as we saw in Porto Alegre, where the budget of a whole city was involved. A good example of the first kind of case is the battle for control over the Delamere Park bowling green.

People's parks?

As tenants and residents gained in confidence, they tried to wrest more control for themselves over the local delivery of services. In the case of parks this meant a serious shake up of Manchester Leisure, the council department responsible for most of the parks in Openshaw, Beswick and Clayton, and a department in urgent need of change. In spring 2001, Delamere Park and Toxteth Residents' Association, after an extended consultation with fellow residents about the development of their local park, insisted that the department should negotiate any change in the park with them. The council had proposed to put up a six-foot-high fence to protect the park's second bowling green from dogs and children. They were backed by the local bowling club, but faced opposition from the residents' association, who convened a meeting with council officials. The topic: how to reach a compromise about the contested fence. The place: the rough, cosy and very masculine veterans' hut in the park.

On the suggestion of the local parks worker who has most to do with the park and local residents, a solution was reached. He suggested a

low-level fence, and residents developed the idea, suggesting it be camou-
flaged by blackthorn hedge – a natural boundary. When the residents'
association chair, Glyn Williams (a determined man, sceptical of all
authority) said he'd better check this with Judith, his wife and secretary
of the association, Ron, secretary of the bowling club and custodian of
the hut, exploded: 'It's two women that run this park, it's just not right.'
For him, this deference to a woman was the final straw. Gender suddenly
erupted as an underlying issue: the protection of the male exclusivity of
the bowling fraternity against what they saw as the threat of powerful
women. Ron felt that bowling itself was under attack, and he was articu-
lating the male bowlers' view of 'community'.

As the meeting progressed, a whole new discussion opened up as the
issue of the fence came to symbolise the exclusivity of the bowling club
and the veterans' hut. Could there be more access to the bowling green
for young people, who had no equivalent place to congregate, and
women? There was a suggestion of taster courses, open days and more
efforts to make bowling open to everyone. Plans for all these suggestions
were agreed along with the blackthorn hedge and a canopy for the
bowlers' hut by the green: the outcome of the meeting was more or less
acceptable to everyone.

But without the self-confidence of the residents' association, things
might not have turned out that way. The opening remarks of Jeff
Staniforth, the senior officer from the outdoor leisure department had
been cryptic and unpromising: 'For various reasons', he had said, 'we
know what works and what doesn't work.' He later expanded this to
'Manchester Leisure's policy is that we're happy if the bowlers are happy'.
The leisure department have a close relationship with the powerful North
West Bowls Council. In the normal course of events Staniforth and his
colleagues would have presented their plan, subjected themselves to a bit
of a protest and then gone away to do what they always intended to do.
But by forcing an open negotiation the residents had moved things on
from this 'traditional' assumption of how a public amenity should be

managed. They now hold the officials responsible for the bowling green accountable to all residents, rather than just the interest group that has lobbied them and built up a cosy connection. It's something that probably could not be achieved and sustained by a local councillor on his or her own. This is a thread running through the East Manchester story: residents grasping for themselves some power over how public services are managed by taking literally the NDC's claim to be 'community led' and driving change themselves.

There are other issues however, on which residents take 'community leadership' seriously and push for change locally, only to come up against national or city-wide constraints. They have found they have few levers of power over this wider decision-making. It is as if participation should know its 'local' place.

Social housing: local participation, national quango, international finance

One of the biggest problems in the area, alongside the dire state of private rented housing, has been the state of neglect of council housing. Faced with a repair bill and debts in the housing account running into millions, and no powers to borrow on the financial market, Manchester Council felt they had no option but to accept the government's bribe of a clean financial slate and new investment via the National Housing Corporation. In order to qualify for this deal however, they would have to transfer their housing stock, subject to a 'yes' vote by the tenants, to an independent, purpose-built company. In effect they would be handing over one of their main means of redistributing resources, through rent subsidy, and of regenerating deprived neighbourhoods, through – if they changed their ways – creative housing management and related social enterprises. The sweetener was greater tenant involvement, and this offered some hope. 'I thought the new company could open things up; nothing could be much worse than what we have now', said Veronica Powell, a member of the steering committee preparing for Eastlands.

Two other tenants who hoped that the new housing company might be an opportunity for some real tenants' control over the management of the estate were Roy and Clare Staniforth. Having set up VORTA (Village of Openshaw Residents and Tenants Association), championing high-quality social housing and the rights of tenants, the Staniforths were among the first tenants also to join the steering committee. They were confident that residents could steer the not-for-profit company in the direction they wanted. In the first phase of the company, the residents had considerable leverage because the council needed them to promote a 'yes' vote for the transfer of the housing to the new company. What is more, the residents brought with them a dowry of around £20 million from the NDC. The residents on the company's steering group made a significant input into the business plan, drawing on what they had learnt in struggling with the council for good housing management.

Several months before tenants voted, in October 2002, on whether or not to transfer stock, the steering committee's decision-making powers were taken over by a 'shadow board'. The committee's job then became promotion of the stock transfer campaign in preparation for the vote (which proved to be an overwhelming 'yes' to stock transfer). The board of the new housing company would be made up of one-third tenant directors chosen by the original steering committee (and eventually the plan was by open election by fellow tenants), one-third directors chosen by the council and one-third independent directors chosen by a process of open advertising. After its initial dowries of public money, the new company would borrow on the financial markets but on commercial terms, and without the financial bargaining power or possibilities of cross subsidy of a city council.[16] The rents it would charge would be set on the basis of a government formula applied to rents across the country and across council and other forms of social housing. Though part of this formula includes the average income of the tenants concerned, it also includes 30 per cent of the rent being based on the market value of the property – a worrying prospect in an area where property values are expected to rise faster than average over the coming years.

When the rules of the National Housing Corporation, under which Eastlands would have to operate, were made clear, several residents on the steering committee were disappointed. Most difficult was the status and obligation that tenant reps would have as company directors. They would, like any company director, have to put the interests of the company first, which might, given that tenants would only make up a third of the board, conflict with their ability to be accountable to fellow tenants and, if necessary, fight for their needs. Most residents still felt they should carry on and make a go of it. But Roy and Clare decided the conflict would be too great. As Roy put it, 'I felt this could cut me off from the community. I'd heard this was the experience elsewhere.' He and Clare decided to leave the steering committee.

The Housing Corporation is a quango. It has a government-appointed board, created to support social housing outside local authorities. It used to be supportive of housing co-ops and innovative forms of social housing that aimed to continue the best practices of council housing – subsidised rents and accountable forms of management – but without the bureaucracy. However, Mrs Thatcher used it to supervise the dismantling of council housing in favour of various forms of privately provided social housing. As a result it became increasingly commercial in its approach, though its staff are supportive to tenants trying to cope with the new constraints. The Housing Corporation requires that new housing companies be run like traditional companies, with all the restrictions that implies.

The corporation is one of many notoriously unaccountable bodies that are steadily taking over the functions of local government. The difficulties that a group of increasingly confident residents are anticipating over Eastlands is one of several examples of an inconsistency running through New Labour's approach to regeneration. On the one hand the NDC programme is promoting community leadership and leading in many cases to the beginnings of a genuine sharing of power between representative and participatory institutions, while on the other hand some of the national institutions which actually hold the long-term power over regeneration resources do not meet stringent standards of representative democracy.[17]

Private housing: participation as power or as public relations?

If residents are to make the idea of 'community led' into a reality they, the NDC and the council are going to have to strike a tough bargain with the private sector, for instance over the new housing developments planned by NEM. For Sandra Black – a self-confessed 'true blue' Tory – and many of her fellow residents in lower Beswick, the presence of the NDC has made it easier to stand up to private developers. Sandra – a victor in the Donaheys 'Weakest Link' – began by getting involved with her local residents' association and has ended up as a resident representative on the NDC board.

Sandra owns her home on Rylance Street but most of her neighbours are still council tenants. On the other side of the street, the hundred-year-old houses were recently demolished in order for the developers to start building. Near Sandra's more modern house is a 500-yard-wide green space, five minutes' drive from the city centre, a prime site for private developers – as is the land on which Sandra's house stands. For the developers it is more economic to have a large site for new housing than to build and design around existing houses. But NEM insist that what happens to the land should depend on the agreement of the majority of existing residents. NEM is insistent too on the need for housing that is both affordable to existing residents and high quality, 'not the little boxes that the volume house builders would want to build' as Tim Presswood, one of the residents' representatives on the NEM board, put it.

NEM has used its bargaining power – most notably the council's ownership of the land and its power to grant or withhold planning permissions[18] – to procure two relatively small companies, Gleeson and Lovell, as developers for the area on the basis that they were willing to consider more 'custom-built' houses and more community influence than

the big 'volume' housebuilders. Residents were involved in the procurement process and agreed to the final choice. At first Sandra was suspicious
of NEM but she pinned down the recently appointed chief executive,
Tom Russell, to a commitment that if the residents voted against demolition, it wouldn't happen: 'It's in the minutes. It's in black and white.'
After such assurances, she and the residents' association agreed to participate in an extensive process of joint work with NEM on their first neighbourhood plan.

A steering group was set up composed of a majority of residents. This
steering committee had clear terms of reference: 'For the avoidance of
doubt, the steering committee can only advise and influence decisions
that are made about the future of Beswick – it cannot override or replace
statutory decisions which must be made by either New East Manchester
or Manchester City Council' its remit stated. Sandra had no objection to
this. Her worries were not about statutory plans that said nothing specific
about demolition or the character of the new housing. It was the plans of
the developers that concerned her. PEP, a long-established consultancy on
issues of resident participation, organised a range of consultations with
the local community, including the Chinese community, the elderly,
young mothers and young people. Gleeson and Lovell arranged for
residents to visit and assess their previous work. Neither Sandra nor her
neighbours were satisfied with what they saw. The fundamental reason
was size. 'They felt so cramped. You need a decent main room, for the
kiddies, for friends, just for yourself to feel comfortable and walk around.'
This raised the issue of costs and price. 'We're prepared to start at low
prices for existing residents, and even bear a short-term loss because we
hope to charge higher prices further into the project, but we've got to be
careful of our costs', the man from Lovells told me.

There is an underlying tension between the needs of the existing
residents and the business goals of the developers. Everybody hints at this,
and increasingly it is explicitly discussed. There are two areas of concern:
the amount of social housing – the more there is the lower the profit –

and the price of the new houses. The council is likely to step in with a system of shared equity to enable residents whose houses are to be demolished to buy the new houses in spite of a gap between the compensation paid for the old house and the price of the new.

There is an important general issue at stake: the right of all to live in inner-city areas and enjoy easy access to the benefits of city life which are fast becoming the privilege of a minority. This means affordable house prices, and it also means finding ways of overcoming the negative equity with which residents are burdened in areas that have become run-down through no fault of their own. Lobbying by councils like Manchester, under pressure from residents like Sandra, has led the government to create a Market Renewal Fund,[19] which will help councils to make new or refurbished housing in high value areas affordable to people whose existing property has lost its value.

Another concern is the design of the new houses; how much power will the existing residents have over this? After several months of 'having their views taken on board' the residents wanted to go head-to-head with the developers and negotiate. 'We have a bit of bargaining power', said Sandra with confidence. 'They need this land and for that they need the support of the people presently living on it. They've got to offer us something better. And if they don't, then no one is knocking us down.' She wants the developers to discuss actual house designs with the residents. For her, it isn't a matter of detail to be decided after the overall plan has been agreed, it's fundamental. She is not satisfied with a participation process unless it offers open community influence over decision-making, and power of veto for local people if they oppose what's planned.

NEM's methods of community involvement have developed in leaps and bounds since the sad consultation in Openshaw Community Centre that wet Thursday afternoon in 1999 when the leaflets had not been circulated. Tom Russell thinks genuine community involvement will strengthen NEM's power to bargain with the private developers for higher quality housing. Whether the developers reckoned on their consultation leading to such real negotiations with the residents is another matter. Whether the NEM and NDC is engaged simply in a clever softening up process, to bring residents to a point where they decide to go along with the developers without having changed anything significantly, will not be clear until the final negotiation on the quality and price of houses. But so far the process has increased residents' confidence in their power to make demands on the developers, which in turn has strengthened the hand of the council and the NEM over both private developers and government.

Young people: 'we don't want to be nobodies'

Youth services are another good test of the responsiveness of the democratic circuitry which theoretically should be connecting the problems and solutions on the ground with the wider political process. The scale of the need for high-quality youth provision in Manchester is considerable: it is estimated that over 750 children in the city are not even on the school register. This means that in each of Manchester's twenty-seven most deprived wards there are approximately twenty-five kids effectively on the streets – not including those excluded from school or playing truant. Moreover, 15–20 per cent of Manchester children leave school with no GCSEs or with one A to G grade GCSE. In East Manchester over 18 percent of sixteen- to seventeen-year-olds are neither at school, nor working, nor on a training course. And over a period when problems for young people have grown, the youth service has been dramatically cut – anecdotal evidence suggests by a half over twenty years.

When official structures fail, local people often take control and organise themselves, especially when expectations are beginning to rise. An excellent example of this process is Higher Openshaw Youth Club, which began when Louis Birmingham, a father of two, went to several major meetings about crime, especially youth crime. His younger brother is addicted to heroin, and he knows the problems youth in the area face. 'But,' said Louis, talking about the meetings, 'no one talked about the need for better facilities for young people.' He decided, with others, to do something about it. With the help of an EMCF participation worker, Linda Brooks, and the headteacher of Higher Openshaw community school, John McAlister, some parents turned a large classroom into a youth club, with playstations, computers, a tuck bar and use of the football pitch. On two evenings a week for the last four years it has been open to everyone between the ages of twelve and twenty-five who lives round High Leigh in Higher Openshaw. The difference it has made can be seen from the thirty kids between eleven and eighteen who turn up regularly to hang out or play football. In its first year one of the gangs that turned up was the notorious Sandywell lads, locally reviled for their joyriding. Early on, the NDC had launched, with the police, a tough, high-profile police operation tagged Excalibur, which was aimed at the Sandywell gang and others, and took considerable public resources and funds. Eighteen months on, however, a tenants' representative concludes: 'It's the youth club as much as Excalibur that's reduced crime round here.'

One secret of the club's success is neutrality 'When they come they don't bring in the problems they have outside', says Louis. Another is mutual respect, which has meant that the building has remained totally unvandalised. What do the kids themselves say? I spent several cold autumn nights discussing what they wanted: 'A house – they could convert a boarded-up one – with sofas and music, warm and dry, with someone there so that there's no bullying or anything.' 'Something as big as this hall.' They wanted easier access to a modern leisure centre for the whole area. And to do something with cars: 'a BMX track', 'motor repair classes'. They were proud of their notoriety: 'We like to be known. We don't want to be nobodies. If you're not known, you're a nobody in life', one of them told me. Jeff Burns, one of the volunteers and himself a father of two teenage sons, was convinced of the importance of providing opportunities as much as administering punishments: 'If you come from the right area you take these kinds of facilties for granted. Here, you miss out on all those opportunities to build up confidence, relate to people, realise your potential.'

Back at the NDC office they are supportive, but NDC youth work had started late. Sean McGonigle is open about the neglect of youth work: 'Tackling fear of crime was relatively easy', he says. 'Working with young people requires more development. Not many people are good at it.' Added to this, government targets link funds for youth provision with crime prevention. NDC youth officer Alun Francis stresses the importance of non-crime-related youth provision. 'Sanctions are important,' he says, 'but so is the development of young people.' 'Curfews on young offenders create obstacles to their involvement with the mentoring and inclusion work we are doing', says Viv Blow who works for the locally based Home Office and NDC-funded mentoring project Discus. 'They have to go through the bureaucracy of getting permission. It puts them off.' Blow also finds negative views towards young people are reinforced by a general atmosphere associating youth with crime. Police Superintendent Dave Jones, who prepared Manchester police force's submission to the Lawrence inquiry,[20] is similarly critical. 'Fear of young people is like racism, it's based on ignorance', he says.

The NDC has committed itself to funding a general expansion of core youth provision with an invitation to young people to influence the nature of the provision. It supported research by Alan Turner, a young person from the Manchester Youth Volunteer Project, on how to involve young people.[21] When I began my research, I thought that the converted house the young people could treat as their own might become real – as real perhaps as the vast construction of the new stadium two miles down the road. A step in that direction was a grant from the NDC for Higher Openshaw Youth Club to decorate its room, buy new playstations and computers, mend the school roof and run summer activities. When I returned in June 2002, however, little had changed. The cramped arrangement with the school continued. Meanwhile, all around them was the build up to the Commonwealth Games. Denise Birmingham (Louis's sister), co-organiser of the club, visited the VIP box at the Athletic Trials as a reward for her voluntary work, along with fourteen-year-old Becka Addy. In Becka's view the trials were 'dead good'. 'But it's not going on for ever', she said ruefully. 'I'd like to see more kids' activities in the area.' 'What about the facilities that will be left? Won't you be able to use them?' I asked. 'They're too important for us', replied Becka.

There have been some moves in the direction of what the young people said they wanted, including a commitment that the new sports facilities will be easily accessible to local people. Also, work is to be got underway on a motor project. In the meantime, though, it's more trips – to go-carts and a course on motor maintenance in Gorton, to theme parks, to the Aquatic Centre – the Commonwealth games pool near the university – for a swim. The NDC will pay. There are tentative explorations of a centre of their own, perhaps shared with another club. But there's always a delay. Things seem to move slowly when it comes to buildings in this beleaguered part of the public sector. The contrast with the speed at which private money moves to harvest profits is revealing: the Asda store was erected in a few months, and McDonalds put up its hut and sign literally days after the superstore opened.

The lack of youth provision in Higher Openshaw – and Clayton, and Beswick – points to a problem. There is no longer any well-funded, fully functional youth service. As a non-statutory council service, it was one of the first local services to be battered by Conservative cuts. It has not been restored by the Labour government. Government money currently available for youth activities is tied to specific, sometimes valuable and creative, sometimes narrowly restrictive activities. The task being given to the NDC in East Manchester was tantamount to 'construct a new youth service, with one member of staff'.

The NDC's budget for youth is considerable: it has spent over half a million a year, of which the NDC itself has contributed £150,000, and it has used the basis of this funding to lever more money from government, Europe and other sources. There is a shortage of people with the right training and experience to do the job, however. Some of the best youth work is currently being done by volunteers, responding to local needs. In Openshaw the volunteers who set up the youth club clearly have special abilities in 'engagement', but they would be the first to agree that they also need training in skills that would enable them to move the project on and follow through the needs of the kids beyond leisure.

Jeff Burns is one of these volunteers. A former taxi-driver, he is now full-time co-ordinator for JOG of a year-long programme, with a budget of £70,000, of out-of-school activities. Jeff sees two yawning gaps in youth services. First is a lack of outreach work: 'One full-time worker and two part-timers covering a wider area which includes Openshaw, is not enough. Youth service funding goes down every year.' Second is a need for amenities: 'There needs to be a sports and leisure facility based here. We always have to go somewhere else, or bring in people to do coaching.' It is an irony that the youth of Openshaw, living on the rim of the multi-billion pound Sportcity complex, have to take day trips out of the area to go go-carting, or get to a decent, affordable gym. 'We need something they can feel an ownership of', says Jeff. He thinks local residents should be represented on the boards that manage the facilities of Sportcity.

Such needs require major resources – they are beyond the financial scope of the NDC. But in Jeff's experience youth don't seem to be anybody's priority. Sometimes it seems the people of East Manchester must continually be scaling their aspirations down, despite the NDC programme. 'I accept there can't be a pool,' says Jeff. 'The money's gone on the Aquatic Centre. But the kids must have something which is specially for their area. Just a really good recreation and leisure centre would be fine.'

The weakest links?

Maintaining the democratic momentum

The processes set off through the NDC, experimental and uneven as they inevitably are, also expose weaknesses in the democracy of the wider political 'system' – including the growing ad hoc, non-system of nationally controlled initiatives and budgets to which the local council and local people have to adapt. The 'community-led' brief of the national NDC programme is targeted on a limited number of small areas. It is not part of a wider expansion of rights to participate directly in decisions about the spending of public money, although the government and local authorities are taking some tentative steps in this direction.[22] This restricted focus of the NDC was always going to be a limit on its influence because some decisions which affect a locality originate beyond its reach and affect a wider constituency. The democratic mechanisms are not in place to link the exceptional – and exceptionally well funded - participatory processes in one neighbourhood to these wider decision-making processes. That would require a city-wide system equivalent to the Porto Alegre model. A decision to reorganise homecare services, for example, would be part of a city-wide strategy. Similarly, if the people of East Manchester were to be granted the right to participate effectively in decisions about local services – about the closure of local housing offices or the building of a local swimming pool – then other communities affected by these amenities would rightly lay claim to the same rights.

There are two issues here. One is that of subsidiarity: what decisions can best be taken locally without damaging consequences for people elsewhere, or without losing any benefits from being part of a city-wide strategy? The other is of participation: how can the diverse and sometimes conflicting views of people in different localities feed into the wider strategic decision-making?

In East Manchester, a taste of real decision-making leads to an irreversible frustration with a reliance on the consultations of the old days, where individuals could put their points of view but could not participate with power in the decision-making. But where does this increase in local power lead? At present in Manchester, the council is opening debate about how to extend popular participation in its decision-making.[23] But across England councils are heavily constrained by the democratic deficit of a national political system which still, though in duly modernised form, treats city authorities as if they were the provincial arms of an imperial centre, obeying its instructions, meeting its targets, 'earning autonomy' only when they please the imperial master. Power is not easily shared by those whose own power is insecure. At present the links between the pressures and demands generated through the NDC and the wider political process depend on the individual leadership of the NDC, senior council officers, the council's political leadership and, sometimes, the local MP Tony Lloyd. Although this is managerially effective, it is not an open democratic system that can be duplicated across this or any other city.

The grant-aided substitute for democratic debate

Another process related to the weakening of local democracy is the stealthy growth of a grants economy – and polity for the allocation of public funds. There's the national lottery handing out £150,000 here, £75,000 there; the European Regional Development Fund (with £54 million for East Manchester over an eight-year period) granting £200,000 to one local business, or agreeing to a community application for £50,000; there's the Single Regeneration Budget, the Youth Justice Board and dozens of other regeneration-related funds emanating from central government. Then there's the NDC itself, though this, as we've seen, works under rules that make it more or less accountable to the community.

This grant 'system' makes its decisions in the shadows, if not in secret. Rarely are representatives on the various grants-giving committees obliged to report back to a wider constituency. It's not that the system is corrupt. On the contrary, most of these grant-giving bodies have clear rules and go out of their way to avoid subjective factors or personal vested interests creeping in. But there is no open local debate, discussion or negotiation. And grant-givers are rarely accountable – at best they abide by their own procedures, which, in some cases can be traced back indirectly to formally democratic decisions in Westminster or in the European Parliament.

There are positives to the grant economy. It is better than nothing, but it stifles debate about the allocation of public resources and about how to raise these resources. This means deeply political issues about priorities for limited resources become administrative decisions, and different sections of the population are propelled into positions of competition with one another, rather than collaboration or open debate.

From grassroots participation to political representation

At its best, the link between grassroots community needs – individual and collective – and democratic politics comes down to good councillors who sort out mainly individual problems and, sometimes, mediate between community groups and council officials. There is also the desultory quarterly East Manchester Members' meeting where councillors listen to reports, snipe at each other across the Labour and Liberal Democrat divide and ask a few inconsequential questions of council staff. When there is an issue which is too political for officers or the NDC because it has wider electoral implications, is controversial and involves councillors outside a single ward, or has repercussions for some wider council policy or planning framework, the councillor concerned normally finds a solution by 'going to see Richard' (Leese, the council leader), as one Labour Party insider put it. The NDC has not radically altered this, though leading residents and NDC officers themselves have more direct access than most, including most councillors, to the council leader. Informal discussions also take place between the leading NDC and NEM staff and the more competent councillors. The local Labour

Party itself does not provide any more vigorous connection between local issues and the wider political process; in the local wards (two cover the NDC area) the party is a small and fairly narrowly electoral affair. Local political parties do not get very involved in community activity, though there is talk that they might – it's clear that that's where the energy and the able people are.

The weak links between grassroots concerns and city-wide politics is partly the result of the electoral system. In Manchester, as in many English cities, there is no serious open competition facing the pragmatic Labour leadership either from the left or the right. The Conservatives hardly exist, and the somewhat ineffectual Liberal Democrats are sufficiently irritating to Labour for Labour to close ranks in electoral periods, but have little impact. Yet there is a wide range of views within the Labour Party, and an even greater range of views outside it, which at present lack representation. A fairer electoral system would nourish the visions developing outside electoral politics, and would give them a greater chance of having an impact.

The blockages facing local pressure at a national level can be seen by following the concerted campaign to get legislation to regulate private landlords. In 1999 council leader Richard Leese wrote to Hilary Armstrong, minister responsible for regeneration, telling her of the barriers faced by the East Manchester NDC in its efforts at regeneration. It was part of the NDC's brief to alert government to wider problems and, in theory, be a catalyst for innovation. Messages from the NDC frontline would, the implication was, be put on a fast track for a solution. One of the most urgent barriers that Leese identified, advised by NDC staff and residents, was unregulated private landlords. He put in an urgent plea for action. His plea was reinforced by Tony Lloyd, who joined with MPs from other regeneration areas facing the same problem. Much lobbying and several meetings with John Prescott took place, and many promises were made. Local residents kept up the pressure. 'They provided pressure both on me and for me', said Tony Lloyd. Eventually, nearly four years after Leese's letter made a simple request for long-overdue legislation, there was a promise of it in Tony Blair's 2002 Queen's Speech. But as yet, summer 2003, there is no action. Whether it is New Labour's reluctance to intervene in any private market, or simply an overcrowded legislative agenda, it shows again the weak links between local community participations and the centres of political power. 'With democratic regional government, something like this would have been sorted years ago', comments Lloyd.

The problem with present forms of political power is not people's apathy or an unwillingness to participate. When there is a chance of having a real influence over the allocation of resources, a real chance to improve the quality of life of a neighbourhood, and when people are aware of it and are at least half convinced that it could make a difference, then they engage. Experiences like East Manchester show the potential, as yet partially realised, of popular participation in the management of public services, budgetary decisions and the use of public assets. It also shows the potential of an alliance of this participatory power with electoral democracy, again partially realised, to exert greater bargaining power over the private sector. But this stress on participation should not let electoral politics and central state institutions off the hook. They have to be reformed to be more responsive to the creativity, and the conflict, that arise from greater participation. It will take a powerful political movement to forge open democratic connections between the growing local participation that is evident in localities like East Manchester and the wider power structures which in the end decide the fate of these neighbourhoods. Mancunians are working on it.

LUTON:
SQUATTING THE STATE

The announcement that a community coalition involving the Exodus collective had won the right to bid for £50 million of the government's New Deal for Communities money was a good enough reason for me to pack my rucksack and get to Luton. From my knowledge of them, if the Exodus people had anything to do with it, this could be 'community led' from the start.

Exodus, an assorted group of squatters-cum-ravers-cum-community leaders from Luton's Marsh Farm Estate had been engaging in 'bottom-up' regeneration before the government's Social Exclusion Unit even began their investigations. Indeed the SEU later visited Exodus for inspiration. Since 1992 Exodus had been running free local raves, organising 'fundays' on the estate for young and old, and occupying and refurbishing derelict properties for community use – especially for the forgotten of the community: the youth.

Other strong and experienced groups from the estate – tenants' and residents' associations, a social and sports club, the local community café, a group of black activists, several churches – were part of the local coalition that had got together to make the bid. This chapter is the story of how the prospect of serious money and the promise that, for a change, local people would not only be consulted but be in the lead, led a diverse and fractious community to get organised and eventually create a precarious experiment in neighbourhood self-management. In the process they radically changed expectations about relationships between the community and the state. They wanted to decentralise budgets, management of waste disposal, youth and possibly other services, and consider how to make the police accountable to the residents of the estate.

For the two years when Marsh Farm NDC was getting into its stride, whenever I was in London I took the train from King's Cross Thameslink to Leagrave. A taxi or a lift took me through a leafy suburban street past Waulud's Bank, the remains of a neolithic settlement,[1] to Marsh Farm Estate, the remains of a 1960's dream of an architecture that would create a community. I got to know the leading players and sat at the back of some of the crucial meetings which led eventually to the creation of the Marsh Farm Community Trust – the organisation which, in theory, would bring everyone together and lead the regeneration of the estate.

Much of what I discovered in Luton – the uneasy relations between council and community for example, and within the community itself – is common to all attempts to rebuild services and employment in estates almost destroyed by decades of neglect. In Luton, as in East Manchester, there was a particular determination by local people that the government's commitment to 'community-led' regeneration should be fulfilled. A genuinely new process was underway, in the course of which Marsh Farm residents were rethinking and trying to change relationships with each other and the council.

All the old political issues of legitimacy and representation were raised in this micro context of a neighbourhood of around 9,000 people (4,000 households). Spurred on by the inadequacies of present democratic structures in the macro settings of both the town council and the national parliament, Marsh Farm residents evolved new mechanisms for democracy. The challenge of the NDC bid forced the growth of a rooted local democracy, more active than the occasional choice of an elected representative. At the same time this creative experiment came up against people with vested interests in the existing hierarchical order and with a mentality that could not cope with the occasional chaos, conflict and uncertainty that goes along with change that is genuinely from the bottom up. Their story is relevant to us all.

Shapers, creators and obstacle makers

Exodus

The Exodus collective first came together when a group of residents mainly from Marsh Farm discovered three huge unused speaker boxes in a garage. They fixed them up in a nearby forest and created the first Exodus party. Three years later they were organising free raves with their own 'peace stewards' taking care of 6–7,000 dancers in quarries and empty warehouses around the area. They took over a derelict ex-hospice and turned it into a thriving community centre and housing co-op known as Housing Action Zone (HAZ) Manor. Eventually licensed by the council to the squatters, the housing co-op welcomed visitors from all over the world. Benedita Silva, a Workers Party senator from the *favelas* of Brazil, warmed to its egalitarianism and poetic spirituality: for her these values stemmed from the liberation theology which was a key influence on her party. For Exodus, it had come from Bob Marley.

One evening in July 1995, Exodus members had returned to the Marsh Farm Estate from a planning enquiry to find a riot of bored and disaffected young people in full swing.[2] At the enquiry the collective had been defending their proposal to turn an empty warehouse into a centre for young people. They came back to find 'burning cars billowing smoke amid the tower blocks of their estate'. A local councillor pleaded with the police not to over-react, as the situation had begun to calm down. But the boys in blue duly arrived, lights blazing, sirens screaming and sealed off the estate. Three nights of violence and running battles with riot police followed.

As it so happened, the Saturday of the rioting was already planned as a night for one of Exodus's fortnightly raves. The collective issued a declaration that a dance was to be held as a 'non-violent demonstration against the use of policing methods that had turned a spark into a fire'. They wanted to try to alleviate the tension and to continue, by direct passive action, a campaign for a permanent community and activity centre in the area. So on Saturday night 2,000 young people from Bedfordshire – including many from Marsh Farm – joined the Exodus rave, six miles away. At 3.30 on Sunday morning Radio Bedfordshire phoned Exodus to say that there was not a rioter in sight on the Marsh Farm Estate. The police were alone sitting on park benches. 'They [Exodus] got the youngsters off the street and got them dancing. It was organised freedom for the kids – the kind of activity missing everywhere else in the country', commented a local councillor, Larry Mcgowan. The *Luton News* christened Exodus 'The Pied Pipers of Hamelin'. It was an extraordinary event, and one which is symbolic both of Exodus's contribution to the community and the confusion it caused the authorities, who became increasingly split over how to react to this group of delinquents turned unique community activists.

There are no adequate facilities for young people on Marsh Farm. On the fringes of the estate is a sports centre surrounded by a high fence and charging unaffordable prices, effectively saying to the local kids, 'This is not for you'. As the local Purley shopping centre has become more derelict, kids turn up there with basketballs and footballs and rather pathetically try to transform it into a makeshift sports club. The estate has a particularly high youth population but despite this there is just one youth club, to which very few young people relate because they don't have any say in how it's run. In 1996 the council employed an outreach youth worker with funding from the Social Regeneration Budget, Debbie Liverpool. By all accounts, she began to get things moving. But after two years the SRB funding was gone, as was Debbie Liverpool. What's left of the youth service is run from the Town Hall.

Exodus, like some of the residents' associations, wanted to get to the root of the problem of youth vandalism by giving the young people of the community some way to express themselves positively. Glenn Jenkins, one of the founding members of Exodus, blames boredom. 'If they were doing something constructive and were enjoying themselves and came home tired every night, they wouldn't be joyriding, setting fires, burgling.'

Some representatives of authority, like Chief Inspector Mick Brown, came to respect Exodus for their work for young people. Others, like the two local Conservative MPs, disliked them because, amongst other things, of the threat their raves posed for the local brewing interests. (Luton is Whitbread country, home to the company's HQ. Samuel Whitbread is the Lord Lieutenant of Bedfordshire. Attendance at the raves was seriously hitting takings at the local pubs. 'Both our MPs were friends of Samuel Whitbread', comments Jenkins acidly.) Another Tory, who for a television programme, *Living with the Enemy*, had briefly lived in HAZ Manor, tried to bring in the police on the grounds that cannabis was being smoked. The police did not respond then, but later when Exodus was about to secure the funding for what would have been the largest environmental task force in the country, the chief of Bedfordshire police used the episode to question and effectively block their receipt of public funds. Taking the smoking of cannabis out of the world of crime and illegality was an important issue for the Exodus collective. Many of the youth on the estate smoked it. In this way this harmless and pleasurable activity was driven underground and associated with exploitative dealers and seriously harmful drugs. Its illegality, argued Exodus, was a major source of social exclusion. Exodus provided a safe and uncommercial context in which young people could be themselves. But there was a general fear on the part of many authorities, of young people getting together on their own terms. This has influenced all official dealings with the Exodus collective and its individual members.

At the same time as the government's SEU was effectively supporting the Exodus collective as part of an innovative proposal for community regeneration, the government's employment services were refusing to fund Exodus's plans to enable the unemployed and homeless to refurbish derelict buildings and rehouse themselves and others. In addition, the benefits agency regularly cut off the dole of those living in the Manor and refused to acknowledge the way their work contributed to the community – this, despite the government making more and more appeals for people to be active in the community. These mutually incompatible state responses pose interesting questions about how far the government's commitment to 'community led' really extends. There was a certain nervousness in Whitehall: 'The establishment are anxious about the involvement of Exodus', said one insider.

As well they might be: the Exodus collective produced experienced leaders who knew how to work in a wider coalition, when to come forward and when to stay in the background. They had learned discipline as part of an organisation that maintained peace and good feeling in raves of over 5,000 people. This was no easy task. It involved facing off drug dealers hoping for a captive market, a hostile council and police, and local gangs, in addition to making sure everything was organised for people to enjoy themselves. Indeed, between 1993 and its break up in 2001,[3] the Exodus collective had succeeded in creating a co-operative way of work and life which was an alternative for young people to the commercialism and exploitation on offer elsewhere in Luton.

Certainly, the ex-Exodus crew were well-prepared for the highs and lows of the NDC process. The NDC was creating new structures. These were intended to embed principles of co-operation, equality and participative democracy in new institutions which could withstand division and conflict. The Exodus members were among the most outspoken residents in resisting overbearing intervention from the council, and at the same time were some of the most persistent and patient architects of a system of collective self-discipline on the basis of rules agreed by everyone.

Jenkins is just one of over forty forceful characters sustained by Exodus in its day. A Puck-like figure, fizzing with ideas and idealism, he, like many collective members, lives on 'the farm' as Marsh Farm Estate is colloquially called. An ex-milkman at the Co-op Dairy and ex-rail driver and shop steward, his philosophy of community democracy is that it is a learning exercise: 'Learning and making mistakes is the only way with a bottom-up process', he says. At meetings he has his say, gently but persistently, while letting the discussion flow. He spends a lot of time talking individually with fellow members of the Marsh Farm Community Trust, listening to them, trying to help wounds heal and encourage the best in people.

Tenants' and residents' associations

Another strong founding force in the wider coalition that came together to bid for the NDC money were the leading activists in the thirty or so tenants' and residents' associations (TARAs). These people were the communication lines between the council and the council tenants, and were sometimes seen by local residents as 'council' or 'friends of the council' because they ended up being local ambassadors for council policy rather than advocates for the residents. The different TARAs were often at war, sending poisonous letters to the council about each other. But there were plenty of TARA leaders whose focus was improving the area rather than pursuing the (dubious) status of hobnobbing with the council.

One of these is Tony Gamble, chair of one of the associations. He started his group because he noticed that those parts of the estate with strong residents' associations seem to get extra amenities. 'I said to my neighbours, "Look that other area has got a little garden for old people to sit in. Wouldn't we like something like that?"' Tony is a stocky man in his late forties. His background is in supervisory jobs, but his CV, from supervisor at Vauxhall to supervisor at the Co-op Dairy, is a catalogue of the closures and restructuring that went on throughout British industry from the mid-1970s onwards, wasting talented men like himself. 'But I've always been busy', he says. When his marriage split up he stayed at home and brought up two of his children, and it was this that made him aware of the needs of the neighbourhood: they were his needs too. He is sensitive to being looked down on or patronised by the council or any other authority. He was determined that 'the New Deal is not going to be another SRB where we were treated as if we weren't important enough to have all the information all of the time'. He added firmly: 'It is meant to be bottom-up and it will be bottom-up.' On this he and the Exodus people were united.

Other local voluntary groups

The Sports and Social Club was another forceful Luton group, good at fighting its corner and getting resources. It was originally set up in response to the riots: 'There was nothing for the kids to do', said its founder, David Crean. Crean's wider commitment to improving the quality of life on the estate stems from his neighbours' support after the death of his six-year-old daughter in a bike accident: 'The way they responded was way beyond the call of duty, even from people I didn't know. My brother came over from Ireland expecting to find me trying to cope on my own. He was amazed at the way the community helped me through. Now I want to put something back.' Now chair of the Marsh Farm Community Trust he has steered it through various periods of turbulence: rival community groups fighting for territory (usually control over community buildings); a council by turns supportive and manically controlling; the presence of the regeneration consultancy Renaisi, who were contracted simultaneously to deliver projects and train local residents to take over their role.

Jean Burns represents yet another group with definite ideas for the future of the farm – community volunteers who are independent of the semi-official TARA system, and aware of the growing number of social problems which fall through the net of state agencies. When the idea came up of putting in a bid to be the Luton NDC, Jean, a shy as well as determined woman, was managing Café 2000, the well-used community café that is one of the few convivial spots in the increasingly boarded-up Purley centre. She decided to get involved. Her special interest is health – especially the issues that often never reach the doctors, such as mental health. People who are facing pressures undermining their health talk about them in the café when they might not go anywhere near a surgery or social services office. She thought the NDC might help in an organised way to spread this kind of vital, non-medical support. 'I want us to be out there listening to people's problems and helping in any way we can', she says. Like David Crean, she is an immigrant to Marsh Farm and has been impressed by the neighbourliness of the place: 'It's like Glasgow, everyone looks out for each other.'

The friendliness of the estate was a continuing theme, often contrasted to its violent and rough reputation. No one can quite explain it. Perhaps neighbourliness is helped by the estate's Radburn design. You park your car in one of the bays round the edge of the compact network of courtyards, pathways and open spaces and enter the estate on foot, not driving. The houses have gardens clustered round small communal yards: on a sunny day you can't help chatting to whoever is out and about. On the south side of the estate, however, there are several blocks of high-rise flats, as bleak and brutal as high-rises everywhere.

The mix

A diverse ethnic mix may be an additional factor in the vibrancy of neighbourly life. The white population is not just local, there's an overspill from London, plus those who came from the north of England and Ireland for jobs in the 1960s and 70s. Then there are also a significant number of people of Afro-Caribbean and Asian origin – 30 per cent of the population. There's no single group who can feel it's their estate, treating others as outsiders. 'Racism is here, like it is everywhere in Britain,' says the Reverend Trevor Adams from the Church of the God of Prophecy, a Pentecostal church based especially amongst the Afro-Caribbean community, 'but it is below the surface.' 'There's every kind of graffiti here but I've never seen racist graffiti', says Juliet Bandoo, who came to Luton from the West Indies in the 1960s. But race is certainly an issue in dealing with the institutions that are meant to be serving the people of Marsh Farm. Amongst the groups driving the NDC trust and or pushing for its resources are strong black and Asian groups and individuals.

Patrick Markland, alias Ricky, runs the African Caribbean Development Forum. His focus is effectively institutional racism in the schools: 'We're like a watchdog and we've found that the practice of schools towards black students doesn't reflect the council's commitment to equal opportunities.' He has also made it his priority to make sure that race issues are addressed properly by the NDC. He believes getting things right on race benefits everyone. 'Most of the stuff we're doing is not just for black people. I'm talking about the overall programme. People don't always seem to understand that we do need to do things specially for black people but that that benefits everyone.' Since I first interviewed him, Ricky has also become the chair of the Race Equality and Capacity Building Group, a watchdog over the NDC trust led by NDC board members. Even the name was originally controversial to the government office for the eastern region (the branch of government supervising NDCs in the south east, and enticingly know as 'GO East'). At first they questioned the idea of having 'race' in the title. 'They thought "equality" in general could cover the issue', says Trevor Adams. 'I had to say that their question proved the need to be explicit.'

Churches

The local churches too have been an important force within the NDC, sometimes unifying the god-fearing, the god-loving, the agnostic, the godless, and even the local Satanist. At the end of one particularly fraught Trust meeting the Reverend Trevor Adams asked if he could give a prayer, and with everyone's somewhat bewildered permission, prayed for the future of the project. The effect was to calm frazzled tempers as people listened to a restatement of common goals. Reverend Trevor has a special commitment to Marsh Farm. Until 1995 he lived in a more affluent part of Luton and drove in on a Sunday and at other times during the week to give a service. But as the centre and surrounding area became more and more vandalised he felt 'there were needs in the community that required our closer involvement'. So he moved to live on the estate. He's enthusiastic about the potential of the NDC to unite the diverse community groups who rarely meet each other, but he is wary of the way the government has set out the topics around which the community must draw up its plans – crime, worklessness, health, education. 'The process should start from what the community says it needs,' he argues. From his experience, a high priority should be given to deep emotional and relationship needs. He describes a different reality to the neighbourly pulling together experienced by David Crean and Jean Burns. 'Every year at least one person commits suicide from the high-rises. When there's a crisis people do come together but in everyday terms there's a lot of loneliness. Besides the café [Café 2000] there are few places for people to meet socially in an easy way. For some people the church provides that social gathering place.'

Luton Borough Council

The final player on this particular NDC stage is Luton Borough Council, which takes different guises. There are friendly local councillors. There are senior officials some of whom opt almost to go native, while others seek to keep control.

Luton Council had no grand visions for Marsh Farm, unlike Manchester Council's vision for the city's old industrial east. Grand visions are not Luton Council's thing: you can tell that by the town hall. On the corner of a busy street, it has the feeling of the watchtower of order and regulation in a bustling market town. It has the air of self-importance common to any custodian of public life, but none of the grandeur and ambition exuding from Manchester's town hall. The modern-day role that Luton Council has taken upon itself is to be expert at chasing funding streams – sussing out what's wanted by the government, European Commission or whoever is the funding body, and submitting effective bids. That's how it was with the NDC – it was assumed, more out of habit than any malevolent intent, that if and when the money came through, the council would be in charge. In fact, NDC guidelines require only that there's an accountable body for the 'probity and regularity' of the local NDC's finances. This backstop role was meant to be the limit of LBC's role beyond providing general support as and when the Marsh Farm NDC asked for it.

The process of the bid

How could the Marsh Farm NDC bid bring together such a diverse compendium of groups and individuals? Before the prospect of £50 million appeared on the horizon, relations between the different groups on the estate all too often degenerated into warring power bases elbowing to get to the front of the queue for council resources. But co-operation was needed in order to have any chance of bringing this serious money into the estate, and co-operation emerged. The process of pulling together to make the bid united the factions – though the sources of division and rivalry still remained beneath the surface.

Some of the other badly neglected estates in the area felt resentment over the Luton bidding process for NDC money – though the council did attempt with some success to channel separate external funding streams in their direction. But on Marsh Farm, the process of putting together and winning the bid brought to the fore positive feelings towards the estate and within the community.

Some of those who got involved have a parochial vision of improving the estate; others, like Ronnie Amanze, a recent migrant from Harlesden and a music producer who searches out and nurtures local black talent, have a more global ambition. 'This could be special not just for the community, but as a launching pad for lots of people to go out and achieve great things.' 'Everyone on Marsh Farm hopes to win the pools or the lottery. This way we have done it as a whole community', says Tony Gamble.

The first meeting: new momentum, new problems

The first public meeting for the bid gathered the movers and shakers together. There were thirty-one of them – dreadlocked Rastas, bald-headed vicars, the middle aged and paunchy, the lean and under forty, men, women (nearly half of them were women): the same group of people that had appeared before a panel appointed by the city council and GO East to present the case for Marsh Farm. Now, on the platform at a meeting of over 200 people, they were taking the first step towards involving the rest of the estate. This meeting, in February 1999, was my introduction to Marsh Farm.

Two years later, as I relistened to the tape of this two-and-a-half hour meeting, I realised that the voices speaking that evening touch on most of the problems which would go on to be negotiated or tripped over as the experiment progressed. Two kinds of relationships were suddenly being shaken up: on the one hand that between LBC and local people; and on the other hand the relationship, or up till the NDC, lack of it, between different local organisations. That evening prefigured so well the democratic experiment it sought to instigate, that I shall summarise what was said that night.

In the first part of the meeting, a sort of dual power seemed to reign: community representatives competed with the council, notably council officers, for control. The proceedings started with the community in charge in the form of the meeting's chair Jackie Gill – a leading activist in one of the TARAs. She explained the rationale behind NDC, para-phrasing Tony Blair: 'In the past regeneration has failed because too much has been imposed from above' – this remark was resonant with the experience of the top-down SRB – 'but experience shows that success depends on communities themselves having the power to make things better.' The stress on power hit home.

Jackie's description of how the community had successfully put forward its case to win the right to be Luton's bid seemed to prove that this was not just another consultation exercise in which the community tagged behind the council. She then asked the director of housing from LBC to make some brief remarks. Brevity was not Mr Gibbins' strong point, however. He presented the NDC as a framework laid down by government within which the community were being given permission to take the initiative – he made it seem like participation by tick boxes. Listing the government's priority problems he said, 'We and you are being asked to find solutions to them with the money available.' He quoted ideas from other areas about how to 'involve the community' and ended up by saying that the involvement of private business would be 'the glue that holds it all together'.

He went on to list the government hoops that had to be gone through: Phase One (drawing up and agreeing the basic vision); Phase Two (drawing up and agreeing the detailed delivery plan); and Phase Three (delivering the plan). The listeners were taken aback by how tight the timetable was: there was only two months for the community to prepare its proposals for Phase One.

The discussion proceeded. No one confronted Mr Gibbins, but just continued on the assumption that they, the community, would be in control. People knew that LBC would be in the background as 'the accountable body', but preferred to think of it as there when they needed it rather than as giving the lead.

The issue of relationships within the community was hardly touched on that night – further evidence that the process of making the bid had built up a sense of unity previously unheard of on Marsh Farm. But Jackie Gill did speak of 'the hostile way we have been treated by outsiders' as a force which had shaped the unity on the estate. Someone asked a question about the influence of Exodus, to which Glenn responded in a low-key way that, as an Exodus member, he too lived on the estate and had children facing a future there. A columnist in the local paper regularly abused Exodus as 'druggies' and ne'er-do-wells, stirring up amongst some residents an atmosphere of suspicion. Beyond this, anxieties about the community, who it was and how parts of it related to each other, were focused by the money; how to create a fair and legitimate way of collectively managing a budget of £50 million over a ten-year period so that the process would lead to something permanent. People also wanted the grant to be a leverage for influencing the running of local public services (the public – mainly council – money already being spent on the estate) and the character of the local economy.

The mix at the meeting was only partially representative of the different ethnic groups and age groups in the area. Asians, young people and pensioners particularly did not come in numbers proportionate to their presence on the estate, and person after person raised anxieties about whether the needs of one or other section of the community would be addressed. One person did speak for the absent youth: 'Youth unemployment on the estate is way above the national average. They're your future so they need to get sorted out. Forget this old dead stuff, tired old minds, games played – that's finished with. There's a whole new generation coming up and they're not here. Sixty-four per cent of the estate are under thirty-five. How many people here are under thirty-five? I just thought I'd make a sound for them.' (The NDC's survey carried out later that year found 26 per cent of the people on Marsh Farm was under sixteen, and 41 per cent of those aged between sixteen and twenty-four were unemployed.)

Also vocal was a volunteer who worked with the 7 per cent of the estate who are elderly 'Some of us here will ourselves be in our sixties, probably seventies in ten years' time. What guarantee can we have from this committee for our safety and our dignity in every aspect of our lives?'

She was speaking about an acute problem: an Age Concern survey of Marsh Farm showed that of the over sixty-fives in the estate, 80 per cent felt afraid to go out alone and 60 per cent felt cut off; 90 per cent of those in sheltered accommodation complained of boredom or depression, one-third had difficulty reading and writing, two-thirds suffered from some form of dementia.

Several people raised concerns about how fully ethnic minorities would be involved. 'I'm not being a killjoy, no way, I love it. I love what's going on, but I want to know how much of the ethnic minority groups, i.e. Asian and Afro-Caribbean, how much are they involved in this?'

One suggestion that took off was that of street co-ordinators. Jackie Jenkins, one of the residents most determined to turn this idea into a reality, explained: 'The aim is that the board of the Marsh Farm Development is in as much contact as it possibly can be with residents, by having a co-ordinator for every street, who feeds the views of his or her neighbourhood to the trust and then feeds information about decisions from the trust back to his or her neighbours.' Speakers argued that before these ideas could be developed, a visible, accessible, physical base for the NDC was needed. It would serve as a sign that the community were in charge and action was underway. They knew the ideal place, a popular landmark that was no longer used – the empty Co-op shop in the Purley centre. There was an atmosphere of get up and go. 'Lets get in there and set up base camp to show that we mean business', said Steve Sovereign, an avuncular Exodus member. 'Something has got to move. We need somewhere immediately where people can go with their ideas, or to find out what's going on, somewhere people are familiar with. Most people won't go to meetings. The Co-op shop would provide an alternative. Also people would own it; they would restore it and run it. It would give people confidence.' As Glenn Jenkins put it: 'Buildings are power.'

But power also lies in the doing. Immediately, the discussion over the Co-op premises raised a fundamental issue of how to improve on the tatty quality of local democracy as it exists. It focused people's attention on the detail of how things are done; 'processes of implementation' became a central point of conflict. It was not that the council were aggressively hostile to the idea of taking over the Co-op shop, which they owned as part of the Purley centre, it was just that for a number of reasons the idea of a community-controlled open office was just not part of their thinking. Michael Mahon, the main council officer responsible, still in his conventional Town Hall mode of thinking (he later became immersed in the inventiveness of the NDC process) explained: 'First, it's an inappropriate use of resources. And anyway it's focusing on the wrong issues. The priorities must be communication, vision and a proper strategy of consultation. Secondly, after Phase Two [of the NDC], we will be providing a proper office and staff. Thirdly, it's a retail area, there's already a housing shop and the charity shop. If more shops move to other functions there'll be problems with passing trade.'

This was a revealing speech, showing how much the council had to learn about genuine community participation and the importance of lateral thinking and the grasping of fortuitous accidents in the way a coalition of groups might put together their vision. There was an importance the council found hard to grasp in the very process – rather than just the outcome – by which a service, in this case a building, got organised. There's a world of difference between a council-provided office and staff, and a community-run centre with no council backing. Rules need to be rethought in the light of changed realities – in this instance for example, retailers were not exactly queuing up for the vast, almost unmanageable space that was the Co-op shop. The issue of space also raised some wider questions: once a democratically legitimate representative body was in place – the permanent elected NDC board – how should its decisions be made real? Should they be handed over for implementation by professional and technical employees? Or should there be some popular involvement in the doing as well as the deciding?

The final 'foundational' issue that evening, the final seed for creating democracy, was how the structures eventually developed would ensure that all projects committed to would help to meet the needs of Marsh Farm community as a whole. Marsh Farm's most recent experience of regeneration was the SRB – originally the brainchild of Conservative Minister Michael Heseltine in response to riots in several of Britain's major cities. Remembering the SRB experience, a woman asked the top table: 'Is this money mainly for individuals or for particular groups, or is it for the whole community?' Her question gets to the nub of what is potentially new about the NDC: under previous regeneration programmes, individual groups made individual bids, often unknown to each other, and usually in competition with each other. The bids were put before a committee on which the local community might be represented, but which was dominated by council officers. The assumption was that the community was already democratically governed by the local authority without any need for renewing democracy from the ground up.

Speakers from the caretaker committee shared her concern. In the words of Reverend Trevor Adams, 'When I was involved in doing the presentation [of the initial NDC bid], it wasn't just for our group, it was for the whole of Marsh Farm'. In Luton, in a place abandoned by existing forms of government, they are taking literally the NDC's ambition to provide for the community as whole.

The need for a deeper democracy and a legitimate leadership

The discussion took place that night against a background of dislocation between an estate with profound needs and its elected representatives at the town hall. Consequently, speakers pushed issues of democracy beyond the matter of simply electing a neighbourhood committee, in other words creating a council in miniature. They wanted to explore how people could more regularly exchange information with this representative committee once it was elected. How could structures be set up which would enable the community to participate more effectively than through elections, while recognising that many people don't want to attend endless meetings or get otherwise entangled in an organisation?

The community was searching for an involvement more thorough-going and systematic than 'Fundays' and information buses; they were looking for a regular, transparent two-way process which would give people definite channels of influence and information.

The meeting had clarified a central issue: how to create democratic self-government for the estate. Before there had been desultory council management of particular services, projects or buildings, but nothing which looked at the estate as a whole. When several people questioned the authority of those on the top table, David Crean said honestly, 'None of us have authority. But somebody had to do it. We've won the right to make a bid. now we're having the public meeting to find out what you want.' Tony Gamble added, 'We are not a committee. We are a caretaker committee.'

Two years on: government hoops; disappointments and dreams

It took two years for the development trust in Marsh Farm to get to the point where it was ready to start spending serious money. This was partly a matter of moving through the stipulated government phases of the NDC bidding process.

Phase One had been a statement drawn up almost entirely by local residents, and involved elaboration of the initial bid into a full statement of their vision. This was necessary to clinch the success of the bid and receive money for managing and administering the next phase of the project. At the end of Phase One some 'early wins' were carried out in an attempt to gain the interest and trust of local residents.

By June 1999, Marsh Farm had passed this test and moved into Phase Two, which was dominated by preparation of the delivery plan which, if agreed, would mean the trust would be self-governing – subject to the council's requirements of financial probity and GO East's application of the national NDC guidelines.

Two years after starting the bid, there were still hoops to jump through. It seems likely that the government was being particularly cautious in Marsh Farm. In some NDCs, community activists needed to wrest control from the local council. In Marsh Farm, however, the impetus was 'community led' from the beginning, and it was GO East and the local authorities who struggled to keep a grip. And struggle they have, using every technical means at their disposal. Most NDCs have delegated authority for grant awards below £250,000. Even after going through all the required phases of development, the Marsh Farm Trust still has to have all its spending approved by GO East. 'Too many of their proposals fail our appraisal requirements', says the officer responsible at GO East. Kevin Segue, the experienced boss of Renaisi, the regeneration consultancy working with the Trust, says that he does not think there are justified grounds for this prejudice against Marsh Farm NDC.

During the period in which the phases were laboriously traversed, I sometimes dropped in to meet up with the Marsh Farm NDC in their office in the Co-op shop – residents had converted it over a weekend, and the council had now granted it a licence. I must have visited on the good days because I would be regaled with stories of people coming in with knives – even of a murder taking place just outside. The Purley centre acted as a magnet for the frustrations of the estate. By April 2002, the NDC had moved, no doubt much to the relief of the administrative team, into what had been the 'education and training suite' of the vast Coulters factory across the road from the Purley centre, where entrance was now via a guarded security door. Empty for some years, the Exodus collective had proposed in 1998 to put the building to use as an imaginative community centre, and had made attempts to squat in the building in order to develop this. Indeed Harry, the security guard at the time of the attempted squat still guards the factory now. He has fond memories: 'I caught Glenn Jenkins trying to get into the building. A little rascal he was. I had to call the police.' Harry is now beaming with delight that his building is alive again – with his neighbours. In a sense, the NDC effectively squatted with permission. Eventually – in 2003 – after completing a feasibility study and winning a considerable tussle with both LBC and the government's regional office – who wanted to bring in an entirely new management of the project – the Marsh Farm Trust has bought the Coulters building. The aim is to turn it into what Glenn Jenkins calls the 'hubbub'. 'Like the old mining villages had the pit, this will be the community's new centre, with community businesses, local services, a café, a radio studio, facilities for youth.'

The new structures in action

The board and its committees

The development of accountable democratic credibility in Luton NDC was tempestuous. Two leading TARA activists were secretary and chair of the steering committee and their roles became an increasing source of tension. Competent and committed though Jackie Gill and Tony Gamble undoubtedly were, they were seen as representative of the 'old deal' residents' groups. These had tended to sit on information rather than spread it, hold on to control rather than share it, and act as if their purpose was chasing money rather than thinking about different ways of running the estate. New ways were needed of managing the money coming into the estate and there was a widely felt need to break out of the cliquishness that had existed in the past. This meant there was widespread support for formalising and opening up the membership of the NDC committee.

The early NDC committee had taken two vital decisions. First, they had engaged solicitors to create a formal legal body – a non-profit making company – which was the Marsh Farm Community Trust, and second they had tried to seal into the constitution guarantees of power for community representatives. They also stipulated the membership (the directors) of any future NDC board: eight would come from partner public agencies such as the council and police, and sixteen would come from the community. Of the sixteen, eight would be chosen by the street co-ordinators and eight would be representatives of community groups, eventually to be chosen through an estate-wide election but in the meantime to be chosen at a well-publicised public meeting of local residents.

In addition to the NDC board of directors it was decided that there would be three complementary committees with delegated powers – the executive committee, the project appraisal committee and the human resources committee. The human resources committee had a difficult job in hand, but a fundamental one for building a lasting form of self-government. Its role was to set up a means of imposing discipline on any NDC directors, staff, grant recipients or committee members who broke the trust's basic humanitarian code of conduct. In July 2001, for instance, a female volunteer had been verbally threatened and physically assaulted by another, male, volunteer; this had been followed up by repeated harassment. Mediation had been tried but had not worked and the issue lingered on, unresolved. The human resources committee was delegated by the board to set up an expert and 'neutral' panel to judge the case and decide on appropriate disciplinary action.

The board on the job

By the time I spent a week on Marsh Farm to observe the NDC trust in action, its elected, community-led board was already in place, with much talent and experience to draw on. As in Manchester there was a strong sense of the need for teamwork, though they were not yet a team. Despite the joint aims set out by the delivery plan, there was not yet a common sense of direction or set of priorities for dealing with the continuing divisions within the community. The board members felt a weight on their shoulders – to many it felt like responsibility without power.

One problem was the controlling hand of the council, some leading officials of which interpreted its role as 'the accountable body' to mean involvement in every financial detail. The board meeting I observed (they are all open to the public), at which the council officer was present, sometimes had the atmosphere of a class of opinionated students eager for the approval of a teacher who was doubtful that she could trust them.

The board were becoming frustrated, and aware that momentum was weak. It was not long before the sixteen community members decided to meet regularly on their own to talk frankly with each other, voice their anxieties, including about each other, and forge a common sense of purpose. Without a regular meeting of this sort they could not, they felt, do their collective job properly. One reason for the loss of momentum was an extraordinary delay between the government's acceptance of the NDC delivery plan, and the agreement of all relevant parties to the funding contract. Finalisation of this contract was necessary to free up the money and put it in the hands of the NDC. Even then spending above £250,000 had to go back to the government office for approval. To make matters more complicated there were three parties relevant to this funding contract – LBC, Renaisi and the Marsh Farm Community Trust.

Renaisi

Renaisi were employed by the trust as experts to help to set up the mechanisms for Phase Three of the NDC bid. Their role would be vital. Originally engaged in June 2001, they expected projects to start getting under way by late July. In fact the funding contract was not agreed until November.

The underlying reason for the delay was the council's concern to protect itself. 'We have to pay the money up front with the government refunding us, so we have to protect ourselves', said Roy Davies, the chair of the council's regeneration committee. While such contracts could be signed in a matter of weeks, in this case there was much delay as LBC tried to pass legal responsibility for virtually everything over to Renaisi – even down to broken furnishing and fittings. In the end, the result of the conflict over the contract was a prolonged legal spat, funded with public money, which blocked the finalising of the funding and effectively took the process away from the community and into the hands of lawyers.

Until the agreement of this contract, there was no money to spend on major projects and only a 'management and administration' budget of £150,000 (much of which went on lawyers' fees) for setting up the trust. There was no money for developing the street co-ordinators, for example, or training residents in the skills of self-management – things that would have deepened the democracy of the NDC. And without the security of the contract, Renaisi could not start training local people. The trust did have a fund at this stage for small projects which could count as confidence boosting 'Quick Wins', but all the major work identified in the delivery plan was stalled for seven months.

Renaisi's role is interesting. Residents were initially focused on involving the community and developing the overall vision. Residents wanted to learn the more technical skills too, but the work could not wait until they did. Since the best kind of learning is working alongside those who have got the skills and are prepared to share them, Renaisi's brief was to work themselves out of a job.

Initiated in the early 1990s by Hackney Council in London to co-ordinate a regeneration project, Renaisi have worked on many projects including NDCs – most notably Shoreditch, which is determinedly resident-led. The structure of NDC bidding means simultaneously getting through government hoops, developing projects, opening up public agencies to residents' proposals, and setting up financial and management systems. Marsh Farm Community Trust brought Renaisi on board to help residents acquire the technical skills necessary to accomplish all this. They were to support the community in a democratic regeneration process which would develop its independence from the council.

Kevin Segue, Renaisi's clearly overworked boss, described their role as facilitation. Renaisi's style combines technical competence with an easy and equal working relationship with residents. But since not all residents are sufficiently confident immediately to drive the process themselves, and others are frustrated at not being able to determine the pace, there is tension. Renaisi have undoubtedly played a key role, without seriously undermining the residents, in negotiating the government hoops. On several occasions they have helped the Marsh Farm Community Trust win national government support when the LBC and GO East placed obstacles in the way of the Marsh Farm experiment. Their presence also buffers the residents from the council, and this creates space for the refining of democratic decision-making processes which everybody can trust and participate in. Some other NDCs have lacked such a space and seriously suffered as a result.

Appraisal

The other mechanism with which Renaisi has helped, although neither they nor local residents feel they have sufficient control over it, is appraisal systems. Every project has to go through three of these: an independent technical appraisal, a community appraisal (in which the council is also involved) and a GO East appraisal. 'At times it seems that the council and the government use appraisal as a form of control', says Norma Douglas, resident director on the board, but she has no resistance to the concept of appraisal. 'We appreciate having to go through questions like "What are the alternative options? How does it relate to the delivery plan? What needs does it meet? What are the risks and how will we face them? Have we discussed it with an advisory group?" That sort of discipline helps you. But the system is so mechanical and inflexible that it can waste a lot of valuable time. It puts off the very people we are trying to encourage.' This is a serious complaint made throughout the NDCs.

NDC appraisal systems are friendlier than their predecessors in the SRB. 'About 75 per cent of the SRB guidelines have been cut. They were so over the top', says one NDC insider. But still the cautious instincts of government officials have tended to want to minimise risks – an awkward stance for an institution that was set up to take risks. One project which nearly got stuck was the Community Outreach Workers (COW). Conceived to give life to the street co-ordinator system, and to generate the ideas and galvanise the people needed to turn the Coulters factory into the hubbub of social enterprises that it was intended to be, COW failed to impress GO East. They objected to its management structure: 'There's no single person responsible', they pointed out. Glenn wrote back, explaining why the management structure was purposefully co-operative and non-hierarchical and eventually, some months after the initial proposal, approval came through. Appraisal remains a useful and undemanding means, however, for government officials to exert control from a distance, rather than having face-to-face negotiations. Such nego-tiations could then lead to the government providing flexible support for innovative and therefore risky projects – precisely the sort of projects the NDC programme was created to encourage. But this would require a cultural revolution in government thinking and methodology.

Training for self-management

Work on street co-ordinators had begun early in the project – soon after Phase One had been agreed – in April 2000. Everyone hoped they would encourage the essential communication between the board and the residents. The co-ordinators would also provide feedback for the advisory groups and this was envisaged as an important part of the flow of creative energy in the trust's organisation. Eight of the co-ordinators would be directly represented on the trust's board.

Over forty people responded to a notice in the Co-op shop asking for volunteer street co-ordinators. The aim was to build up to a team of a hundred and divide into north, south, east and west areas with two co-ordinators for every eighty houses. In this way it was hoped that from the choice of two, every resident would have someone they would feel happy to have as their point of contact with the trust. There was some argument about the role of the co-ordinators. Some saw them as a possible network for distributing leaflets and a regular NDC newsletter. Glenn Jenkins and Bruce Hannah were wary of this. 'Their work is above all word of mouth, finding out what people want, discussing with them proposals that are coming to the trust, being a human transmission belt for people's ideas, keeping the trust on its toes', said Bruce. Circulating trust publicity was, after all, something the children on the estate were eager to do in exchange for some extra pocket money. In fact the kids are now regularly called upon on a Saturday morning to put out a 'jungle call' – a mass distribution of leaflets – advertising future events.

It proved difficult to sustain the momentum for the street co-ordinators on a purely voluntary basis. It's an ambitious idea, one which attempts to deepen the idea of regeneration far beyond the conventional model of a 'board'. Street co-ordinators would create the networks on which real neighbourhood democracy depends, like the CRC co-ordinators in Porto Alegre. Their work would mean that decisions about public resources – buildings and expertise as well as money – could be influenced by everyone on the estate. Members of the Trust could see the importance of this. 'Putting our roots back down into the community was to us as important as drawing up the delivery plan, legalising our structures and organising our administration systems', said Jackie Jenkins, who had been quick to volunteer for the streets where she lived. She was already, in effect, doing a co-ordinator's job – listening to problems, working on solutions, devising strategies. But there was no money to pay her. In the first two phases of any NDC there is little money available to pay those involved in the crucial work of what could be called 'building community democracy'. Consequently as other pressures, especially the completion of the delivery plan, built up, the street co-ordinators project was put on hold. It was constantly discussed, however, because it was clearly needed. The breakthrough came in February 2002 when GO East approved the scheme.

I dropped in on the April 2002 meeting of COW. It was a self-selecting group, made up of respondees to a leaflet distributed to everyone on the trust's mailing list and to every household in Marsh Farm. The group was already beginning to develop a self-discipline. The fact that they were funded by the community, i.e. the NDC, added to their sense of responsibility. The street co-ordinators' prime need was training in democratic self-management. There was a wealth of ideas – a builders' co-op, a music studio, a crèche, a catering co-op, a photography group. The question was how to turn these new ideas into lasting social enterprises. What was needed was training in the theory and practice of effective co-operative organisation.

The Organisation Workshop

A series of fortuitous, accidental connections led COW to become aware of the work of Brazilian Clodomire Santos de Moraes and his concept of the Organisation Workshop. Moraes had developed this concept from the training methods used in the Peasants Leagues that had resisted the dictatorship in Brazil in the 1960s. Self-discipline, unity of purpose, division of labour and efficient planning, delegation, co-ordination and organisation of time were matters of life and death in that context. In the 1970s Moraes had applied these methods to self-reliant co-operative peasant agriculture in the Honduras, with the backing of the UN's Farming and Agriculture Organisation. It was a success, and the participants in these workshops then reproduced this experiment across Latin America. The basis for an extensive network of training or 'capacitation' in self-management, the Organisation Workshop has now been in use for some two decades in Latin America and twelve years in South Africa.

It was arranged for one of the most experienced teachers of Moraes' ideas, Ivan Labra, to visit Marsh Farm. Labra and Marsh Farm immediately clicked and he was invited to run an Organisation Workshop which would be open to all trust members. On the day he arrived to start his week-long course, the boardroom of the Coulters factory was packed. 'We should have done this at the beginning', said several people, buzzing with enthusiasm during the breaks.

Ivan began by spelling out the global political context: an unusual thing to do in an age where community organising has been deeply depoliticised. The gap between the rich and the poor was growing, he said, and there was an anxiety about this in elite capitalist circles, mainly because of the disorder and disequilibrium it could produce. He quoted James Wolfenson, the director of the World Bank, as saying that 11 September was a response to poverty. In turn the World Bank's response, along with other international bodies and left-of-centre national governments, was to give money to poor communities, though holding back from any serious redistribution of wealth (echoes of the New Labour motivations for the NDC programme itself). But any new resources, argued Ivan, should be distributed directly to the poor, otherwise it would get siphoned off into the hands of consultants – 'people like me', he joked. The poor, however, were usually not sufficiently well organised to build for the long term.

All this connected with the experience on Marsh Farm. 'We've been a disorganised community – without being organised we'll go back to the old system'; 'We didn't know how to do it, no one told us', were some of the comments. Ivan moved the group on at a sharp pace through a discussion of constraints on direct delivery of local services to local people (where possible, by local people). Communities lacked experience of handling and deciding on the use of money; they lacked an efficient framework for members' participation; they lacked power to deal with bureaucracy, politicians, private consultants and autocratic leaders. He asked the group to reflect critically on concepts of 'community', 'development', 'empowerment' and 'power', with the aim of overcoming these lacks. The focus was all the time on creating the conditions, whether in organisations or consciousness, which would move people away from seeing themselves as passive victims of social processes, towards seeing themselves as subjects guided by self-consciousness: 'as active agents of change.'[4]

The emphasis of the Organisation Workshop method is learning by doing, so after two days' theory the course moved on to practice. COW formed themselves into a 'facilitators enterprise'. They would spread the workshop method to other people in the community and social enterprises proper. The task was to identify which social enterprises proposed for the Coulters building were suitable for development through the Organisation Workshop. People from the chosen projects would then work with COW to refine their proposal before applying to it the Organisation Workshop skills. Projects chosen included the crèche, the environmental task force, a cafeteria, a printing and publishing business, a social club/media suite and a community garage. COW undertook to identify the human and material resources required for each enterprise and work up a project application for it.

It was a heady week that had brought about many positive results on different levels. It had enabled people to consolidate half-worked-out insights about organisation that they had gathered during the first two years of the NDC; it had kick-started the process of finding social enterprises; it had instilled in the group a sense of inner self-discipline that had been lacking before, from being punctual to raising problems and doubts openly in the meetings; and it had enabled people to discuss values, an issue that came up again and again. The ex-Exodus people had been badly burnt in the final collapse of the collective by assuming, rather than explicitly stating, common values, and agreeing them. Bruce Hannah reflected this when he said, 'Values can be a danger. I've been part of a group with values but they turned out very different and it fell apart.' There was a general feeling though that common values are important and that the community had lost them. Ivan and Trevor Adams agreed: 'Values are our standards and we must discuss them, but it is resources and concrete activities that bring us together.'

The workshop also helped to create more equal relationships – one aim of the Organisation Workshop is to create a concept of community that favours dissolved leadership, a framework that relies on all members – and created a new energy and unity of purpose just at a moment when momentum was beginning to drain away from the formally democratic structures. It was suggested by attendees that all trust members and associates be encouraged to do this week's training.

Conclusion: an alternative source of buzz

The kind of energy which this outward-looking, confidence-building approach generates is illustrated by one final example: Dave Baptiste, convenor of the drugs and substance abuse group. He came to Marsh Farm in the 1970s, attended college and then did all sorts of jobs. 'Things looked good and Marsh Farm was a good place for young people. There were lots of us.' Then came the 1980s and unemployment. 'We became a group of lads who hung around together, got drunk, smoked weed, were into petty theft. We were all black.' They became connected with a group of older men, who organised pay parties and dealt in serious drugs. 'We got into fights with them. We took guns with us. Shots were fired. no one got hurt because we realised how serious it was.' But two of them got arrested. 'I realised it was a dead end and I had to get a new life.' He went to London, educated himself in martial arts and boxing and eventually became a professional boxer in Europe. In the meantime, his girlfriend had become a drug addict so he came back to look after his daughter. He bought a flat in Marsh Farm, heard about the trust, knew something of Exodus and came to offer his considerable energies and organisational skills to the problem of drugs. 'The old methods don't work because they don't recognise that people need an alternative source of a buzz. Through achieving something for example, doing something where you can buzz off other people.' The trust, full of kindred spirits, will give his ideas a hearing and maybe try them. Given a taste of alternative opportunities, young people might feel, like Baptiste did fifteen years ago, that drugs or crime are a dead end.

Glenn Jenkins too believes in nurturing this sense of responsibility in everyone. He argues this can be achieved through an active local democracy with a direct involvement in service delivery. Take, for example, the youth service: 'In the absence of figures from Luton Borough Council, I guestimated 50p per week per household from our community charge is spent on youth and community services', says Glenn. There are 4,000 households, so around £2,000 a week is spent on the youth service: on buildings and youth workers. 'The youth workers are great people but young people are not relating to what they are doing. The buildings are hardly used. Young people need to be in charge of how the money is spent. They need a youth forum where they could decide how money should be spent. They'd learn about democracy and responsibility in the process. Some of the £2,000 could pay youth workers to facilitate this, the rest would be for their own ideas and projects which they would manage.' Glenn's idea is that eventually youth workers, like Renaisi, would work themselves out of a job, though some kind of supervisory role would always be necessary.

One thing is certain: the present youth service is failing, and innovations like Glenn's proposal, which are rooted in the experience of those it is trying to help, are needed. But a responsive political system is also needed if such proposals are not to remain a pipedream. The whole of the Marsh Farm experience is like this – probably much of the experience of trying to improve the quality of life on all the neglected estates and neighbourhoods of twenty-first century Britain is like this too.

The old systems of local government have failed – partly through their own mistakes, partly through forces beyond their control. The only alternative to escalating chaos, followed in all likelihood by the authoritarianism of either the state or the far right, is an organised democratic participation in the management of public funds backed by real redistribution of resources to the poorer communities. Serious redistribution has not been on the government's agenda but their Social Exclusion Unit has at least recognised the importance of real power over whatever public funds are made available to be a necessary condition for people taking participation seriously. In pursuing its commitment to participation, however, it cannot assume tailor-made communities – identikit models produced by the Home Office's Active Citizenship Unit. The benefits of community leadership – the local knowledge, the local ownership of the regeneration process – cannot be had without pain, division and much raw conflict, including conflict with those in power. To adapt a quote from the US black civil rights leader Frederick Douglas, 'Those who profess to favour community, and yet deprecate conflict and risk are men who want crops without ploughing the ground. They want rain without thunder and lightening. They want the ocean without the awful roar of its waters.'[5]

A good number of the residents of Marsh Farm believe there is too much at stake to allow division and conflict to defeat them. They continue to improve their processes – their values, their relationships with each other and with outside agencies as well as their structures. They keep refocusing on the bigger picture of the quality of life on the estate. They would say they still have much to learn about self-management. But the most fundamental learning, or relearning, will have to go on in public bodies: especially learning the ability to work with the unpredictability and initial chaos – generally organised chaos – of genuine democracy. Public bodies will have to allow for a more thorough ploughing of the ground, more showers of rain and the continuing roar of the ocean before the people of Marsh Farm have the quality of life and control they are struggling for.

NEWCASTLE:
OUR CITY IS NOT FOR SALE

A phone call from Kenny Bell, UNISON branch secretary in Newcastle and an old friend, conveys a sense of urgency. 'You remember the alternative plans of the shop stewards at Vickers? People are raising the idea of alternative plans again, for the whole of the West End [of Newcastle, where Vickers workers and their families used to live – a few still do]. It's in response to council plans for demolition. There's a meeting at the civic centre next week. You should come.' Community organisations can lie low for years, immersed in a mundane routine of meetings and community advice, rarely appearing on the political surface of the city. Aroused by an injustice they can then explode.

In June 1999, the grand banqueting hall of Newcastle's civic centre, was the crucible for such an explosion. Tenants from the old riverside community of Scotswood poured in through the hall's padded leather doors. Teenagers, determined-looking middle-aged women, a smattering of older men who had seen their riverside workplace, the engineering shops of Vickers Elswick, demolished, were here to protest against the wholescale demolition of their community. Residents, vicars and shopkeepers from neighbouring Benwell and from Walker in the east of the city, just up from the walkways and restaurants of the quayside, were protesting too. The council's glossy A4 *Going for Growth* pack announced a city-wide plan 'for a European city of the future'. Scotswood, along with parts of Benwell and Walker, were coloured red for 'unviable'. No other option was presented. The 'masterplan' was given added authority by the claim that the internationally renowned architect Richard Rogers had been a joint author.

The first that the residents had heard about their fate was through the local press. 'We sat in the Community Project in Scotswood all morning gradually taking in the information as it came in from journalists', remembers Father Nicholas Henshall, whose church St Margaret is at the heart of Scotswood. 'Eventually we had a list in our hands: every street in Scotswood is to be flattened.' What made matters worse was that local residents had been working with the city council's community develop- ment staff on their own plans for the area. The basis of these discussions had been that although some demolition was necessary – everyone was agreed on that – Scotswood had a future. Gwen Hind, who had been on an 'awayday' funded by the council, recognised the residents' handiwork in the new plan in a ghostly sort of way. 'Everything that is in *Going for Growth*', she says, 'is what we wanted anyway, except that they have left out the community: the people who live there now.'

It was not the idea of regeneration that the people of Scotswood opposed. 'We know change is necessary and we want it to happen', said Gwen. It was the brutal character of the change and the contempt with which existing working-class residents were being treated that aroused such anger. It became clear that *Going for Growth* meant not just new private homes, but a new privately managed community including schools, street lighting, health centres, parks and shopping malls. The 500-strong meeting at the civic centre brought together people from across the city. They agreed to form the Newcastle Community Alliance (NCA). That night a new source of power was born, one that aspired to ensure the people who lived in the city determined its future.

A distinctive part of this alliance, and a factor which gave it added clout, was that Newcastle's protesting residents had allies in the unions inside the civic centre. Public-sector trade unions also often lie low, apparently on the defensive, sunk in routine, rarely setting the pace of public policy. But they too can be roused to take more strategic action. This can happen, for example, when management takes action that undermines workers' ability to give the public a good service. Management, politicians and most of the media seriously underestimate the strength of the ethic of public service that motivates public-sector workers.[1] These workers talk of their desire to 'do something useful', 'do something for the city' as a significant reason for taking a job with the local authority. They have as strong a pride in doing their job properly as the skilled engineers who used to work along the banks of the Tyne.

Privatisation at every turn

Newcastle Council's UNISON branch is one of the largest union branches in the north of England. One consequence of its size is that in a predominantly working-class city most people will know someone in the union at 'the civic'. Union members have a sense of loyalty to the city and its people. This kind of ethic led UNISON to throw its considerable strength behind the Community Alliance. But it wasn't just the council's regeneration strategy as set out in *Going for Growth* that was quickening the pace of activity in room 145, the hectic UNISON office. There were a variety of other concerns. Talk was also of what to do about Private Finance Initiatives (PFIs), in particular for street lighting and schools, council house stock transfer, and about the proposed outsourcing of Information Technology and Related Services (ITRS), the department responsible for collecting council tax and housing benefits and for providing the public with 'customer care'. In addition, there was the issue of the Byker incinerator, whose toxic ash (with levels of toxicity reaching that of the ingredients used in chemical warfare) was spread across the gardens and allotments of the city's east end. Despite residents and UNISON representatives gaining what they thought was an influence over the council's waste strategy following a powerful, locally driven protest, the council was still considering rebuilding the incinerator as a 'Reclamation Plant' and to bring in the private multinational contractor Sita (who already ran the council's disposal operations and managed the incinerator) to run the government-required recycling programme. By autumn 2002 unions and community groups were organising a demonstration and publishing a pamphlet under the banner, 'Our City is Not for Sale'. Privatisation, in its many guises, had brought together council workers and local people.

At the beginning of Newcastle's rebellion against its council's *Going for Growth* proposals, Kenny Bell was asked to speak to a meeting of homecare workers. 'There were about 250 workers in the room – I thought I was going to talk about terms, conditions and contracts, but speaker after speaker was standing up saying "We don't care about that. What we are here to tell you is that our jobs are being privatised."' This was a dedicated workforce: most of them have committed their lives to working in homecare. Their concerns were not just the potential impact on their jobs – they were increasingly concerned about the impact on clients. Many of those they had cared for in the past had been moved to the private sector and were talking of a whole catalogue of problems – carers not turning up on time, those needing three visits a day getting a different carer each time, sixteen-year-old students turning up without adequate training to put to bed people in their eighties.

At that meeting, a campaign was launched involving the homecare workers, unions, clients and clients' organisations (such as DAN, the Disabled Action Network). The emphasis was not primarily on the transfer of work from public to private, but on the quality of care. As a positive public focus, a charter for homecare was drawn up – a very basic set of demands about the quality of care that both clients and workers would expect people to receive. 'It's an explosive issue', says Kathy Collins, the GMB steward, herself an ex-carer. 'Thousands of people in the city get homecare. Councillors are susceptible to the debate about it because they can see the networks of relatives and the number of people affected and what this might mean electorally.'

Soon UNISON and the GMB were confronting management plans for privatisation on every front. As the different campaigns each gathered momentum it became clear that a source of unconventional power – workers defending not just their wages but the public nature of their work – was being mobilised. The anti-privatisers' stand won support across the city. It had a momentum of its own, independent of any formal political process, and eventually it had a considerable impact on the balance of power within the council's Labour Group.

The Real Politik behind the scenes

The man driving Newcastle Council's plans for regeneration and private financing and contracting was the new chief executive, Kevin Lavery. At thirty-six one of the youngest chief executives in the country, he had arrived fresh from a consultancy with Price Waterhouse and research into the US experience of contracting out local government services. Lavery was eager to have the power to put into practice his strategies for *Smart Contracting for Local Government Services* – the title of his book.[2]

His first conclusion in the book was that the management of local government needs to be 'depoliticised'. For him politics meant politicians, and he had absolutely no comprehension of the submerged politics of the city in which he found himself. Newcastle people felt loyalty to place and public services, and had a heightened consciousness of people's daily interdependence and an expectation that the council and the Labour Party were there to protect them – all of which was incomprehensible to Lavery. All this was still near to the ground, however, and bespoke an indigenous political culture that had not surfaced for ten years in the formal politics of the city.

The formal electoral politics of Newcastle were clear but not particularly democratic: the Labour Group held an overwhelming majority –

albeit with a still small, but steadily rising, Liberal-Democrat vote. There was a weak centrist leader, Tony Flynn, dependent on the king-maker and real centre of power, Kevan Jones, chief whip for the Labour Group, a councillor in the east end of the city and officer of the GMB, the union which made or broke many of the region's leading politicians. Jones, to judge from the columns of *Private Eye*, was a political baron in the worst north-east tradition. Peripheral to him and his clique were a group of left councillors who were competent and respected but marginalised. This arrangement, albeit murky, Kevin Lavery could deal with. He could rely on Jones to keep political control through a variety of forms of patronage – from tickets to the director's box of Newcastle United through to the salaried posts of membership of the council's executive or a chair of a scrutiny committee. And he could rely on Flynn to talk up the plans for reform to a cabinet which contained few if any independent spirits.

But what Lavery did not understand were the unions, the community groups, and the Tyneside history which had regularly brought the two together in defence of communities and workplaces. Nor was he aware of the independent left tradition in the region that had helped to form community and union leaders like Kenny Bell and Gwen Hind. Leading left councillors, community organisers, committed intellectuals, radical socialist clergy – all were alien phenomena to him. And political labels could not be easily stuck on any of them.

Lavery attempted to do his work within the framework of the simple political caricature spread by the thin but pervasive culture surrounding New Labour: 'Old Labour' versus 'the modernisers'. He saw himself as a missionary come to a backward land, not an ideologue but an evangelical pragmatist, working very much with the grain of government policy. To him the story was simple: the bureaucratic inertia of the 'sleeping giant', as he described Newcastle Council, needed the wake-up call of an influx of private-sector partners. He followed a US model of the city manager, adding a greater sense of strategy, and he assumed he could see it through.

In 2000, for example, the city drew up a bid to be the '2008 City of

Culture'. For the leading councillors this was a coveted prize, a symbol of transition from an industrial working-class past to a vaguely defined classless, consumerist future. The City of Culture bid stated that 'redevelopment is underway to transform the character of old industrial areas such as Scotswood, Benwell and Walker'.[3] This was before the council had even told the people in these areas what might be in store for them, let alone been forced to consult them.

By September 2001, two years on from the meeting at the civic centre, Kevin Lavery had resigned to take up a £200,000 a year job with Jarvis, a company specialising in PFIs. For all his analysis of smart 'outsourcing', he had been outsmarted by those who believed in doing a better job under democratic control – not one service had been outsourced while he was chief executive. Over the same period Kevan Jones had become an MP. *Going for Growth* meanwhile was being renegotiated in response to popular pressures in Benwell and the East End. The flattening of Scotswood continued though, through a combination of deceit and refusal to consider alternatives. Richard Rogers dissociated himself from the original document; while not wishing to take sides, he stressed the independence of his architectural work and the preliminary nature of his company's involvement in Newcastle. It looked like his reputation had been used. 'The problem,' he said, 'is that the council has blurred our very draft masterplan, with their plans. We have offered no solutions. We made no specific proposals for demolition.'[4]

Awakening the public-service ethic

By the time Lavery left, contracting out, smart or otherwise, was on hold. The sleeping giant was roused but this process, in part through the pressure of UNISON, had made some council managers more assertive in defence of publicly delivered and publicly accountable services. Some managers were shaken out of their routines, reminded why they had come to work for the local authority in the first place.

Lavery's problem was not simply that the natives rebelled, but that they advanced on him with spears in one hand and alternative plans to modernise public services in the other. If it had been just a matter of facing down protest then possibly, with Kevan Jones at his side, Lavery could have placated the ringleaders until the emotions calmed down. But the rebels had discovered that they could create effective forms of power to back up their plans. This chapter is the story of how these forms of power developed, the lessons learnt by those who built them, and the places they may take them next.

Kevin Lavery's significance is that he brought New Labour's message to a group of council managers many of whom were committed to keeping public services public, but who had taken the public-sector ethos for granted. He was faced with a politically conscious trade union leadership which had been rethinking how simultaneously to defend and improve public services ever since Mrs Thatcher first put the public sector on the defensive. UNISON had begun to create strategic alliances with politicians and senior managers which challenged the culture of the council. As a result, the way some of the services were managed began to be more dynamically public; the involvement of all levels of staff became more openly valued; and it began to create a positive relationship with service users and local communities. This is not to say, however, that this was the case throughout the council. In other services – waste, for example – departmental vested interests, including long-term contracts with private contractors, meant that senior officers were resistant to change. Moreover there was the constant pressure of a government for whom partnership with the private sector was an essential part of the definition of efficiency, and who had no comprehension of the possibilities or means of internally driven transformation. In addition, behind the government stood the international pressures to open public services up to the private market, in particular through the General Agreement on Trade in Services, GATS. GATS is an open-ended treaty, agreed behind the closed but besieged doors of the World Trade Organisation in 2002.

It aims to achieve 'progressively higher levels' of liberalisation of services, presumably until all those activities provided as public goods become potentially profitable commodities in which private companies can trade and invest. It is an international time bomb for local democracy.[5]

Given these challenges, local successes will always be partial and precarious. The Newcastle anti-privatisers knew that although their campaign was born in their city, if it remained restricted there, it would always in the longer run be vulnerable.

Keeping it public

The exemplary success story in Newcastle is the most strategic of the campaigns – to keep council control over ITRS. The city's workers and, under pressure, managers and politicians committed themselves to defeating the privatisation of these vital services, and in the process became an active force for improving public provision. In September 2002 Newcastle City Council made the landmark decision to accept the bid from its own management and workforce for a ten-year contract worth £250 million, one of the biggest in the country. They rejected a bid from British Telecom for a Joint Venture Company in which BT would have been the leading shareholder. Eighteen months previously an in-house bid had been out of the question.

What turned things around? When BT made its bid for ITRS, the council was under financial and ideological pressure, struggling to serve its citizens. BT presented its 'public/private venture' bid as a possible solution. The council would be only the junior partner, but there would be money to invest in modernising this crucial infrastructure – that was the conventional wisdom. The story took a new turn when UNISON pushed a new player onto the stage in the form of a strategy for internal reform of public services. This presented a challenge to the prevailing myths that the sole possible contenders in this contest were, on the one hand, 'old-fashioned' public management, characterised as inefficient, weak and in the thrall of overweening unions, and on the other, the dynamic private sector, arriving like a knight on a white charger to rescue ailing public services.

This alternative solution was driven initially by a new kind of strategic trade unionism. Union efforts were supported by the Sheffield-based Centre for Public Services (CPS), a rigorous research organisation headed by the dedicated and convivial workaholic, Dexter Whitfield. The CPS has a long record in collaborating with trade unions, community organisations and public bodies, and much experience in pulling together academic research and insights from 'best practice' in the public sector, scrutinising the record of private companies and developing strategies for defending and improving public delivery of public services. This combined well-argued intransigence and practical commitment to change, and revived the confidence of senior managers within the council in the values of public service. In addition, a mutually supportive alliance between UNISON and a group of councillors who had consistently opposed privatisation provided a catalyst to the Labour Group backing in-house provision.

The stakes were high. For a private company the proposed ITRS contract was major. The £250 million they paid for it would buy them an annual profit of up to £12 million, plus a foothold in the north east which, the logic went, might lead to contracts with others in the dense cluster of public agencies in the region. For the council, ITRS is the engine of its financial and communication systems internally, and externally its links with suppliers, the users of its services and the people of Newcastle. It is, however, a 'back-office' sort of operation, dealing with council tax, payroll, debt collecting, benefit payments – nothing glamorous or (visibly) related to the identity of the council itself. Lobbying organisations for the private sector played on the 'backroom' nature of what are in fact vital services that influence the effectiveness and character of everything the council does. The pro-privatisation lobbyists appealed to impatient politicians or weary senior managers with arguments along the lines of 'We'll take all the back-office burdens so that you can concentrate on the frontline services'. In fact, many local councils in Britain have already handed over effective control for these services to private companies, acquiescing to the government argument that the public sector does not have the capacity to modernise itself.

Pressures to privatise

The scenery against which the seduction was attempted in Newcastle included regimes set in place by the New Labour government. Although they did not impose privatisation in quite the blatant way that the Conservative's Compulsory Competitive Tendering (CCT) legislation had, nevertheless these new measures were increasingly directed towards 'outsourcing', effectively privatisation. New Labour's first shot at this was the Best Value regime that replaced CCT. This required councils to challenge their existing way of delivering services and explore how it could be done better – 'better' being generally defined as cheaper. Best Value guidelines did encompass the possibility of internal reform, and contained welcome emphasis on consulting service users and even public service workers, but in practice the insistence on 'markets of services', and targets of 2 per cent savings per annum over five years – a quantitative measure which easily squeezed out more qualitative assessments of service improvement – favoured 'outsourcing' to private companies. Certainly that was Kevin Lavery's interpretation, though departmental managers, where they had the freedom, often took a different approach.

The other legislation driving local councils into the hands of private companies is the severe restriction on capital spending, borrowing on the money markets or creating bonds. These activities are restricted on the grounds that they increase the Public Spending and Borrowing Requirement. As a result, councils approach private companies to negotiate finance and inevitably have to offer something in return, such as a degree of control of the project in question (future ownership, for example, as with PFI hospitals), or a high rate of interest on money borrowed.

Finally, legislation makes it difficult for councils to have anything more than a 20 per cent share in any independent company. If a council has a larger percentage shareholding than this, any borrowing that the company does is counted as borrowing by the council and hence increases its deficit. This means that in any 'joint' private/public venture, the private sector will normally have the controlling share. The only way of avoiding this is to bring other public bodies into the venture and thus dilute the power of the private shareholder.

The backdrop for the battle over ITRS in Newcastle also figures, centrally, a dramatic black hole in the council's finances – partly a legacy of the Conservative's reduction of central government grants, not restored by New Labour. Newcastle, like other predominantly industrial cities, received a double punch from the Conservatives: traditional industries were abandoned to the whims of the market and regions dependent on them were not supported to restructure. People were driven out and as they left, there was a fall in revenue for councils, since both council tax and government grants were dependent on the numbers using council services. In 1999, Newcastle council's budget showed an overspend of £1,505 million. The pressure on all council managers therefore was to save money. 'It was a pressure which would have us think short term and lose the wider picture', says Fred Stephens, head of ITRS.

Strategic counter-pressure

As we've seen, it was UNISON that initially provided the counter-pressure. Its ability to do so flowed from a number of distinctive features in the thinking and action of this unusually political (with a determinedly small 'p') kind of trade-union branch.

First, it looked at developments within the council strategically, as a whole. Then, as the comprehensive nature of the Newcastle version of

New Labour's programme of private-sector-driven modernisation became clear, in winter 2000, the union branch decided on an equally generalised counter-strategy. 'Very quickly after discussions amongst the shop-stewards committees [in different departments] we realised we would not win if we picked out just a single privatisation proposal', said Kenny Bell, a strategic activist to his core. 'We realised that while we would fight on an individual basis we had also to run a generalised campaign, raising the understanding of our members regarding the consequences of what was going to happen.' The bible of this approach was a thorough piece of work carried out by Dexter Whitfield in close collaboration with stewards and helpful managers, many of whom were themselves members of UNISON. The title was not one to catch the eye – *Outsourcing the Future: A Social and Economic Audit of Privatisation Proposals in Newcastle*, but the picture it drew of the threat to public services and their democratic control was dynamite.

As proposals for privatisation came thick and fast the branch decided on a general campaign to support the arguments in the CPS pamphlet with action. First, they proposed strike action by workers likely to be directly affected by privatisation: 'This was the best way to draw attention to the seriousness of the threat of privatisation and open the debate about how to stop it', said Bell. This became a regular tactic, but only one of a number. Others included lobbying, careful use of the press, and the spreading of information and arguments far and wide. The first use of strike action came on 10 February 2001. On this occasion it was only UNISON members who were involved. Fifty housing staff who feared that council plans to transfer the housing stock away from the council made their jobs insecure, voted to walk out. As a result of UNISON's campaign explaining how council housing transfer was part of a more general attack on the public delivery of council services, thousands of other members also took action. This success led the branch to follow with a more ambitious day of strike action, proposed for 28 September 2001. Spearheaded by workers in the sectors to be privatised: street lighting and ITRS, preparations included information campaigns and political lobbying. The workers were balloted and voted to strike, and this time found themselves supported by all the unions – the GMB, the building workers, UCATT, the engineering workers, AMICUS, and the Transport and General Workers Union – who encouraged every worker, as far as they could within the law, to join the strike.

This consciousness-raising and education campaign was successful. 'A mass meeting showed support from members in all services, way beyond what we anticipated', said Gill Peirson, one of the younger members who had decided to become an activist in response specifically to the privatisation issue and its consequences for democracy. Gill was not the type for whom routine trade-union meetings would be a natural habitat, but this campaign inspired her. 'We found fantastic support from community groups we'd worked with', she added. The press were sympathetic too – possibly following their readers. UNISON had worked hard to win this media backing.

The next step was to consolidate the breadth of support. 'We needed to explore whether we could bring all these separate developments under one umbrella and try to get more linkage and a strong coalition', said Bell. This led to the creation of the Public Services Alliance, bringing together as many organisations as possible in defence of the public sector, including a brave band of six Labour councillors who faced disciplinary action and threats of expulsion for speaking out against privatisation. Here was another feature of the branch's approach: a drive to create wider alliances rather than take on the employer or the government in heroic isolation. Politically it has been effective, personally it has taken a toll. The extra round of meetings for many activists has caused partners and co-parents to remark, only half in jest, 'You're behaving as if you're single'.

Not everything went smoothly. At eight o'clock on the night before the day of strike action, the council obtained an injunction declaring the strike illegal on the basis of Mrs Thatcher's unrepealed legislation against unions taking supportive action. The management attempted to contact every employee to tell them to report for work, but as John Field, branch publicity officer, remembers: 'On the day, thousands of members stayed away from work and lots of people turned up saying, "Hang on, some of my colleagues/mates are not in work, I'm not prepared to come in", and walked out again.' Despite the injunction, the day of action was judged a success. 'There was a massive public outcry in the local press about the council using anti-trade union laws. It showed the breadth of public support', concluded Bell.

Certainly it had a dramatic effect on the future of the ITRS. A week after the protest, the second company competing for the contract, CSL, withdrew from the procurement process, citing UNISON's opposition to its desire to transfer staff from council employment as the main reason. The city council issued a press release claiming that 'UNISON Intransigence Damages Investment Opportunity', but the protest also began to shift the balance of power against those who condoned press releases with such an anti-union flavour. Politically it was a watershed.

Three weeks after the would-be day of action, a number of resolutions on the future of public services came before the Labour Group. There was a defensive and ambiguous one from the executive, a firmly anti-privatisation one from Don Price, previously deputy leader of the council when the left had a very brief moment of power, and a strongly pro-local government amendment from Sir Jeremy Beecham, the widely respected ex-council leader who, Roy Hattersley-like, appears increasingly left-wing as the national Labour Party leadership moves so dramatically to the right. What came out of an unusual set of alliances was a shrewd use of words: 'This Labour Group reaffirms its commitment to public services delivered by public employees as its preferred option for the Best Value services for the people of Newcastle. Our aim is to achieve this through improved "in-house" services not privatisation ...' The resolution went on to acknowledge that the council must comply with Labour government legislation requiring councils to examine alternatives to 'in-house' provision and to consult the users of services, but it stated that the council would use alternatives to in-house provision if and only if 'a full "in-house" option has been prepared and there are still significant improvements to the service which cannot be achieved "in-house".' Since early on in the negotiations over ITRS, Kevin Lavery had said an in-house bid would not be prepared, this clause in the resolution was for UNISON and the Public Services Alliance a bottom line. The resolution continued: 'Group calls on the Government to lift restrictions on … departments carrying out work for other local authorities and resolves to consider joint operations with other councils.' It concluded: 'Group further agrees to support a campaign to persuade government to move away from the privatisation agenda.' All this was pretty radical for a group whose leadership only a few months previously was threatening expulsion to councillors who spoke up against privatisation. The resolution was passed overwhelmingly.

Don Price, familiar with the moods of the different factions who make up the Labour Group, explains what turned them around: 'Traditional Labour councillors, right-wing on many issues, realised the chief executive's privatisation plan went against their fundamental values. They were getting a lot of feedback from manual workers telling them they were crossing a Rubicon if they supported the privatisation proposals. They could see their base of support ebbing away.' Other factors were important too, including evidence, contrary to the assurances of the chief executive, of viable alternatives, as well as the calamitous examples of private sector inefficiency that were starting to emerge emerging, such as the collapse of privatised housing benefit systems in London.

The conversion of the Labour Group on this issue was fundamental to the success of the subsequent campaign for keeping ITRS in-house. It gave political legitimacy to UNISON's arguments for in-house provision, and it gave backbone to managers committed to keeping public services public. The achievement of this political shift illustrates two other features of branch strategy: explicitly political goals combined with an awareness of the limits of the union's own political role. As far as these activists were concerned, the defeat of ITRS privatisation was a political not a technical issue (as some of the top management claimed) and if they needed to push, press, inform and embarrass elected politicians into taking a stand, then they would, but not in order to substitute for them. 'There's no way that trade union activity in itself could have stopped the steamroller', commented John Field, the UNISON branch's press officer.

The union as messenger

Two tactics were important in persuading Labour councillors to start to turn the steamroller round. The first was for UNISON to keep the group of dissenters fully informed about what senior management, usually with the cabinet's rubber stamp, was up to. It's an odd situation where the union is keeping the politicians informed, but it's a product of the new cabinet system of local government. The old committee system, though not ideal, at least allowed ordinary councillors to have direct involvement in some areas of decision-making. All key decisions are now made by the cabinet, a fairly obedient group, usually elected on the leaders' recommendations, 'Most backbenchers are completely in the dark', says Don Price, agreeing that the work of UNISON was indispensable in exposing the full extent of the plans for private contracting. 'Our contacts with UNISON were also vital to demonstrating that there were viable alternatives', he added.

The second tactic for getting Labour councillors on board was to build public support for alternatives to privatisation, so that the councillors could no longer be complacent about their base. With turn-outs as low as 10 per cent in some wards, any signs that so-called apathy might be turning into active challenges to council policy, forced councillors to think before they nodded. The support for the day of action and rally proved to be a wake-up call. 'What really started to get it home to the Labour Group was the electoral threat', said Kath, the GMB steward for homecare workers. She herself seriously considered standing against Labour. One influence on her was that 'at meetings of 200 or so homecare workers, people would themselves raise the questions: "Why are we supporting Labour? Why are we giving money to Labour?"' 'In the build up to the 2001 local election, the debate was alive about taking bats home, standing alternative candidates', commented Kenny Bell. It was a strategy which the branch encouraged, aware of its potential to stir into action traditional members of the Labour Group. The Public Services Alliance gave the debate a concrete focus by involving all members in drawing up a Public Service Manifesto. 'The idea was that in local elections the manifesto went out to every candidate asking them to give it their support', says Kenny. 'It gave us a good start to develop an independent political stance but one that united people around a realistic but radical set of policies.'

These features of branch strategy created a favourable environment for the focused campaign to keep ITRS public. By October, BT was the only suitor in the field. It assumed that its favours – investment finance, 'business re-engineering skills' and a commitment to the staff that they would remain council employees, seconded not transferred – would be welcome. In fact, so far as BT was concerned there was no serious in-house bid on the table. This situation called forth other features of the UNISON branch's distinctive approach. The branch leadership and the twenty ITRS stewards began to pursue a 'twin track' strategy, on the one hand rigorously scrutinising the detail of all privatisation proposals, and on the other presenting alternatives.

Dexter Whitfield and the CPS backed up the scrutinising. Because the CPS works with many unions and local authorities it can keep each one well informed about the lessons to be learnt countrywide. Dexter's detailed scrutiny of BT was decisive in influencing several of the managers of ITRS to commit themselves to the in-house bid. 'Dexter's was one of the best critiques of BT's first offer. It was spot on', said Fred Stephens.

As soon as BT became the favoured partner, Dexter provided a profile of the company. His analysis revealed that BT needed the stability and low-risk profits that a deal with the public sector offered because it was under pressure from financial markets due to a £30 billion debt. This was a result mainly of the minority stakes it was holding in foreign companies while it transmuted from a British utility into a communications multi-national. The Newcastle contract would be with its loss-making Ignite division, whose sale had already been mooted in the financial press. At the same time that BT was negotiating with Newcastle, Ignite was facing ultimatums to break even or face closure.

If Newcastle Council was a sleeping giant, BT was one that had lost its way. Certainly, it appears to have changed direction suspiciously often. In 2000 it had restructured to create four business sectors: Ignite, BT Openworld, Yell and BT Wireless; by 2001 two of these were sold and it had embarked on yet another restructuring. The cost of 'rationalisation and restructuring' in the financial year ending March 2002 was a staggering £4,525 million, which included a £2,202 million bill for writing off Ignite's European assets (a result of 'streamlining') and call-centre rationalisation.[6] BT's pitch to the council included its expertise in 'change management', but the record documented by Dexter Whitfield of the consequences of these changes did not impress.

Another background factor Dexter highlighted was the series of catas-trophes experienced by the services across the country that had already been contracted out to private companies. After Andersen Consulting won the computer contract for National Insurance, for example, over 100,000 pensions faced underpayment of their pension plus a delay on their rebate. Siemens won the contract for the Passport Office; waiting time tripled. Siemens also took over the computer contract for immigra-tion and nationality and built up a backlog of 76,000 asylum cases and 100,000 nationality cases. They were penalised £4.5 million. And so on.

A central part of UNISON's campaign was to stress the importance of change and argue for the in-house bid not as a means of preserving the present situation but as an alternative, and more effective, strategy for change. They were clear that employment, wages and good conditions could all be protected, indeed could best be protected, by changes – as long as the unions were involved at every stage. UNISON made a special point from the beginning of the campaign against privatisation to stress that it was also working positively for change to come from within the council. UNISON's document, 'No Corporate Takeover',[7] spelt out how the union and management should change to deliver improved services. 'What we have learnt,' said Kenny Bell firmly, 'is that the status quo is not an option.' He continued 'I think this is a general issue, not just for Newcastle. If we are actually going to defend services then just arguing for the status quo is not going to engage the public. Much of their experience of the services we want to defend is not the best.'

The unions were determined to be involved in negotiating every management move to change. That had to include the process of procuring a contractor or partner. The unions insisted on an involvement in every aspect of the process, even apparently technical matters like the OJEC notice, which announces to would-be partners or contractors the city council's intentions. Not normally the material of class struggle, for Newcastle UNISON everything that defined the criteria for judging bids and partners mattered. UNISON insisted that the OJEC notice for the ITRS contract included the plan to develop an in-house bid, and ensured that the broad criteria for accepting a bid included 'community wellbeing, quality employment, vision'.

The importance of being involved in the procurement process was a lesson learnt during the Thatcher years, while dealing with competitive tendering. UNISON'S effective strategy at that time was to keep services in-house and improve their quality by negotiating the specification for each tender. In close consultation with service users during these years, they argued for the specification to include details about the quality of service required and the conditions of employment. Such requirements made it difficult for private companies, accustomed to emphasising cost-cutting, to compete with an innovative in-house bid. It is well known that the profit in privatisation, especially in local government services, comes from cutting labour costs. In the course of these CCT negotiations, over a ten-year period management and unions built up an accord, bonded by a common interest but driven by a respectful tension over their different roles. The result was that not one tender went out to the private sector – quite a record. In this way public-sector trade unionism differs from the more fundamental conflict that divides management and unions in a private company, where the company is required to put the interests of its shareholders first. 'There are times when we have a common interest with management in good quality and democratically accountable public services. It's important to co-operate with them, and sometimes to push them, without losing our independence, our accountability to our members, and our ability on questions of principal to face up to a conflict', explains Kenny Bell.

But winning an in-house bid against a multimillion-pound transnational company is very different from seeing off the regional or national companies that proffered the CCT bids of the 1980s. For one thing, there was a huge problem of confidence amongst council management and staff: did they have the capacity and vision, and the financial basis, to make an in-house option work? The political groundwork had been done, the principle of an in-house bid was on the table. What was needed now was to infuse it with drive and energy, to make it happen.

The senior manager responsible for the procurement process for the ITRS contract after the departure of Kevin Lavery was Barry Rowlands, a solid, powerful-looking man who held his cards close to his chest. The unions had worked with him during CCT. He was known to be inclined towards public provision but unlikely to take risks to defend the principle – well adapted, in fact, to the apolitical culture encouraged by New Labour. But he was ready to do business with the unions. UNISON was, as we have seen, committed to change and probably had more energy and ideas for the in-house bid than many managers, but no ambition to do management's job for them. 'We never considered drawing up our own proposal for an in-house mainly because if management didn't "own" the in-house bid, it would not succeed', said Ian Farrell, shop steward for the ITRS.

The twenty or so ITRS union representatives did have extensive discussions amongst themselves though, and developed clear ideas about what they would like to see in an in-house bid. These reps first gained the confidence to take some responsibility for the future of the service by studying the private bids and then meeting with their would-be employers, CSL and BT. 'We'd got really on top of the arguments with briefings and seminars beforehand', said Lisa Marshall, the union rep from the housing benefits section. CSL's slick PR and personnel team seem to have been somewhat taken aback by some of the questions put to them, particularly when asked to justify their financial model. This process drew some new blood into the union fold, people like Tony Carr who did not see themselves as trade unionists: 'The union wanted a staff-side exchequer rep. I'm not a union person but they've created a mechanism for getting involved in the process and I'm pleased with their approach. It's not extremist. We talk, we argue, we recognise there's got to be change. The union has kept up the pressure, seeing councillors and pushing at joint meetings.' Looking through UNISON files, Tony is right: the pressure is constant. In March 2001, an e-mail from branch secretary Bell complaining that the management is giving no leadership on the in-house bid. In July 2001, a letter requesting a meeting with top management to clarify the timetable for the in-house bid, and so on.

Building confidence

For Tony Carr and other union reps, the first real sign that management were taking the in-house bid seriously was a series of workshops on the bid in May 2002 – one for management, one for staff and one jointly. 'It was these that gave us the confidence that an in-house bid was in our grasp. There had been an atmosphere coming from management that we just weren't capable of improving things ourselves.' The final joint workshop tested and built up commitment to the in-house bid. It started with basic questions such as 'Why are we in this position?', 'Do we have the capability and willingness to change?' and 'What would happen if we did not change?' and went on to agree guiding principles for the in-house option, consider the assessment criteria for all proposals, and finally to discuss opportunities for improving the benefits from the in-house proposal.

These workshops were unique within the council: a structured mechanism for genuine staff involvement. And the staff made sure that they were not a one-off. They were followed up by three kinds of involvement; informal staff input into the detail of change within each department, regular meetings of 'the core team' which consisted of the twenty or so staff reps and the nine managers who made up the ITRS project team, and further regular meetings of the core team with leading councillors. 'We were insistent on this political involvement, even if it meant being chaperoned by management', said Tony Carr.

Prior to the workshops and any serious consideration of the in-house bid, there had been ad hoc staff involvement in the Service Improvement Plans (SIPs) drawn up to prepare for the change. 'Staff were involved in the initial ideas for improvement in most departments – the council tax department was not so good – but the final plans were drawn up by management, or possibly BT', says Kenny Bell. BT were involved in this way because they used the SIPs for their bid. The unions learnt to be insistent on joint mechanisms for every bit of the process.

The unavoidable impetus for change came when the computers on which the ITRS relied reached the end of their working life. Like changing a carpet, the future positioning of everything else was suddenly in question. A new, standard system would cut costs and create opportunities for improving communication with service users. It would also mean retraining and some loss of jobs. Essential to the staff involvement was an agreement with the union that all staff displaced would be re-deployed and retrained without loss of pay. This agreement helped create the co-operative atmosphere of trust that made the workshops produc-tive. It was not a guarantee but it was a commitment. 'It always has to be monitored,' commented Ian Farrell, 'that's one of the jobs of the trade union reps.' Reps developed a dual role: the normal monitoring of wages and conditions and taking up of grievances, and the organisation of the staff's input into the process of change.

The debate in the workshops about why radical change was necessary revealed the distinct perspectives of management and staff. There was a degree of mutual blame: management was accused of lack of leadership and poor project management, unions were accused of having too much power. But there was a more interesting difference of emphasis. 'We stressed the need for integration between departments and between back office and customer services', said Farrell. 'We see things service-wide because that is how we are organised, it's where our strength is. Management tend to have a much more departmental view.'

Another distinct emphasis coming from the staff, especially those dealing with the public, was caution about over-reliance on new technology. Take Lisa Marshall and Jean Dunlop – working on housing benefits and debt collection respectively, they are 'back-office' workers, employed to discuss problems with people on the phone. A fear of too much displacement of human contact by mechanical solutions was one factor in their opposition to a joint venture dominated by BT. As Jean put it: 'It's about retaining control in order to be able to follow things through with someone, build a rapport.' 'We'd lose a lot if we lost the ability to talk to people directly', Lisa added. 'We give out a lot of advice, about debt management, other agencies. We get a lot of people from vulnerable groups or with problems of literacy, or just old biddies wanting to sort out their benefits. You just can't get away from people's feeling that they want to deal with a person. They want to have a name. CSL were saying they would simplify the process, by which they meant effectively get rid of this direct access. There was talk of creating portals so people just keyed in their details and it was all processed outside of Newcastle.'

This issue of relations with the public became central to the way that staff regarded change. There was discomfort with the split between 'back-office' and 'front-of-house' services. In the past the two areas of work had been closely linked, but the gradual cost-cutting automation of back-office work together with the rise of image as all important, sharpened the distinction. From what the Newcastle reps could see, BT's approach would widen this gap.

'We went to Liverpool [where BT already had a joint venture with the council] and the front of house was all very glossy and people seemed happy with the changes; it was from the back that the grumbling came. We don't want to be second-class citizens', says Tony Carr. Newcastle ITRS workers wanted to use the new technology to improve communication and make the human factor more effective, not cut it out. 'We've all had that experience as a user of a service when they ask you what you want, and all you really want is a person. Also as a worker you get satisfaction from getting to grips with the details of someone's problem, through human contact, and then solving it with the help of technology,' added Carr. 'There was a fear that with BT we'd end up working in call-centre conditions, like automatons', says Jean Dunlop.

Staff felt they understood the needs of the public for council services in the way that a private company could not, and that this was a strong reason for keeping IT services within the council. They looked at how each service could be improved through use of the technology and through greater integration of presently separate departments. A good example of an improvement which could be made best under public control was the closer linking of the Customer Services Centre with different council and ITRS services. 'We understand the council as a whole, we can integrate these services much better than a company coming in without that knowledge', said Farrell.

Without setting out to, the workshops had effectively denuded the corporate emperor, BT, challenging each of its claims to be the best agent of effective change. The workshops fortified the council workers and boosted their confidence to challenge BT's critique of the in-house bid.

BT, for instance, boasted a management free to 'take hard decisions'. Council workers replied that if they meant they would hammer the unions, that would rebound on the council, and be expensive and counter-productive. The in-house option aimed to work more efficiently with the unions, giving them the commitments that staff need to feel secure enough to take on change. Again, BT, peacock-like, displayed its extensive corporate feathers, stressing its capacity to provide economies of scale. The in-house option countered: 'We can form partnerships with other public bodies. We can share IT facilities for wages, council tax, housing benefits with Gateshead, North Tyneside and other councils in the area. That's value for money, public-sector style.' BT suggested its involvement would be good for the image of the city, maybe attracting further investment. The in-house bid, however, could envisage that an efficient, publicly run IT service would achieve this positive change by building up confidence in the council's own abilities – even widening the scope of the council and the rest of the public sector to develop the regional economy.

Some truths were told during these half-day discussions. Outside the context of the normal hierarchies and work groups, both management and staff were able to drop some defences and acknowledge room for improvement. In the management workshop voices were heard admitting the need to develop an ability to work 'across functions'. The staff, for their part, were clearly committed to making changes and they wanted to get on with it.

Management moves

By May 2002, when the workshops got underway, people who had a real commitment to improved public delivery led the management team. People like Fred Stephens, who had moved from the private to public sector to avoid the continual pattern of structural vacillations following on the whims of private directors. He feels proud to work for the city council and is not against buying services and skills in from the private sector when necessary, an approach he describes as 'horses for courses', but he is clear that private companies have very different motives. 'Their prime motivation is to make a profit and to pay a dividend to their shareholders, whereas we are focused on serving the citizens. And we know the services that Newcastle City Council delivers have a direct impact on people's lives.' Pragmatic, describing himself as 'definitely not a political animal', Stephens still has a strong commitment to the irreplaceable role of the public sector.

Another such manager was Alan Bertram, head of services in Housing and Community, who took the lead in preparing the in-house bid. His day-to-day responsibility was for the smooth working of housing benefits. His profession was accountancy and since leaving school he had chosen to pursue this profession 'in the service of the public'. In his cautious accountant-like way he was firmly committed to 'the huge value that there is in the public delivery of services'. With a long inside knowledge of how to make a complex system like a large city authority work on limited resources, he was not the man to be impressed by private-sector claims of management skills.

The two events that led managers such as these to commit to the in-house bid, while at the same time working with BT, were Kevin Lavery's departure and the resolution of the Labour Group in favour of in-house provision. From then on management knew that their political bosses were serious about an in-house bid, not simply as a foil for the BT bid. But there still needed to be 'a big culture change' to overcome widespread resistance to change within the council workforce. One development that shook management out of their cautiousness was UNISON's decision to sign up for such change as integral to the framework of an in-house bid. The union would not have done this for a Joint Venture with BT.

Another underlying factor pulling management towards the in-house bid was a creeping disillusion with BT. One senior manager pointed mischievously to a postcard he kept on his desk that summed up his feelings towards the company. It was produced as an advertising gimmick by a rival telecoms company and said 'Don't Trust Them'. BT was already attempting to bring into the process its own favoured suppliers, rather than the most economic (keeping things 'in-house' for BT, in fact).

In June 2002, the two bids came in. Alan Bertram did his sums and concluded that all the savings achieved by the BT proposals and more could be achieved in different ways in-house. The savings on staff proposed by the in-house options were considerable – 153 jobs to go over six years – but not as large as BT's. For the in-house bid, financial institutions had agreed to play their part in the leasing arrangements to cover the capital investment necessary for new hardware, and expertise would be bought in, where necessary, to transfer skills to the council. On the other hand, with a Joint Venture with BT, management would probably take away more knowledge from the council, for example about the workings of local authorities, than it brought to it. And of course, as Fred Stephens put it 'the profits BT had to take out of their deal in order to satisfy their shareholders made theirs a very unattractive proposition'.

A landmark for public-sector reform

In September 2002, Newcastle's cabinet agreed to accept the in-house option. This led to the creation of a new council organisation, which would bring together all the IT-related services, called City Service. It might prove to be a quirk or it might prove an example to set a trend. The cabinet's decision and all the work pressing for and creating the in-house bid means that it can no longer be assumed that putting a strategic service out to tender will lead to a private company, usually a major transnational corporation, taking control. Few, if any, local authorities have started the procurement process, something increasingly required by the government, and then drawn up an in-house bid to compete within it. The language is so inert and stodgy – 'in-house bids', 'procurement processes', 'strategic delivery services' – that it is difficult to convey the importance of what has happened here. It is the first time that the people's commitment to carrying out a public service, with co-operation between departments and between management and staff, has been given a value and recognised as able to deliver a public service more efficiently than a company working for profit can. By the 'first time', I mean the first time since Tony Blair's mantra 'it does not matter who provides the service, what matters is what works', took a grip on the battered and defeated public services of Britain's local government. Newcastle's story provides a model for improving public services quite beyond Blair's political imagination. It's a model that has been born out of a struggle in which people – staff and managers – believe it *did* matter who owned and controlled the service. It mattered for reasons to do with the efficiency of the service, because for a public service efficiency is closely connected to democracy.

Whether Newcastle becomes a trend depends in part on whether its public delivery of ITRS succeeds. In comparison with this, winning the bid was easy. Two developments are important here and will influence the spreading of Newcastle's example. The first is staff involvement in a process of change which is being negotiated between management and a union committed to public-sector reform, committed also therefore to the spreading of this example. The other is the development of a subregional and potentially regional public-sector alternative. This is significant because the north east is likely to become the pioneer of regional government, thereby gaining some autonomy from central government, and some limited powers to carry out and promote its own policies.

The agreement on staff involvement and 'employee relations' in the new City Services builds on processes developed during the creation of the in-house bid. There is an explicit recognition that 'staff are stake-holders' and a commitment to make this real with thorough-going representation. There is a recognition of the need for both speedy decisions and rapid resolution of disagreements around change proposals, but there is also acceptance that there might be conflicts of principle which require access to disputes procedures. All this reflects the (normally) creative tension between a common commitment to high-quality public services, and readiness to take action if staff conditions, jobs or public delivery is under threat. It keeps both Newcastle UNISON branch and senior management on their toes.

How the new public City Services works in practice will depend a lot on attitudes brought to it. Staff reps are hopeful and excited but apprehensive at the same time. Pat Carr is the rep for IT itself; his members include the team working on the old mainframe computers. Their jobs will be completely transformed, and some will be made redundant. He's enthusiastic about the new development but he's also anxious: 'At last we'll be planning our own future. I just hope that our co-operation isn't going to be used as a stick to beat us.' He accepts that new senior jobs need to be recruited by open competition but is worried about 'how down the line this will be' and wants new jobs ring-fenced for existing employees who will lose their present jobs.

He sees real potential in the new organisation. 'It won't be hidebound and will be based on industrial democracy.' One of the directions he wants to push in is: 'using IT to get people's opinions and feedback about services. At present all the council's information is one way. In a situation where we are seeing democracy wither on the vine, we must find a way in which people can have an influence. The local politicians should be pushing for that.' But Pat is also worried about the democracy in his own workplace. He thought the workshops were good but 'a bit isolating'; the membership was not sufficiently involved. He thinks management should do more to involve staff, beyond the reps in the process of change. 'We the trade union reps shouldn't be a conduit for management: they need to have their own communications systems.' So change is going to be a constant negotiation not with 'dinosaurs' – New Labour's caricature of public-sector trade unions – but with people full of drive for improving the service in a way that is responsible to those who use it.

Though the union will try to develop the Newcastle experience into a wider trend, such learning from an innovative but gritty experience faces a major obstacle: fear. The union had issued a press release celebrating the success of the in-house option. Management were furious, at one point threatening disciplinary action. Fred Stephens was explicit about why: 'We need to keep a low profile because of the Performance Review.' Barry Rowlands was more defensive: 'The success of the in-house bid was the outcome of proper procurement procedures. It's nothing to do with privatisation. The union gets it wrong when it says it's political.'

The government's Comprehensive Performance Assessment Review is the latest in its inspection regime on local government. It is run by the Audit Commission, with all its authority as a neutral evaluator. Regarding neutrality, however, notions like private tendering for public services, at one time seen as highly political, can become in another era normal, by virtue of habit. In 1998, a year after New Labour gained office, outsourcing was just one possible means of achieving Best Value. The final decision would, most people assumed, be taken ultimately by the politicians. By 2002, however, the Audit Commission's Comprehensive Performance Assessment Review had defined outsourcing as in *itself* a positive indicator of good value. Barry Rowlands and Fred Stephens were afraid that by celebrating the success of the in-house bid, the council would lose marks in the Performance Review and therefore the funds dependent on top marks – it must be a bit like being back at school.

The extent to which democracy has been eroded and with it the chance of spreading alternative models of improvement of public services is revealed in the story of the Audit Commission's 'Best Value Review of Construction Related Services' (CRS) in Newcastle. One of the problems facing local democracy is a bureaucratic invasion by harmless sounding acronyms and worthy sounding titles, so that most people no longer notice what is actually happening under these epithets. But this story deserves the spotlight.

In 2002, the council carried out a Best Value Review of Newcastle's construction services. The Audit Commission inspectors assessed the results. They were not happy, mainly because in their view there was not enough 'market testing', i.e. putting services out to tender, and not enough 'outsourcing' to the private sector. In other words the Best Value inspection regime carried out by the Audit Commission for the government, no longer posited Best Value as neutral between public and private but laid down outsourcing as itself a criteria of good value. This brought the Audit Commission and its political masters, the government, into direct conflict with the democratic procedures of Newcastle council. This was starkly demonstrated by one of the overheads in the presentation that the Audit Commission inspectors gave to councillors and senior officers. The overhead showed the resolution passed by the Labour Group on 15 October 2001 stating its overwhelming preference for services being provided by 'public employees'. 'This is a problem', explained the inspector. 'It is in direct conflict with government policy.' In effect, managers were being told that a higher authority annulled the political framework within which they thought they were working.

Newcastle UNISON may have helped to defeat one global corporation, through a combination of a positive alternative and a strong industrial and political campaign, but the organisers rushing in and out of the union office know that they cannot defend public services successfully in just one city. 'We've got to get more informed about the international pressures that are driving this government, and about the companies that are hovering to move into our services. We need to be part of a wider movement', said Ed Whitby, a rising young politically minded activist.

From local to global

In the middle of the struggle over ITRS, Kenny Bell had the opportunity to go to the World Social Forum (WSF) for 2002 in Porto Alegre. His funding came from a progressive trust, the Barry Amiel Trust, and the UNISON branch. Also Veronica Dunn, UNISON national president but also a leading activist in the Newcastle branch, was so keen that Kenny should go that she contributed some of her presidential personal allowance.

He went to the WSF with an agenda: 'to make contact with public-sector trade unionists from across the world, learn from their experiences, make contact with intellectuals, research what's going on with the WTO, GATS and the leading privatisers like BT – and just to enjoy the spirit of such an amazing event.' He returned home with a much clearer, pressing sense of the global agenda being driven through by the WTO. Having spent some time with people from across the globe who had been on the sharp end of WTO rulings, he was stunned by the similarity between their experiences and Newcastle's: 'Whether you are talking about electricity cut-off in South Africa, privatisation of water in Columbia, the threat to public transport in India or the break up of local government services in Britain, there's a global free-trade agenda behind it.' Such an awareness could be paralysing, but the vibrancy and solidarity of the WSF made him aware that every attempt to implement this agenda is facing a resistance that is growing and is coming mainly from a new generation, not the dwindling battalions of the traditional left. 'We went on a demonstration of 50,000 people campaigning and marching against a free-trade agreement between the US and Latin America. The majority of them were workers and young people.'

To transport something of his inspiration home to share with the rest of the branch, Kenny brought back from Brazil a twenty-foot banner announcing in red on white: '*Globalismo lutte, globalismo esperance*' – 'Globalise struggle, globalise hope'. It was signed '*Via Campesina*', the name of the global farmers and peasants movement whose banner it originally was. This banner now covers one wall of the UNISON office in Newcastle Town Hall, sharing inspiration duties with the equally large, though more homegrown banner, 'Our City is Not for Sale'. In the months since Bell came back the message of the two banners have become increasingly connected. Through his report back and information about GATS, union members and others in the Public Sector Alliance could understand more clearly the international pressures driving the determined, relentless efforts to privatise services in their city.

International organising is beginning to take shape. UNISON has realised that across Europe public-service trade unionists are facing very similar market pressures. 'Corporate chief executives are roaming the world as part of the privatisation process. We have to get organised at that level.' So a group of activists across the region organised to get elected on to the regional international committee of the union. It was almost moribund. Their budget had been cut to £300. Ed Whitby and his colleagues got the committee galvanised again and argued for UNISON throughout the region to develop an international perspective on their work, appointing an international officer for every branch.

Their first focus was to organise a delegation to the European Social Forum (ESF) in Florence in November 2002. It was an initiative that had its origins at the Porto Alegre WSF. Europe, along with the US, was the last continent to organise a means of continental co-ordination of the various networks and movements challenging neo-liberalism. In Newcastle, twenty-eight trade unionists, mostly from UNISON, signed up for Florence within weeks of the first announcement of the event. 'I wanted a greater understanding about European and world-wide issues and where we fit in the big picture', said Gill Peirson, one of the first to sign. 'I wanted to bring information and understanding back to Newcastle to help our members and build our campaigns', 'Greater co-ordination', 'More information about similar experiences in Europe', 'Greater contact with people facing similar problems' – all the delegates to the ESF gave similar reasons for taking the coach to Stansted, a cheap flight to Ancona and then a four-hour train journey before they could taste their first sip of Florentine coffee.

The ESF presented the Tynesiders with 60,000 people from over twenty-five countries, running hundreds of workshops in at least six different languages and representing thousands of different organisations. June Saines, the branch administrator, and Gill Peirson went ahead to set up camp for the delegation (and to check out the best bargains in boots and bags). The Newcastle contingent had the air of a major expedition with delegates being well briefed beforehand, and priorities having been worked out back home for attending designated workshops at the Forum. Every morning the group met to give a shape to a day that could otherwise be very chaotic. At the end of each evening their growing entourage converged on the appropriately convivial Bacchus Bar to swap experiences and hammer out finer points of political strategy.

Forming a small cohesive group and touching base regularly is the best way to engage with huge and extraordinarily diverse international gatherings like the WSF and ESF. In this way the Tyneside crew made the most of everything the event had to offer, despite making comments such as 'I'm new to this trade union lark', or, like Gill Peirson: 'I'm not a political activist'. They were impressed by the organisation, which had gone into the Forum. 'The only organisational improvement I can think of is to get people to say beforehand what seminars they want to go to' said Derek Muse, frustrated by the overcrowding of the workshop on GATS. 'I certainly didn't feel an outsider,' he added, 'which is more than can be said of UNISON meetings I've been to!'

Perhaps the biggest leap in consciousness – and reality – arising from the ESF was a sense of a Europe-wide movement. As Gill puts it: 'What we are facing in Newcastle is happening everywhere. That's what really hit me.' 'The sheer volume of people gave me a sense of a growing movement that is very real', said Lee Turner. For Kenny Bell, a more hardened politico: 'Florence really illustrated the potential for a European left and laid the basis for more networking, sharing ideas and experiences, and co-ordinated action.'

On their return, co-ordinated action to stop GATS became the focal point of the energy generated in Florence. The long-term consequences of GATS are drastic. If it is allowed to go through, it will open up all public services, in Europe and worldwide, to private corporate investment. Most human activities will become, in the fullness of time, profit-oriented commodities. The ESF became the launch base of a pan-European campaign to expose and halt the secret progress of GATS through the corridors and lobbies of the European Commission. The Tyneside delegation came back determined to mobilise their labour and trade union and community movements to join actions to stop it and to brief activists on its consequences.

Back on the domestic front pressures were building. On the issue of waste and the Byker incinerator, council management led by Barry Rowlands had offered the contract for recycling to Sita, rejecting out of hand the idea that the council's own refuse workers could handle this new work, as if they had never been through the successful experience of an in-house bid for ITRS.[8] Elsewhere management was putting out proposals for not-for-profit trusts for leisure services; the campaign to defend and improve council housing was building up; construction services were offering 'framework contracts' to private companies which effectively gave them blank cheques by granting them overall contracts for a development with the power to subcontract as they wished. 'A housewife's work is never done', says a feminist poem. The same applies to the work of a public-service trade union branch dedicated to defending and improving public services. The truth is, however, that the power to defend and improve services lies beyond any individual trade union branch: it also lies with the public, organised in some way; with other unions, co-ordinated in some way; and with politicians, activated in some way. And it lies with a sense borne of practical experience, that local campaigns are connected with a wider movement of people organising internationally on the same problems. The Newcastle example shows the power that is created by making well-organised connections between these otherwise disparate forces. It also shows how precarious such power can be.

This precariousness lies with the weak political representation of the alternative ideas for public services of the UNISON branch and the Public Service Alliance. This posed a dilemma. The campaign to defend and improve public services was broad based – drawing on people inside and outside the Labour Party and the Green Party, supporters of the Socialist Workers Party and other small left organisations, and independent activists. The Public Sector Alliance had to find a way of influencing electoral politics without grouping round any single banner. The solution was to draw up a manifesto on which they could all agree, and then to campaign for different parties and candidates to support and adopt it. In effect, this manifesto would become their banner. It's a novel way of seeing electoral politics and has echoes of the PT: the movements set the pace, develop the policies and then creates or in the case of Newcastle bring together a diverse electoral voice. It is their next step on to new political ground.

FROM BESWICK TO BRAZIL:
DEMOCRACY NOW!

I want to return to the foundation stone on which Tom Paine built his argument for democracy. It became the touchstone of my journey:

> It appears to general observation, that revolutions create genius and talent; but those events do no more than bring them forward. There is existing in man, a mass of sense lying in a dormant state, and which unless something excites it to action, will descend with him, in that condition, to the grave. As it is to the advantage of society that the whole of its facilities should be employed, the construction of government ought to be such as to bring forward, by quiet and regular operation, all that capacity which never fails to appear in revolution.

The people I observed for several years in Porto Alegre, Marsh Farm Estate, East Manchester, and Newcastle (and more briefly in many other places besides), were all, it seemed to me, applying this 'mass of sense', previously used within families, neighbourhoods, trade unions, voluntary groups and (exceptionally) political parties, to the process of government – democratic self-government. They were trying to create a form of government that would through its very character – its power structures and decision-making processes – employ fully the capacities of others like them in the future.

Now, I write these conclusions at a time (April 2003) when the gulf has rarely been greater between decisions made by those in power and the wishes of the people; it is the nadir of representative democracy. George Bush and Tony Blair, two world leaders each elected with the support of only a minority of their country's voters, have felt sufficiently above international law to unleash the world's biggest military machine supposedly to disarm a dictator already under effective pressure from the United Nations Arms Inspectors.[1] Their ally, Jose Anzar of Spain, gave his support against the wishes of 90 per cent of his population. They have treated democracy with contempt.[2]

But the resistance organised to try to prevent this political catastrophe moved closer to creating a much-needed source of global democratic power than ever before. No longer can the issue of public opinion be relegated to the post-decision clear-up and spin operations. Before the global anti-war demonstrations political journalists discussed every relevant factor, other than the views of the public. After these insistent expressions of public opinion Kofi Annan's press officer remarked that there are now two superpowers: the US and world public opinion. People's consciousness of power, and of democracy, has changed. Millions have witnessed for themselves what it is like to be powerless even when in the majority. And the experience has got them thinking – grappling with the problem of how to build a new power for genuine democracy in the face of the military and corporate interests of the United States. A mass of sense, it seems, is truly being awakened.

The era that preceded this awakening and inspired this book began in 1998 with demonstrations outside and inside the World Trade Organisation in Seattle. They were demonstrations that exposed the secret constitution of the global economy which was permitting companies from the developed capitalist economies to sell and invest wherever they liked, on whatever terms they chose – while the markets of the North were closed to the developing economies of the South.[3] The movement that stalked the global elites from Seattle to Dohar and beyond, encamping, demonstrating, arguing, lobbying outside every summit and every major international negotiation created a new global bargaining power. Through a growing network of organisations – and more recently the World Social Forum – it has become like an unofficial interrogator questioning the legitimacy of the new world order and providing a constant reminder that there are alternatives. This opened up hopeful new possibilities. Were there local processes, with their own dynamics, that could give this global challenge sustainable roots? How could such local power together with global action exert a pincer movement of democratic control over the national governments that have been both architects and accomplices of the new global power structure? Such questions set me journeying.

As I looked, I soon faced the issue of the state, or at least of state institutions. In a locality, any struggle for democracy becomes engaged with the state, whether they want to or not. But it's not a simple question of the state versus the people. To varying degrees in all the places I visited people had become aware that they were losing a tug-of-war over institutions they had previously taken for granted: city finances, local council departments and services, indeed, in the case of Luton, the whole infrastructure of an estate. All were either about to collapse through neglect or corruption (the latter most explicit in Porto Alegre) or to be taken over by private companies. Elected politicians had neither sufficient power nor the political drive to save them on their own. But through different combinations of political parties, community movements and active trade unions, people are beginning to create new forms of democracy aimed at transforming those aspects of the state that are susceptible to public pressure and making it more responsive and accountable. Not only this, in small ways they illustrate how one set of state institutions can under greater democratic control be a source of leverage over other less accountable ones, and also over private interests that in some way or other depend on the state. In that sense, winning political office is never winning power – like climbing mountains, reaching one point just gives you a better vantage point from which to make an assault on the next.

My hunch was that my journey would be one of political discovery. My starting point was a belief in the creativity of practice. Not surprisingly, this conclusion is less a rounding up of arguments than a summary of new ideas and new departures stimulated by what I found. The idea of bargaining power for democracy is the first. Flowing from this is the notion of 'political follow-through' – the way that people can make the power they have generated in order to gain a degree of control over their daily lives percolate upwards to challenge the out-of-control elites who shape the future of the world.[4] Finally is the idea of international democracy emerging less through a traditional 'follow-through' – working up the political hierarchy – and more through an increasingly dense web of international connections created horizontally in the course of mobilising bargaining power of every possible kind (see also the resource section).

Bargaining power – a new force for genuine democracy

Like the global anti-war movement, people in places like Porto Alegre, East Manchester, Luton and Newcastle are grappling with how to achieve democratic control over the decisions shaping their future. They are not creating blueprints for a new politics, but rather they are developing a new bargaining power – for sustained leverage over local state institutions, private developers and, even to a limited extent, over national governments and the global market place.

The idea of 'bargaining power' evokes particularly the traditional conflict between workers and bosses, but the usefulness of it as a concept is to highlight the *many* sources and levels of power through which to bring about social transformation. The struggle for real emancipation is about more than workplace power relations – important though these are – and there are many more sources of bargaining power to be mobilised in order to achieve it. Consider the complex chains of dependence on which societies are structured, each one providing the basis for a different kind of bargaining. All parts of the state depend on other parts – different institutions, from local government to the International Criminal Court, can be part of the bargaining power on other institutions less responsive to democratic demands or humanitarian considerations. Corporations depend on national, regional and local governments for access to markets, funds, investment locations and so on. Elected politicians depend on voters who can generate demands backed by sustained organisation in between elections. Within each different level and institution in society exist possibilities for bargaining power that can be mobilised to achieve democratic change. The list is continually added to as people find new ways of resisting in their own daily lives, and make them collective and public: from action around corporate brands to direct forms of personal international solidarity with people facing military occupation.

The realisation of these multiple sources of bargaining power is in good part a response to the failings of electoral democracy. Sixty-three years after everyone had the right to vote in Brazil, over 34 per cent of that 'everyone' survives in poverty. Seventy-five years after British people won the right to vote, one-third of us live below the average wage, and 3.8 million of our children live in poverty – on government figures. From the White House and Whitehall down to the Newcastle Civic Centre or Porto Alegre Prefeitura, powerful private interests embed themselves in the state and bias its behaviour in their favour. Departments of state also develop their own bureaucratic interests. The combination leaves the elected representatives as strangers or accomplices in institutions only formally under democratic control. With 'outcomes' like this, what power the vote? Though still important, the evidence suggests that on its own representative democracy is now not enough. Democracy is a constant struggle, not a finished state of political being.

The declining strength of electoral democracy is not new, but two recent developments reveal how weak democracy has become relative to unaccountable sources of economic and bureaucratic power. First is the dismantling by Northern governments (led by the US and the UK) of the web of regulations that required multinational corporations to at least appear to behave as if they deferred to democratic constraints. In the absence of these regulations, corporations have sought to maximise their profits, manoeuvring against elected governments without restraint and with blatant confidence.[5] Experience of this contempt has become part of people's everyday life. Second, the end of the Cold War also meant the end of a moral cover for rampant capitalism. Under a culture that held up the alternative as the command economies of the Soviet bloc, scrutiny was muted. When the Cold War ended, though this meant new markets for corporate predators, it also meant that they strode the world morally naked. And people's imaginations were freed to discover their own alternatives. It took a little less than ten years for a new generation to emerge with its own anti-capitalist morality and visions of another world.

Participatory democracy: embedded bargaining power

The new political thinking of the social movements of the late 1960s and 70s provided a glimpse of the need for deeper forms of democracy that would reinforce electoral democracy and help withstand the pressures of private interests and public bureaucracy to which politicians had proved vulnerable. The radical politics of that era challenged the dominant assumption on the left that the party, through the state, had a monopoly on the power to bring about social transformation. It began a shift that has continued in practice ever since, to an understanding of multiple, interrelated sources of transformative power. Underpinning this shift was a more complex and potentially democratic understanding of knowledge, capacity and human creative potential, as discussed in detail earlier in the book. In practice more than in theory, these movements put participatory democracy on the long-term political agenda.[6]

In the course of my journey I found people developing what were lasting institutions of participatory democracy. These were not neat, finished institutions, however, but permanent sources of active bargaining power over private and public institutions beyond their immediate reach: in this sense participatory democracy is 'embedded' bargaining power. Porto Alegre illustrates this best: popular pressure is a permanent part of the democratic process in the city; it is both a bargaining power for the people over the state apparatus and a source of sustained power with which the elected council can ally in negotiating with the private sector and the federal government.

The argument is still sometimes put forward that participatory democracy should be the basis for a whole political system, a replacement for parliamentary democracy. However, this weakens the case for genuinely participatory processes, the importance of which lies in an ability simultaneously to both challenge and complement existing representative arrangements. Representative democracy's legitimacy stems from the minimal but equal participation of all through the vote, whereas the legitimacy of participatory democracy lies in the high degree of activity of what is likely to be a minority through institutions that are transparent, open to all and based on mutually agreed rules. Representative institutions based on one person one vote determine the principles and general direction of an elected government. They set the broad framework. The processes of participatory democracy provide ways in which the people, rather than simply officials, can play a decisive role in elaborating the detail of how these broad policy commitments are carried out. An open, rule-governed process of popular participation appropriate to the task at hand – proposing the detailed priorities of the budget for example, or managing a local public facility – has a much stronger democratic legitimacy than a group of officials working behind closed doors, often doing their own deals with certain social groups and economic interests. Participatory democracy also plays a vital role in monitoring the work of the executive and state apparatus, able to go where politicians never do, able to know what politicians rarely investigate. Again, the legitimacy comes from the intensity of the activity and the transparency and openness of the process. The participatory institutions generate self-confident expectations and this in turn leads to pressure – in the form of lobbying or campaigning – on the representative elected bodies, who make the final decisions.

Formally, representative democracy does have the final say. But since representatives must each seek re-election in a multi-party system, they have to be responsive and sensitive to the proposals drawn up by their constituents. Using a pictorial metaphor, the strong democratic control of participatory democracy, though actively involving only a minority, appears painted in vibrant colours in contrast with the washed-out water colour of representative democracy alone, based on the participation of all, but only weakly. In its complementary role, participatory democracy has the potential to move societies further towards the democratic ideals of popular control and political equality.

But, it must be asked, what is new about this idea of embedded bargaining power? Surely liberal democracy has always conceded that civil society organisations play an important role? It is conventionally accepted that a strong civil society keeps elected representatives on their toes, and does so through organised interest groups all of whom press their causes on government, sometimes through political parties, sometimes through independent lobbies. Sometimes, certain special interest groups – most notably unions and business, but locally also residents or voluntary sector organisations – have been drawn into corporatist arrangements with government, gaining a special political status so that the government negotiates with them over decisions affecting their interests. This sort of deal, however, has often undermined the credibility of both groups: the non-governmental organisations seen as both too close to government and as pursuing their own special interests; the government seen as favouring one group or two groups against others, or organised interests against 'the people'. One of the frustrations and flaws of representative democracy is that civil society has grown in size and developed in terms of structures and internally democratic forms, but finds itself nevertheless marginalised in its impact on the formal political system – or invited in and then ignored, or used to give the formal system unwarranted legitimacy. Participatory democracy provides a real alternative, or complement: a distinct and organised public sphere in which the demands of the people can be articulated, developed and negotiated between each other, and finally negotiated with the local or other relevant state institutions.

Representative democracy, as we have noted, already has legitimacy, although this is now in serious crisis. In order for participatory democracy to attain its own legitimacy and be able to reinvigorate democratic politics as a whole, certain conditions need to be in place.

First, if any form of participatory democracy is to achieve legitimacy as a source of power over decisions concerning the government of a locality, it needs to be open at its foundations to everyone affected by such decisions – even if only a minority participate. Openness is not just a formality; it needs to be worked at, in the way that, for example, the CRC in Porto Alegre or the outreach team in Luton worked at it. Not everyone may directly participate, but everyone needs to be in contact with someone who does.

Second, there need to be mutually agreed and openly negotiated rules. In all four places I visited the issue of rules was very important in the development of the participatory process. Agreed, inclusive rules had not in all cases been arrived at. Their mutual negotiation was a signal to those involved that they had real control over the process, and any breakdown would lead to a revisiting and revising of them.

A third condition, always difficult to preserve, is the autonomy of the participatory process from the state. Not that it can be entirely separate, as the whole rationale of participatory institutions is eventually to share decision-making power with government, to exercise some control over the work of state institutions and to monitor the implementation of government's decisions. But these relationships depend on equality:

participatory institutions need to have their own life and dynamism, and know that the elected body respects this.

This egalitarianism leads to a fourth condition: the genuine sharing of knowledge. We have seen how a process of democratisation through which users and service workers can contribute their knowledge to improving services is an unexplored strategy for public service reform; an essential part of an effective and democratic alternative to privatisation.[7] A further basic condition then, is that real resources must be at stake, resources which could make a positive difference to the lives of the community. The process must get results. It must not be seen as just another consultation exercise that leads nowhere.

An implication of all these ways of rethinking government is that the administration of public policy is not neutral. The process therefore matters. Popular participation is not only about who takes the decisions about the allocation of resources but also about how something is done. The disposal of waste is a good example. An environmentally sustainable approach which sees waste as a resource – an embodiment of accumulated energy and materials – is totally different from an approach which regards waste as something to be got rid of. The former, guided by reuse and recycling, requires widespread popular participation as a matter of daily life. That participation isn't an extra, and it's not about going to meetings and attending committees. This approach is about a publicly accountable and therefore improvable system that supports the household making the voluntary act of separation of their waste.[8] The same importance of daily democratic processes to the nature of the work could be applied to education, transport, social services – indeed every public service.

Finally, there's no doubt that the feasibility and legitimacy of the participatory process is enormously enhanced by the existence and electoral success of a party that believes in it. The PT is the pioneer in this respect, though parties influenced by the new left of the 1970s such as the German Green Party and the Danish Socialist People's Party created more limited experiments in this direction.[9] But an increasing number of parties of this form are emerging, and in the South more than the North: Akbayan in the Philippines is one example, the Democratic Labour Party in South Korea another. In a sense these parties are able to use their electoral legitimacy to emphasise the importance of the participatory process. Their message is that without the active participation of the people, the programme on which the party was elected cannot be carried out. Hence, when they are in government, they seek to work with popular movements in ways that create mechanisms of support, collaboration and pressure – including on themselves.

The end result of these conditions is that the organs of representative government lose some power to the new participatory sphere. But the new system of managing public resources through a combination of electoral and participative democracy involves an overall gain in democratic legitimacy and as a result, potentially, in power. People are more likely to feel that they become, in Tom Paine's terms, 'proprietors in government'. This sense of popular ownership is in itself a source of power, as evidenced by the unprecedented gains achieved by hard bargaining with would-be private investors, spurred on by the participatory process, in Porto Alegre and Newcastle.

This understanding of participatory democracy as being embedded bargaining power breaks down the traditional liberal division between politics and economics. For not only does the idea of embedded bargaining power provide political institutions with a means of standing up to the pressures of private capital, it also points to ways in which political institutions can ally with economic pressures for democracy. Alliances with cooperatives, the social economy generally, trade unions, public and trade union pension funds can all bring about the wider economic democracy without which participatory democracy is always unfinished and under threat.[10] Moreover, the notion of bargaining power involves seeing social movements as causing ripples well beyond their apparent focus: the green movement or the peace movement for example when in alliance with others are able potentially to exert power over the economy as well as over politics. Both movements raise fundamental questions about the purpose of production in huge swathes of the economy: the defence industry; the food, waste, energy and chemical industries. Recent democratic social movements have rarely been 'single issue' movements. The demands they raise require radical changes throughout society – and come up against vested interests that will resist those changes. The need therefore is to make organised connections with groups who have power and potentially a common interest at every point in the process. But all this would involve another book ...

Political follow-through

If participatory democracy is potentially a basis of effective forms of democratic bargaining power over both state apparatuses and concentrations of private economic power, local efforts at popular control must be able to percolate upwards through the political system, if only to transform it and break up its hierachies in the process. Conflicts between the demands and policies emerging from the participatory process in one locality and those in another, or between those of a city council and those of a government, must be able to be overcome. For a fully democratic government in the Paineite sense – i.e. forms of government that fully utilise the capacities of the people – there must be open democratic processes connecting local 'community' participation to the wider political process. In other words, there must be channels for political follow-through.

Take the following two examples of extensive local participation that have minimal impact on the wider political system. Many neighbourhoods in the US are as organised and as participatory as any in the world, and yet few of the demands and ideas coming from them rise up the political system; neither does the extensive participation. There are two main reasons. First, the problem is money and the costs of standing for office. Most people can afford to stand for election for their block, but when it comes to standing at a country or city level, the scale of finances needed – and the lack of any state provisions to create an even financial playing field – is prohibitive to all but a small minority. In addition, many services are provided through the private market rather than the state, so action around these services does not lead to any attempt to call state institutions to account.

In Cuba and Mozambique, by contrast, blockages to political follow-through came from the one-party state, the absence of political pluralism (though this has changed recently in Mozambique). In these countries there have been extensive and democratic forms of popular participation. Priorities and proposals are often thoroughly debated in neighbourhoods and workplaces. The problem is, such proposals are then brought to the regional party and government body – in neither place were the two distinct – appointed by the central party/government leadership. Such a regional body, since it is not elected in competition with others in a multi-party system, is not under effective pressure to be sensitive to the demands of the people. Genuine participatory democracy requires representative government to be maximally open to consideration of the demands coming up through the participatory system. It needs political pluralism, a fair electoral system, freedom of information, effective scrutiny of the executive and a free press, all guaranteed in a written constitution. Many countries, including the US and UK, are in different ways, significantly lacking in these regards.

Tony Blair's Third Way also fails to provide for follow-through for the community involvement that it endorses. The packaging of the Third Way ideology has fallen apart, but its content, including assumptions about relationships between community, the state and democracy, remains the orthodoxy in Britain and a significant influence on international institutions like the World Bank and the IMF. What is common to all its levels of policy are the circumscribed patronising limits within which popular participation is encouraged. More sophisticated than the

'*Je participate, Nous participatons, Tu participate, Vous participate, Ils decide*' mechanisms ridiculed on posters in Paris in 1968, now the orthodoxy (no doubt conceived and implemented by ex-68ers) is that 'I participate, we participate, but they decide over what kind of issue we can decide'. Decisions about the wider allocation of resources whether at a city-wide, nation-wide or global level remains with 'them'; there are no formal mechanisms for feeding back the ideas, controversies and knowledge arising from participatory processes. Such mechanisms would require a linkage of community participation to political democracy. It would involve taking participation out of the realm of good managerial practice into the sphere of democratic politics. It would radically change the character of politics, requiring national and international politicians to face the demands of the organised poor. A striking absence in government policy towards NDCs has been any recognition that innovations in neighbourhood participation might reveal the need for wider democratic reforms.[11] Thus, whether in relation to this regeneration programme in Britain or the participation programmes of the World Bank, 'community' has become an evasive substitute for political democracy. It allows its advocates to talk the talk of society without facing up to the conflicts of interest involved in policies that would make society just. 'We must talk about "us" not "I"', said Tony Blair, but his programme avoids the controversial issues of redistribution, regulation or any concrete action against powerful interests. In its limitless malleability but inherent spinelessness, it is a perfect framework for those political parties who depend on the votes of the poor but govern according to the pressures of big business.

In reality in Luton and East Manchester, people did not obediently stay in their 'community' box. The NDC experience, painful and messy, created a momentum that led them to follow up issues and make wider connections in their search for solutions. A real momentum – a 'mass of sense' – has been set in motion, but it needs structures through which it can exert influence and be of use to society. Instead, it too often finds bureaucratic brick walls which obstruct and absorb its energy and threaten to consign these innovative experiments to becoming little more than community quangos.

A further threat to democratic political channels is the break up of systems of public funding and provision in favour of private corporations or mutual and not-for-profit organisations dependent on the private financial market. In Britain, for example, democratic control of services will be increasingly vested in PFIs, public-private partnerships and contracts and legally binding 'targets' set between government and private companies, mostly large corporations such as Serco, Balfour Beatty and Sita. It is doubtful that legal contracts can effectively and sustainably impose a set of ethics – those of public service – onto powerful organisa-tions that are themselves driven by the ethic of profit. Contracts with private partners may stipulate 'consultation', but if this really meant the public's views had to be respected and acted on, most private companies would either walk away or later seek to subvert the agreed conditions. Contracts between public officials and private companies are inappro-priate mechanisms for democratic control. Many aspects of a high-quality service cannot be legally summarised. More often than not, lawyers delete references to things that are difficult to codify, let alone make legally binding. In addition, genuine democratic control by users as well as politicians requires open access to information, yet most private companies refuse this on grounds of 'commercial confidentiality'. Access to information is self-evidently a fundamental condition of democracy.

The challenge of resisting privatisation has drawn unions into expanding their own agendas in ways that often add up to a practical vision of participatory democracy. Their involvement in community campaigns, for example, strengthens and broadens the possibilities of developing a bargaining power for change. Their emphasis on alternative strategies for public-sector reform leads to new possibilities of political follow-through, particularly in relation to the public-sector workplace. The opening up of the normally highly secretive procurement process in Newcastle, in which the unions pressed for the evaluation of bids to be based on considerations of social need, employment and public account-ability in addition to the conventional job description is a good example of this. UNISON's work always aimed to increase the control that lay in the hands of elected councillors, but it did so by developing participatory processes that resulted in an improvement in the quality of the city's public services. It alerted voters to the damage done by privatisation thereby awakening greater popular pressure on councillors to keep control over their officers.

The Newcastle experience also illustrates a dynamic by which a local initiative can generate its own political follow-through, though to be sustained this requires wider political support. The Newcastle Public Service Alliance has begun to address the question of influencing local elections, and has also become involved with the European Social Forum. The conditions that made these developments possible were significant sources of its own industrial and political power, a wide range of contacts both across the city and region and beyond Tyneside, and a broad political perspective, under constant debate and refinement. A distinctive feature of the Newcastle UNISON team and their allies in the PSA, also evident elsewhere, is their willingness and confidence to move into the unknown, fuelled by demands and ideas originating in their own circum-stances. They moved onto new territory by creating consciously experi-mental structures. In the course of this experimentation they came up against more permanent and entrenched existing systems, often defensive of their own power – council departments, government offices, multina-tional corporations and the like. UNISON responded by searching out new sources of power to deal with every new blockage: it sought out new alliances, new information, new industrial and media tactics. Whenever a conflict significantly changed the balance of power, this opened up new thinking about alternatives and where to go next. Each new assertion of power gave people the strength to break old habits by which people unthinkingly maintain the status quo. It becomes an escalating process: going beyond established structures widens people's focus and through this people gain the confidence that previously unimagined alternatives are possible. Changed consciousness is as important as a new structure. Where the two can develop simultaneously people are able to gain in understanding, self-confidence and a sense of direction.

A new kind of party

This developing cycle – the exercise of power, the facing of new constraints, the search for alternative strategies, the expansion of consciousness, the move to a new assertion of power – can be a delicate process to maintain. In Newcastle, it depended on a well-resourced, politically minded but also open-minded union branch with a long historical memory and a wide range of city-wide, regional, national and international contacts. There are important signs that unions are opening up to a wider view of their role,[12] but the most obvious means of generalising such follow-through is a new kind of political party. What is needed is a party that does not simply use participatory rhetoric but is committed – through its structure, its culture and its way of arriving at its policies – to allying with and nurturing the power and consciousness of independent movements and initiatives.

In order to highlight some of the issues here, it is interesting to compare the relationship between the ANC and the township civics in South Africa with the relationship between the Workers Party and social movements in Brazil.

In the struggle against apartheid, the civics were the organisations through which the people of the townships mobilised. They were based on street-by-street representation and they took responsibility for organising social welfare, public health, conflict resolution and environmental protection, as best they could in desperate conditions. They provided an ideal, almost ready-made, base for a new kind of local government. Through an adaptation of their structures – making them able to negotiate with ANC-dominated municipalities just as the Porto Alegre urban movements negotiated with the PT – and in close alliance with the highly politicised trade unions, the civics could have been the basis for the strengthening of the ANC by creating deeper means of popular control over the state apparatus, something urgently needed in a post-apartheid South Africa. The popular legitimacy and knowledge of a trans-formed movement of civics and trade unions could have supported the ANC's elected representatives with the bargaining power they needed in the face not only of conservative officials, but also the growing pressures of multinational capital backed by the IMF. The initial Reconstruction and Development Plan (RDP) drawn up for the economic and social reconstruction of the country did propose exactly this kind of demo-cratic, participatory role for the civics and the unions, and for a brief moment it flourished. But it was not sustained. The ANC negotiators with the IMF submitted to pressure and pursued a constrained and constraining parliamentary model, very much on traditional British Labour Party terms. In time the civics became more marginal. I remember twice interviewing Moses Mayekiso, former leader of the militant Alexandra civic, and of the metal workers' union. The first time was in Manchester when he was attending a meeting of local authorities during the last phase of the battle against apartheid. He was buoyant and confident, clear of his role: campaigning for the civics as the foundation for local democracy. The second time we met was in South Africa, in his office as an MP and secretary of SANCO, the national organisation of civics. It was soon after the ANC had become the government. His office was isolated, down a long corridor in an annexe of the South African parliament in Cape Town. He seemed a different person, still charming and shrewd but unsure what his new role was, feeling that SANCO and the civics were being ignored, as indeed they were. He seemed to symbolise a missed opportunity.[13]

As I write, however, the temporarily dormant tradition of the civics may be re-emerging. In the face of privatisation of the townships' basic infrastructure, and the failure of the ANC government to deliver on promises for basic services like water, sanitation, education and housing, a militant anti-privatisation movement has emerged. It takes direct action – for example to connect electricity supplies – and it is beginning to challenge the ANC on its own electoral ground.

The contrast between the ANC and the Brazilian Workers Party, with its commitment to sharing power 'with the movements we came from', is striking. The difference is that the PT (or at least a strong tendency within it) has consciously spurned the idea that it has a monopoly of power. It is under pressure so to do. Brazilian social movements – the landless movement, the neighbourhood organisations, the trade unions – fiercely protect their autonomy at the same time as electorally supporting the PT. There is always a danger that when parties who work closely with social movements gain office, they seek to constrain those movements rather than encourage them to act independently to create further sources of democratic power. There are some signs of this appearing now that the PT is in office. Tough struggles lie ahead.

Across the world, from Scotland to South Korea, an increasing number of parties are emerging that are in effect the electoral voice of coalitions of social movements. They see many sources of power to challenge capitalism and create in its place an equal, democratic and environmentally sustainable society. Akbayan in the Philippines is a recent example of a party whose roots and present support lie in social movements, and which is growing in popular appeal. It was founded in 1999, after several different meetings of organisations of labour, including overseas Filipino workers, peasants, the urban poor and feminists. One of its leaders, Professor Joel Rocamero, a former guerrilla leader, describes how: 'The social movement groups affiliated with Akbayan are our most important link with our "leftness". Unions, urban poor and community organisations deal with day-to-day problems of the poor. They "pull" the party towards these concerns, dragging rickety old knees like mine to demonstrations and pickets, criticising our representatives in the legislature, in local governments.'

There is a debate in Akbayan about how it should relate to social movements. 'Everyone agrees that mass movements should be autonomous of the party', continues Joel. 'Some think, however, that the party should play a more active role in mass movement affairs, for example to help federate peasant organisations already affiliated with the party. My problem with this is partly practical, we don't have the capacity to play this role at this time. When we have that capacity I would worry about the party subverting the autonomy of social movement groups.' This commitment to safeguarding the autonomy and strength of democratic social movements is combined with a serious commitment to electoral work. Gaining representation and political leverage for the movements was after all the reason for forming Akbayan: 'My argument was that we can't leave political power in the hands of the bastards', says Joel. 'Electoral politics is the distinct instrument of the party, it's "added value" to the power of the movements. It is our means of accumulating power. We respect and uphold its integrity and we work hard at reforming our corrupt, inefficient electoral system.'

There are a huge number of new issues raised by these hybrid movement/party organisations.[14] A fundamental one is differing approaches to time: the tension between the deadlines for decisions versus the time to let developments grow, innovations mature, solutions evolve, to let people make mistakes and learn lessons, to allow diversity to flourish. In part this is the tension between the imperatives of the existing political system. On the one hand is the agenda and timetable set by those in power and on the other the conditions that favour the emergence of new, cooperative, ways of organising in which everyone plays a full part, and which encourage the development of new solutions requiring thorough investigation and experiment. Those seeking to bring about change need to engage with the dominant political system but not be dominated by it. They need also to be rooted in the changes that people are bringing about through organising and resisting in their own daily lives. It is difficult to operate on both timetables at once. That is why a division of labour between movements and electoral parties is important, while at the same time they work for maximum dialogue, mutual learning and coordination. It means a politics that is willing to cope with uncertainty and is not constantly straining for a programmatic unity that would restrict the creativity of the process for no good reason. A good metaphor is the jazz of Charlie Parker or Miles Davis: an underlying structure with which everyone is familiar, and then improvisation whose character is impossible to predict or orchestrate. Such jazz also depends on strong personal bonds and a generosity of spirit. Certainly these are all ingredients of the World Social Forum, which over three years has enabled this new politics to gain a positive global identity, through harsh conflict as well as warm embraces.

New departures: from the local to the global

While I was plodding the streets of Beswick, Openshaw, Marsh Farm Estate, Newcastle and Porto Alegre, an extraordinary international movement was coming into being. While I was attending local residents' meetings, shop stewards' discussions, different stages of the participatory budget cycle and so forth, a bolt of political lightening was being released. It began with the 40,000 strong World Social Form in Brazil in 2001, which by winter 2003 had spawned social forums in every continent. In November 2002, around 30,000 people converged in Florence for the European Social Forum; in January 2003 around 10,000 gathered in Hydrabad for the Asian Social Forum. Porto Alegre itself has hosted two more meetings of the WSF, in 2002 and 2003, and each time 20,000 more people than previously have attended.

Through my association with the Transnational Institute I was lucky enough to be invited to join the first stage of this process, but I had mixed feelings. I arrived in January 2001 for the first World Social Forum at Porto Alegre's familiar airport – now resplendent with posters proclaiming that 'Another World is Possible' – having spent the previous cold winter's evening talking to the 'Sandywell lads' at Higher Openshaw Youth in East Manchester. They too fantasised about another world – for them it meant a proper sports and leisure centre, jobs as architects and accountants, 'to be somebody'. But a connection between the changes demanded at this global gathering and a realisation of the opportunities these kids dreamed about was yet to be made. I myself fantasised about a mass delegation of disempowered young people attending the forum, drawn from cities like Manchester. It could be as large as the trade union delegation from Argentina, as vociferous as the landless movement from Brazil. That was a little optimistic but by the following year I had companions from Newcastle UNISON and East Manchester Community Forum on the plane with me as I flew again to Brazil. They had raised the money from supportive organisations, and travelled with the enthusiastic support from people in their areas who were keen to connect with and learn from the international contacts.

By 2002 the Organisational Workshop method pioneered amongst social movement activists in Brazil was becoming part of the Marsh Farm Community Trust's daily reality in Luton. In November that year twenty-four members of the Newcastle UNISON branch attended the European Social Forum. At the Commonwealth Games in Manchester, the EMCF organised a World Peace Mosaic, inspired by a project at the WSF, composed of clay tiles inscribed by people with their messages to the world. The mosaic is due to become a permanent feature of Philips Park. At its centre is Nelson Mandela's remark: 'Our deepest fear is not that we are inadequate. Our deepest fear is that we are powerful beyond measure … We were born to make manifest the glory that is within us, It is not just in some of us – it is in everyone. As we are liberated from our own fear, our presence automatically liberates others.'

In their own ways, local initiatives are tapping into the global movement, and bringing it home. This is one function of the WSF: to provide an organised space through which organisations worldwide can connect and exchange ideas, lessons, information and mutual inspiration. It is striking that every delegate is in some sense active and organised; it is one of the reasons why such a vast event doesn't dissolve into chaos – everyone feels a responsibility for the whole. Moreover, they are experienced at organising themselves, rather than waiting for a lead. The contrast with equivalent Soviet mass gatherings like the World Festival of Youth, organised throughout the post-war years until the revolts of 1968[15] made it unsustainable, is striking: at the WSF everyone is independently organised, coming together with their own diverse agendas; at the World Festival of Youth everyone followed the agenda of their party or state. The other function of these international gatherings has been to coordinate action on an issue on which everyone is in practice in agreement. Internationally simultaneous action against the Iraq war in February 2003[16] is a good example; action at the WTO against GATS is another. Diversity combined with unity: the networks, movements and new parties that have been emerging over recent years show a combination of firmness of principle and flexibility of tactic and organisational form which bodes well for their future development.

Above all, what inspires optimism is the organised internationalism of recent political innovations (see the resource list for a sense of these dense, practical international networks). One of the reasons why social democratic governments were so vulnerable to the neo-liberal right was their reliance on the nation state, their own nation state, as *the* agency of social change. When the forces of markets dominated by multinational corporate capital proved too much for any one nation state, their strategic thinking and ability to organise on an international scale was so weak that they effectively became awestruck by the apparent immutability of the corporate-dominated global market. Recent movements, building on older foundations, are showing an ability to combine their extraparliamentary organising on an international scale with attempts to create new political institutions, locally and nationally. Local initiatives are connecting with international networks. But these local roots need nurturing: global action needs local bargaining and vice versa.

The historic protests against the Iraq war brought these levels together. They demonstrated the emergence of a new democratic power that has yet to become fully aware of itself. We cannot predict the variety of ways that this self-consiousness might develop, but in the course of writing this book I have witnessed efforts to create an ever-growing range of sources of democratic power, from the local to the global. I have found an intensity and density of activity for democratic change at the base of society that simply is not compatible with the democratically hollow forms of power that persist at the top. It is clear too that these democratically hollow institutions are not a pushover. They rule by other means. Economic and military violence are the last resorts of those who fear the capacities of the people. This only makes it all the more urgent that all of us who do believe in democracy work to create lasting economic and political institutions which every day bring forward the capacity that, as Tom Paine observed, 'never fails to appear in revolution'.

NOTES

Foreword   Wanted: new forms of political power

1 Martin Wolf, *Financial Times*, 29 January 2003.

2 See *The Global Civil Society Yearbook 2003*, Cambridge 2003.

3 See Sue Branford and Bernard Kucinski, *Politics Transformed: Lula and the Workers Party in Brazil*, London 2003, for an excellent brief history of Lula and the Workers Party.

4 Consulta is a Zapatista word for a democratic consultation in which delegates are sent to thousands of villages and towns to communicate developments and seek feedback. They then bring back these views to a conference where decisions are finalised. Drawing on this notion the NPI has sought democratic consultations with communities, individuals, and organisations working for long-term goals of social justice, ecology and democracy. It has been keen to hear people's vision for a better society and learn about their work with progressive organisations. After some 'trial' Consultas the NPI developed three versions: one aimed at a general audience; one for people involved in organised politics, especially the NDP; and one for community groups. Because of the radically decentralised structure of the NPI, the lack of resources for training, and national and international events which altered the direction of NPI energies, the broad-ranging Consulta campaign originally envisioned never took place. But Consultas remain an example of the NPI's notion of how to implement a more participatory democratic process, and a tool they may use in the future.

5 See www.rabble.org, and Judy Rebick, *Imagine Democracy*, Toronto 2000.

6 Including the tactic whereby the whole of the leadership of the Taiwan Communication Workers Union shaved their heads as a protest against privatisation. Since men in Taiwan shave their heads only upon the death of a parent, this was a way of demonstrating the seriousness of the threat posed by privatisation.

7 The conference on Globalisation, Trade Unions and the Environment was itself international, with guests from the British-based Red-Green Study Group, who have published an influential pamphlet *What On Earth is to be Done? A Red-Green Dialogue*, Manchester 1994.

A 'mass of sense': knowledge, power and democracy

1 'The rights of man', in *The Thomas Paine Reader*, London 1987, p. 277.

2 *Ibid.*, pp. 278–9.

3 International Institute for Democracy and Electoral Assistance (IDEA) *Voter Turnout Since 1945: A Global Report*. According to IDEA, voter turnout has decreased globally over the past ten years by almost 10%, both in established democracies and newly democratised developing countries. The only region in the world with an increase in voter turnout during the past ten years is Central and Eastern Europe. The report includes statistics from more than 1,600 parliamentary and presidential elections in over 170 countries. Voter turnout information is available at www.idea.int/turnout.

4 See Daniel Lazare, *The Frozen Republic: How the Constitution is Paralysing Democracy*, New York 1966.

5 Joseph Schumpeter, *Capitalism, Socialism and Democracy*, London 1942.

6 Seymour M Lipset, *Political Man*, London 1960, p. 32.

7 From Schumpeter, *Capitalism*, p. 295. See also Anthony Arblaster, *Democracy*, 2nd edn, Buckingham 1994, Chapter 4, for an analysis of this narrowing of democracy.

8 See Richard Barnet, *Global Reach: The Power of Multinational Corporations*, New York 1974.

9 See Sheila Rowbotham, *Promise of a Dream*, London 2001, and Tariq Ali and Susan Watkins, *1968: Marching in the Streets*, London 1998.

10 'Growing trust in public service: why Reggio Emilia's pre-schools are world class', Brendan Martin, www.publicworld.org.

11 See the book that coined the phrase and laid out this analysis most congently: London–Edinburgh Weekend Return Group, *In and Against the State*, London 1980.

12 Quoted by Robin Pauley, *Financial Times*, 5 May 1984. See also Ken Livingstone, *If Voting Changed Anything They'd Abolish It*, London 1988, and Maureen Mackintosh and Hilary Wainwright (eds), *A Taste of Power: the Politics of Local Economics*, London 1987.

13 In the early 1970s, when demands for greater popular participation started rearing their alarming heads, a worried member of the US ruling elite, David Rockefeller of the Chase Manhattan Bank, founded the Trilateral Commission to bring together the elite of the three industrialised continents of the capitalist world. Its report on the threat the new movements posed for parliamentary democracy aimed to put ruling institutions on the alert. It organised annual gatherings of leading politicians, industrialists, financiers and academics to provide a mechanism to develop common responses. This was just a sign that potentially profound change was underway. It was also a sign that an international establishment was forming to control the impact of this unrest. Interestingly the Trilateral Commission led to the establishment of the Davos-based World Economic Forum.

14 See Geoff Eley, *The Left and the Struggle for Democracy: The History of the Left in Europe*, Oxford 2002.

15 This generational conflict and its political expression were most intense in Germany, presumably because of the unfinished business left over from fascism. See W. Hulsberg, *The German Greens,* London 1988.

16 Paul Foot, *Harold Wilson*, Harmondsworth 1971; Ralph Miliband, *Parliamentary Socialism: A Study in the Politics of Labour*, New York 1964; Greg Palast, *The Best Democracy Money Can Buy*, London 2002.

17 Labour Party Conference Report 1944

18 Aneurin Bevan, *In Place of Fear*, London 1945.

19 See Ralph Miliband, *The State in Capitalist Society*, New York 1969, and *Parliamentary Socialism*.

20 Interview with the author.

21 The World Development Movement, *'Still Sapping the Poor': Analysis of the Impact of Structural Adjustment by Charles Abruge*, London 2000. Updated 2001.

22 See Mary Kaldor and Ivan Vejvoda (eds), *Democratization in Central and Eastern Europe*, Oxford 2002; Mary Kaldor, *The Imaginary War: Understanding East West Conflict*, Oxford 1990; John Keane, *The Power of the Powerless: Citizens Against the State in Central Eastern Europe*, London 1985; Hilary Wainwright, Patrick Burke and Mark Thompson (eds), *After the War: Democracy and Movement Politics in the New Europe*, Amsterdam 1991.

23 Friedrich von Hayek, *The Use of Knowledge in Society in Individualism and Economic Order*, Chicago 1948.

24 *Ibid.*, p. 87.

25 I have developed these arguments in detail in an earlier book: *Arguments for a New Left; Answering the Free Market Right*, Oxford 1994.

26 Though my argument draws mainly from observing the distinct way in which these movements approach knowledge, in their practice more than in theory, they developed critiques of the arrogance of professional knowledge and the methods for sharing it. The argument is also grounded in an awareness of the revolution in the philosophy of science and social science from the 1960s onwards. This was an intellectual revolution which both influenced, and in its later phases was influenced by, the new social movements. At the risk of being crudely schematic, it can be traced back to the later Wittgenstein and to Karl Popper, as author of *The Logic of Scientific Discovery* rather than a Cold War polemicist. Wittgenstein's stress on the social character of knowledge and Popper's challenge to the conventional assumptions of the linear, cumulative character of scientific knowledge were taken up by Imre Lakartos, Paul Feyerband and Thomas Kuhn. Kuhn demonstrated that the character of science as a social institution was, like any social product, subject to the erxercise of power. These and other developments in the philosophy of science proved to be a vital resource for a generation of social scientists radicalised by 1968. There was a paucity of tools of critical analysis in conventional social science. Social scientists like Roy Bhaskar, William Outhwaite, Ted Benton, Kate Soper, Andrew Collier and others started systematically to explore questions of method. They were also influenced in this process by the work of Herbet Marcuse and Jürgen Habermas, and Louis Althusser and the debates around his work. This led them to reconsider the basis of scientific knowledge, and this work generated a distinct intellectual school of 'critical realists'. The conceptual tools they have developed help to overcome the lag between the philosophical refutation of positivistic theories of knowledge and science and the persistence of these theories in underpinning state, party and economic organisation. Concepts alone, however, can never achieve institutional change, though they can help to clarify the practice of the movements with whom they share their origins. See K. Popper, *The Logic of Scientific Discovery*, London 1959; L. Wittgenstein, *Tractatus Logico – Philosophicus*, London 1961; T.S. Kuhn, *The Structure of Scientific Revolutions*, Chicago 1970; I. Lakatos, *Criticism and the Growth of Scientific Knowledge*, Cambridge 1967; J. Habermas, *Knowledge and Human Interests*, London 1971; L. Althusser, 'On contradiction and over-determination', *New Left Review*, London 1968; E.P. Thompson, *The Poverty of Theory*, London 1979; R. Bhaska, *A Realist Theory of Science*, Sussex 1978, and *Reclaiming Reality*, London 1988; W. Outhwaite, *New Philosophies of Social Science*, London 1987; K. Soper, *The Idea of Nature*, Oxford 1994.

27 A.H. Wright, *G.D.H.Cole and Socialist Democracy*, Oxford 1979, p.55. Taken from Beatrice Webb, *Our Partnership*, Oxford 1948 (entry for 29 Dec 1894).

28 See Wright, *ibid.* See also: Logie Barrow and Ian Bullock, *Democratic Ideas and the British Labour Movement 1880–1914*, Cambridge 2002; Sheila Rowbotham and Jeffrey Weekes, *Socialism and the New Life: the Personal and Sexual Politics of Edward Carpenter and Havelock Ellis*, London 1977; June Hannam, *Isabella Ford*, Oxford 1989; the work of E.P. Thompson, especially *Poverty of Theory and Other Essays*, London 1978; an essay by Kate Soper in her *Troubled Pleasures*, London 1990; Raymond Williams, for example *What I Came to Say*, edited by Neil Belton, Francis Mulhern and Jenny Taylor, London 1989. For historical examples across Europe see Geoff Eley, *Forging Democracy*, Oxford 2002.

29 See Anne Phillips on the limits of participatory democracy in the women's movement, *Engendering Democracy*, Cambridge 1990.

30 See Hilary Wainwright, *The Lucas Plan: A New Trade Unionism in the Making*, London 1982.

31 Paulo Freire, *The Pedogogy of the Oppressed*, London 1970, p.12.

The journey: reclaiming democracy

1 Marco Aurelio Garcia said this in a speech to the 1999 PT Congress in Bela Horizonte. Marco Aurelio is now Lula's main adviser on foreign affairs.

2 See Jane Foot, Democracy or Management? Competing Discourses of Community in Modern Local Government, MA Thesis, City University, London 2001, unpublished.

3 See an interview with the author in *Red Pepper*, July 2002.

4 See Colin Leys, *'Market Driven Politics': Neoliberal Democracy and the Public Interest*, London 2001.

Porto Alegre: public power beyond the state

1 *Folha de São Paulo*, 13 May 2001.

2 Paulo Freire, *The Pedogogy of the Oppressed*, London 1970.

3 Census Bureau in Brazil (IBGE), 2000.

4 The classic historical reference book on Lula – and the PT more generally – is Margaret Keck, *The Workers Party and Democratization in Brazil*, Yale 1991; a useful shorter 'handbook' on Lula's history and PT politics is Sue Branford and Bernard Kucinski, *Politics Transformed: Lula and the Workers Party in Brazil*, London 2003. See also Emir Sader and Ken Silverstein, *Without Fear of Being Happy: Lula, the Workers Party and Brazil*, London 1991; and on the Landless Movement, Sue Branford and Jan Rocha, *Cutting the Wire: the Story of the Landless Movement in Brazil*, London 2002.

5 See Boaventura Dos Santos, 'Participatory budgeting in Porto Alegre: toward a redistributive democracy', *Politics & Society*, 26:4, December 1998, 461–510; Archon Fung and Erik Ohlin Wright (eds), *Deepening Democracy: Institutional Innovations in Empowered Participatory Governance*, London 2003; Daniel Chavez and Benjamin Goldfrank, *The Left in the City: Attempting Participatory Democracy in Latin American Municipalities*, London 2003; Rebecca Abers, *Inventing Local Democracy: Grassroots Politics in Brazil*, Boulder 2000.

6 Isabella Bebem's father had been a brave senior pilot who opposed the military coup. After refusing to carry out a mission, he was murdered in circumstances that remain mysterious. The memory of the dictatorship and the fight for democracy are still potent. It was formative in the political outlook of many of the activists I met on my tour of the participatory process. Isabella was one of them.

7 For more details about the international pressures on the Brazilian government, see Alfredo Saad-Filho, *New Dawn or False Start in Brazil? The Political Economy of Lula's Election*, London 2003; Branford and Kucinski, *Politics Transformed*; Sue Branford, 'Breaking the chains of Brazil's slavery', *Red Pepper*, March 2003.

8 See Sérgio Baerlie, 'The Porto Alegre thermidor: Brazil's "participatory budget" at the crossroads', in Leo Panitch and Colin Leys (eds), *Socialist Register*, London 2003.

9 CIDADE/PMPA, *Participatory Budget Research*, Porto Alegre 2000.

East Manchester: no neighbourhood is an island

1 The reason for Manchester's favourable position in receiving NDC money was a bid in 1997 under the Conservatives' Estates Renewal Programme for funds to regenerate East Manchester. Estates Renewal was a conventional 'bricks-and-mortar' housing improvement policy which was still in place in the early days of the New Labour government. Manchester's bid would normally have been successful but Hilary Armstrong, the new minister responsible for regeneration, turned it down with a wink and a promise that something better was in the offing. Hence from the beginning Manchester council has had a strong relationship with the Department of the Environment, Transport and the Regions.

2 The Settlement was a community project that was part of a long-established national movement which originally aimed to spread the educational resources of universities into the poor inner cities, and in the process introduce students to the problems facing working-class neighbourhoods. Toynbee Hall in the East End of London pioneered the idea. For its early history see David Englander and Rosemary O'Day (eds), *Retrieved Riches: Social Investigation 1840–1914*, Aldershot 1995, pp. 21–4, 176–7.

3 One of the most vibrant East Manchester initiatives, though outside the NDC area, is the independent charity Manchester Environmental Resource Initiative or MERCi (pronounced murky). The project started in 1997 when, after several years of activism against roads, airports and GM foods, Cath Miller, Jane Pickering, Chris Walsh and Helen Woodcock decided that protesting wasn't enough. Activists also wanted somewhere which would allow them to be integrated with local people. Having taken up premises in an old cotton mill, Bridge-5 Mill, on the banks of the Ashton canal, MERCi have walked their talk, creating a home for many diverse campaigns and activities, meeting rooms, a cafe and a roof garden. The buzz reverberated outwards, including as far as Beswick, Openshaw and Clayton. It began with £100 in the bank, and last year had a turnover of £1m. Now that the building is in working, living order, some of the restless MERCi mob are moving on. There are also plans for a community business centre. 'Our aim is an economic strategy which the community can control and ensures money circulates as much as possible within the local economy', says Walsh.

4 94% of the population in the whole of the NDC area – based on the 2001 Projection by Ward – is white. 1.1% is Black Caribbean, 1.0% Black African, 1. 1% Black other, 0. 4% Indian, 0.2 % Pakistani, 0.9% Chinese, 0.2% Asian other. The equivalent figures for Manchester as a whole: 82.6% white, 3.5% Black Caribbean, 1.2% Black African, 1.7% Black other, 1. 5 % Indian, 5.7% Pakistani, 1.1% Chinese, 1.9% Asian other.

5 NEM's areas beyond the NDC are Ancoats, Miles Platting and parts of Newton Heath and West Gorton.

6 For example, Libby Graham, the NDC's woman of all trades (doing the job of at least three men) is a veteran of both independent community organising and attempting to change council structures from the inside to make decision-making more genuinely open to residents affected by those decisions.

7 This is in addition to the money already spent on maintaining public services. New government initiatives with their own budgets have also come in since: Sure Start, On Track and more. The area has become a pilot for just about every new initiative.

8 In setting the NDC's brief, the government, according to Geoff Mulgan in correspondence with the author, wanted to avoid such significant proportions of NDC money being spent on housing. However, given the neglected state of council stock and the inadequacy of funding from elsewhere, the pressure to spend large proportions of the NDC budgets on housing – across NDCs – has proved impossible to resist.

9 Their main job is to check that spending meets the targets laid out in NDC delivery plans. In Manchester, perhaps as a result of the leading role of the city council in creating the NDC and a long-established understanding between the council and the government's North West Office, this office has played a less active role than is typical for NDCs.

10 Turnout rose to 38% in the Bradford ward in 2002, mainly due to an intense battle in which Labour fought hard, with help from Labour activists across the city, to fend off a determined but ineffectual challenge from the Liberal Democrats.

11 For example, London Docklands, Liverpool and Bristol. In most cases but by no means all, turnouts for NDC elections were higher than for local authority elections. See *NDC Elections: A Study in Community Engagement*, published by the Neighbourhood Renewal Unit, 2002/3, www.neighbourhood.gov.uk.

12 Specific projects include mental health needs, teenage mothers, older people and drug users. The older people's group, for instance, concentrates mainly on supporting older people during the housing renewal programme, by providing access to housing of their choice and housing-related support. But it doesn't stop there: a group of its members visited parliament and also attended a national Help the Aged conference, with much positive feedback. There are hopes to secure funding for a more long-term older people's service which would remain independent of the existing main local service providers. In the field of mental health much enquiry into the experience of youth workers, if not youth, has taken place to find out what would help them meet the mental health needs of the young people they work with. For adults there is a mental health group which meets regularly to offer 'leisure, learning, social contact'. People are referred by the new Primary Care Mental Health Service or they refer themselves. 'There is, intentionally, no tight clinical definition of the project's target group', says a report. In this way it is similar to Outlook, the drugs project. There is also a Schools Mental Health Programme which audited schools in the area to reveal widespread concern over working with pupils with emotional and behavioural problems without the support of specialist mental health services. Teenage mums are the subject of much activity and input – many aspects of teenage pregancy are addressed in a range of responses, including a plan for purpose-built flats around a central yard. Support and information packs on teenage pregnancy and related issues actively solicit the input of the girls themselves; they are invited, for instance, on an NDC-funded weekend away to talk about how best to help mothers like themselves, and to plan and design new outreach material. There is also a teenage parents mentoring scheme which trains volunteers with relevant life experience and matches them with younger parents in need of support.

13 In spite of all Manchester's economic growth, the city has levels of those claiming unemployment (13,000) and economically inactive (80–90,000) that are amongst the worst in the country. The city council acknowledges that Manchester residents face one of the worst labour market positions in the UK.

14 See Ash Amin, Doreen Massey and Nigel Thrift, *Cities for the Many Not the Few*, Bristol 2000.

15 NEM also employed another company, Urban Strategies, a Canadian-based urban design team that had previously worked with the city council on Hulme and the city centre. But Grimleys was the local company and so effectively 'fronted' the work.

16 It's true that councils also borrow on commercial terms but they are in a position, with large assets etc., to strike more favourable terms.

17 The Housing Corporation does not meet the democratic standards established by the Democratic Audit. See Stuart Weir and David Beetham, *Political Power and Democratic Control*, London 1999, and *Democracy Under Blair: A Democratic Audit of Britain*, London 2003.

18 NEM's main bargaining powers are first the council's ownership of the land on which the developers would like to build and therefore its power to grant or withhold planning permission (both in outline and detail), and second the views and pressures of local people which can determine whether or not the council grants planning permission.

19 The Market Renewal Fund will be an £800m fund over three years to renovate tens of thousands of empty homes, mainly in the north of England. The fund is used to compulsorily purchase privately owned properties, compensate homeowners in negative equity, demolish substantial swathes of terraced property, and pay for new build that people in houses whose value has fallen can afford. The Market Renewal Fund spans local authority boundaries and aims for a mix of tenures. It has generally been welcomed, though the amount of money is considered inadequate for the scale of the problem.

20 On 22 April 1993 a young black man, Stephen Lawrence, was murdered by racists in London. The police enquiry made no arrests and no one was brought to trial. On 31 July 1997 Jack Straw, then home secretary, ordered Sir William Macpherson, an ex-high court judge, to report on the police handling of the case. Published in 1999, The Macpherson Report labelled London's police force 'institutionally racist' and condemned officers for 'fundamental errors'. Public and media attention focused for a moment on 'institutionalised racism'. The report was the first official acknowledgement of the racism that permeates British society on every level.

21 Alan Turner, Manchester Youth Volunteer Project, 'Researching into Youth Involvement in East Manchester: Problems of Youth Engagement', Manchester 2001.

22 Local Strategic Partnerships (LSPs) were set up by the government to deliver their Neighbourhood Renewal strategy and to bring together the proliferating partnerships which now exist at a local level. Initially they were set up in the 88 areas covered by the Neighbourhood Renewal Policy. Started in 2001, they operate all over England, normally within the same geographical boundaries as boroughs or district councils.

They are intended as structures to bring together key 'stakeholders' in towns and cities so that they can make coherent decisions about services for their area. These stakeholders are usually drawn from the local authority, other public service providers and the private sector, as well as the community and voluntary sector(s). There have been criticisms of LSPs – for example that awareness of LSP-related funds amongst the communities who are supposed to be represented at the decision-making tables for this money is variable, and that LSPs are too often manipulated by local authorities to be little more than a consultation opportunity for senior people across the public and private sectors. It's hard to gauge whether the genuine commitment to community building which is undoubtedly present in many of those who work in LSPs can survive the layers of bureacracy which threaten to submerge the scheme.

A year after the LSP programme had been launched, the Urban Forum carried out a survey of community and voluntary organisations and found that in only 19% of LSPs was there any community involvement and in these only a minority of participants were satisfied with the process. In Manchester there is a strong commitment by community organisations to turn the LSP into a genuine forum for negotiation over real resources to meet community needs. Many of those involved have been influenced by the experience of Porto Alegre as the result of the extensive work on applying principles of participatory budgeting by Community Pride.

23 Report by Manchester City Council's Select Committee on Regeneration, Chair Joanne Green, 2002.

Luton: squatting the state

1 Jackie Jenkins, *Marsh Farm ... Where Luton Began, Our History*, Bedford 2003. The Marsh Farm Community Trust are hoping to create an interactive centre at the Waulud's Bank site 'where local schoolchildren can come and get involved in "hands-on history"' (author's conversation with Jackie Jenkins).

2 In September 1995 *Red Pepper* carried the cover line 'Rave or Riot?' Inside, Jim Carey, a writer and film-maker who had been following Exodus from its beginning, told the story of the riot and the events that followed.

3 The Exodus collective dispersed after a number of its members, especially those living in HAZ Manor, came under intense pressure from the police. Chief Constable Brown, who was interested in a dialogue with the collective, had been removed and his replacements attacked as if to destroy. They arrested leading HAZ Manor member Paul Taylor, known as 'Biggs', under every conceivable charge, from drug dealing to murder. Glenn Jenkins' mother was attacked by police and her licence as a publican revoked, ruining her life's work. 'Eventually Biggs and my mum were cleared,' explains Glenn, 'but this and other harassments left serious scars and tied up key members in endless legal battles just at a time when the collective's membership was growing.' There was a significant dilution of the common spirit. Many Exodus supporters had waged jobs. They lived outside the manor and the farm, although they frequently went to both to contribute to the refurbishment, organise the raves and so on. An ethic of the collective was that for those on the manor and the farm on benefits, these were pooled and the work shared. For over six years this survived on the basis of trust and honour. 'We had structures and principles,' says Bruce Hannah, looking back, 'but no means of

enforcing them. No means of self-policing.' Under the pressure of the police harassment and the difficulties over money, tempers frayed and friendships were stretched to the limit. The trust and honour began to evaporate. 'They are not sufficiently deeply imbued in us to do without agreed ways of policing our own rules', commented Glenn. A group led by Biggs rebelled against the way of life and cooperative organisation of the manor and the farm, with the end result that those who still believed in the original ideal left the manor to develop their ideals in the wider local community. Some people stayed. The manor now takes paying tenants. 'It's still painful to think about it. My emotions are very mixed', says Glenn. 'But it doesn't feel like a defeat. We practised and learnt many techniques which have proved really critical for bottom-up, DIY ways of organising society.'

4 Tilakartan and Rahman, *The Animator in Participatory Rural Development*, quoted by Ivan and Isabel Labra in their manual, *The Organisation Workshop Introduction to the Social Scale Capacitation Method.*

5 Frederick Douglas said: 'Those who profess to favour freedom, and yet deprecate agitation are men who want crops without plowing the ground. They want rain without thunder and lightening. They want the ocean without the awful roar of its waters.'

Newcastle: our city is not for sale

1 See 'Public Voices', the *Guardian's* annual report on the views of public service staff published every March since the last elections.

2 Kevin Lavery, *Smart Contracting for Local Government Services: Processes and Experience*, Boston 1999.

3 See the following articles by David Byrne: 'Tyne and Wear UDC – turning the uses inside out – active deindustrialisation and its consequences', in R. Imrie and H. Thomas (eds) *British Urban Policy and the Urban Development Corporations*, 2nd edn., London 2000; 'Newcastle's "Going for Growth" – governance and planning in a postindustrial metropolis', *Northern Economic Review*, Summer 2000; 'The reconstruction of Newcastle: planning since 1945', in R. Colls and B. Lancaster (eds), *Newcastle upon Tyne: A Modern History* (forthcoming).

4 'We will not be moved', interview with author in the *Guardian*, 4 September 2000.

5 For two good briefings on GATS see Scott Sinclair, *GATS: How the WTO's New 'Services' Negotiations Threaten Democracy*, Ottowa 2000, and *Serving*

(Up) the Nation: A Guide to the UK's Commitments Under the WTO General Agreement on Trade in Services, www.wdm.org.uk.

6 See Dexter Whitfield, *Public Services or Corporate Welfare*, London 2002, and *What Future for Public Services*, www.centre.public.org.uk/briefings.

7 Newcastle UNISON's ITRS Evaluation Team assisted by the Centre for Public Services, 'No Corporate Takeover of Council Services', Newcastle 2002. The CPS has also published *An Investigators Handbook: Guide to Investigating Companies, Organisations, Government and Individuals*, Sheffield 2003; *Mortgaging Our Children's Future: The Privatisation of Secondary Education*, Sheffield 2002; *Our City is Not for Sale: The Impact of National, European and Global Policies*, Sheffield 2002.

8 By October 2001 union reps had heard that management was putting the contract for collecting and recycling householders' separated waste, out to tender. They tried to have discussions with management about an in-house bid, on the ITRS model. Sita already had all the other waste contracts for Newcastle. If Sita got kerbside recycling this would consolidate their monopoly and reduce the council's bargaining power. The unions thought they would be better able than a private operator to meet the government's increased targets for recycling. Moreover, they feared a private contractor could be the first step towards privatising the whole refuse system. But the council's management dismissed their concerns and rejected the proposals.

The following month, the unions were told that a tendering process would not take place, as prices, including Sita's, were too high. Mysteriously, nearly a year later they were told that the contract would go to Sita. There had been no new tendering process. Management said they had costed an in-house option; it would cost millions more than Sita.

GMB and UNISON commissioned waste consultant Robin Murray to help them formulate an alternative, which was turned down flat. The unions responded with industrial action, argument, research and political lobbying, and the council deferred signing to Sita and gave them a month to submit a more detailed proposal. The result was a detailed plan including a suitable depot, the negotiation of long-term contracts for the transport of recycled paper and glass, better collection methods, and models demonstrating that the union option was financially viable.

The council hired their own – costly – consultant who had had little operational experience of recycling. When the unions presented their full case to a meeting of councillors and management, they were told they had to leave the room for this consultant's comments. Sympathetic councillors later reported that the unions' plans had been grossly misrepresented. The vote against the union plans and for Sita was 5 to 3.

There seems to have been systematic bias in favour of Sita. The unions' concerns reveal a contrast with the process by which an in-house bid was agreed for ITRS. First, the in-house bid was over £300,000 cheaper than Sita's; second, the union's proposals for extensive community involvement meant it was more likely to raise recycling levels and to win funds from the Department of the Environment; third, there was no financial assessment of Sita, even though the company was said by the financial press to be in difficulty. A fourth concern was that the monopoly of waste contracts Sita would hold would put the council at a disadvantage in further negotiations.

Compared with the ITRS story, the (unfinished) waste story illustrates the dark side of local government. Whereas in ITRS, union pressure awakened the public-service values of many senior managers, over waste it came up against conservatism and stubborn vested interest. In addition, senior management's approach to waste was untouched by the politics of sustainability: for them waste was not a resource but simply rubbish to be disposed of in the easiest possible way. There is one thing in particular that senior management could not understand – that recycling depends on a positive relationship with the householder. The crucial issue with kerbside collections is householder participation, and they need to be able to trust those for whom they do the voluntary work of separation and preparation. Community involvement is of material relevance.

Here is an interesting case then where a community, trade union and political alliance, drawing on wider national networks and expertise, provided a real force for modernisation in a direction that was green and democratic. But it met with an implacable wall of cosy relationships with the private sector and low-level corruption which is at the root of so much local authority inefficiency and unaccountability, and which is effectively protected by new pressure to contract out rather than to encourage those who are pressing for change from within.

From Beswick to Brazil: democracy now!

1 One of the most revealing signs that the processes set in motion by the UN, most notably the United Nations Monitoring, Verifications and Inspections Commissions, were a meaningless ritual as far as the US were concerned is

Arms Inspector Hans Blix's report to the Security Council, the day after he had in effect been told to clear his desk. On 17 March 2003, three days before war was declared, UNMOVIC published an 83-page report suggesting the weapons inspectors in Iraq were making progress, though there was a lot more to do. UNMOVIC's Draft Work Programme specifically stated that there was no cut-off date for the completion of inspections. Elsewhere in the report the authors state 'there has been a good deal of destruction of missiles and missile-related equipment'. While problems clearly remained, the report shows a group of professionals competently carrying out their job and confident of completing it.

2 This contempt applies also to the Iraqi people. Hours after the US claimed victory in Baghdad, Jon Snow, Channel 4's persistent interrogator, put to Foreign Minister Jack Straw that as Saddam's regime was clearly hollow, it did not need a war to bring it down. Straw's response was 'How else were we to know?' A month earlier Tony Blair had refused to receive a letter from anti-war Iraqis who were long-standing opponents of the Baath regime. He preferred to treat the Iraqis as passive victims in need of a saviour than as people with long traditions of opposition, debate and disagreement, Unlike the leaders of the US-funded Iraqi National Council, they had no vested interest in an US/UK installed regime so they were intending to tell the Prime Minister the truth: that regime change could be brought about Eastern European fashion, without violence, led by the Iraqi people with the help of UN pressure. See 'Iraqi's speak out', *Red Pepper*, February 2003.

3 See pamphlet *After Seattle: Globalisation and its Discontents*, London 2000, published by Catalyst, an independent think-tank. See also the work of Susan George, Dot Keet and Walden Bello on the Transnational Institute website: www.tni.org.

4 See George Monbiot, *Captive State: The Corporate Takeover of Britain*, London 2001, and Greg Palast, *The Best Democracy Money Can Buy*, London 2002.

5 See Sheila Rowbotham, *The Past is Before Us: Feminism in Action Since the 1960s*, London 1989.

6 The 'Port Huron Statement' of the American Students for a Democratic Society, drafted by Tom Haydn in 1967, was the classic case of that era for participatory democracy. See Alexander Bloom and Winnie Breines (eds), *Takin' it to the Streets*, Boston 1995.

7 Real openness is also a question of time. Full equality of the right to participate requires radical changes in the economy of time, whether it is an extension of principle of paid time off work to participate in public life, or a

general reduction of working hours enabling people to play a fuller public role where they wish to do so.

8 The form of popular involvement will vary according to the task. The key issue is the sharing of power, of citizens' representatives and front-line workers having real power in the decision-making process. Swedish unions have developed models for worker and user involvement in public-sector management as part of a model for making public services more efficient and more democractic. See Brendan Martin, *European Integration and Modernisation of Local Public Services: Trade Union Responses and Initiatives*, London 1996, p. 37, and at www.publicworld.org. For a more profound discussion of this example, see Robin Murray, *Zero Waste*, London 2002.

9 See Chapter 7 in Hilary Wainwright, *Arguments for a New Left*, Oxford 1994.

10 See Robin Blackburn, *Banking on Death or Investing in Life?*, London 2002; 'Alternatives to competitiveness', in Daniel Drache, *Getting on Track: Social Democratic Strategies for Ontario*, Montreal 1992; Diane Elson, 'Socialising markets, not market socialism', in Leo Panitch and Coline Leys (eds), *Necessary and Unnecessary Utopias: Socialist Register 2000*; Pat Devine, *Democracy and Economic Planning*, Cambridge 1988; Michael Albert, *Parecon: Life After Capitalism*, London 2003.

11 At a press conference to launch the first public report on the NDC programme, I asked Lord Falconer, then the minister for regeneration and very enthusiastic about the whole experience, a question: 'Given that you consider community-led decision-making a success, is the government exploring possible changes in the political structures of local government to make more of it possible?' To summarise, his answer was 'No'. During the conversation that followed it emerged that the NDC experiences he was particularly proud of were those where community activity, supported by NDC money, had cut costs but improved delivery of services. It is true, of course, that community cohesion can itself directly contribute to resolving problems like vandalism, petty crime and the state of the environment. These are important achievements, but they don't define the scope of 'community-led decision-making'. When the government did attempt to create a new structure for local partnerships with councils, the Local Strategic Partnerships, they did so without any direct learning from the NDC experience, and with very under-developed notions of community involvement. See the Urban Forum Report 2002: www.urbanforum.org.

12 See Jane Wills, *Union Futures: Building Network Trade Unionism in the UK*, London 2002, and *Community Unionism and Trade Union Renewal in the UK:*

Moving Beyond the Fragments at Last? (Transactions of the Institute of British Geographers), London 2001, pp. 26, 465–83.

13 See Mzwaneli Mayekiso, *Township Politics: Civic Struggles for a New South Africa*, New York 1996.

14 See a useful discussion of some of these in Leo Panitch, *Renewing Socialism: Democracy, Strategy and Imagination*, Boston 2001, chs 1, 5, 6 & 7.

15 For a full description of the work of the second World Social Forum, see William Fisher and Thomas Ponniah, *Another World is Possible: Popular Alternatives to Globalisation at the World Social Forum*, New York 2003.

16 For useful background on the war on Iraq and the 'war against terrorism' see: Tariq Ali, *The Clash of Fundamentalisms: Crusades, Jihads and Modernity*, London 2003; Andrew Cockburn and Patrick Cockburn, *Saddam Hussein*, London 2003; Peter Gowan, 'New American century?', *Spokesman*, 76, 2003; Milan Rai, *War Plan Iraq: Ten Reasons Against War on Iraq*, London 2002.

RESOURCE:
ACTIVIST AND RESEARCH NETWORKS

The following list sets out a selection of important activist, campaign and research networks spanning both the local and the global. This is not an exhaustive directory. It is based on groups and organisations that I think make vital contributions in efforts to claim or reclaim democracy and common resources from corporate or military power, or which form key nodes in networks from which one can find more information and get involved. Also included as activist networks are a selection of left and/or green political parties I think deserve a mention for their aspirations towards grassroots participation and alternative, redistributive and emancipatory agendas. The list is divided along thematic lines and ordered according to scope, with the wider themes listed first. We also, where possible, help to show where and how organisations interconnect. A full and constantly updated directory will be placed on the *Red Pepper* website (www.redpepper.org.uk).

The ideas in this book will be developed further through the 'new politics' project of the Transnational Institute (www.tni.org, see page 242). Suggestions for developing the directory are welcome, as too are both responses to the ideas and accounts contained in the book and reports of readers' own experiences or observations of new forms of democracy. These can be sent to newpolitics@ redpepper.org.uk

Compiled by Stuart Hodkinson with special thanks to Leila Deen, Hazel Healy and Kelly Edwards.

The local – UK networks

The global – international networks

THE LOCAL – UK NETWORKS

Anti-capitalism – green – socialism

Earth First!, www.eco-action.org/ef/index.html
A radical, innovative, militant and biocentric environmental movement composed of countless small, bioregionally based groups across the country and the world that take direct action to protect nature. The international website links to the global network of EF groups (www.earthfirst.org).

Globalise Resistance (GR), www.resist.org.uk
PO Box 29689, London E8 2XR
(t) (+44) 020 7053 2071, office@resist.org.uk
A membership-based anti-capitalist mobilising organisation which has become an important protest network for mainly the socialist/Marxist left. Takes national delegations to numerous international protests, and is a co-organiser of the English mobilisation for the European Social Forum (ESF).

Green-Socialist Network, http://members.lycos.co.uk/leonora/gsn.html
15 Linford Close, Harlow, Essex CM19 4LR
j.ennis@gold.ac.uk
A new network of environmentalists and socialists advocating green-socialist policies across the left political and (extra-)parliamentary spectrum in the belief that social justice and sustainability are inseparable.

Wombles, www.wombles.org.uk
wombles@hushmail.com
Standing for White Overalls Movement Building Libertarian Effective Struggles, the Wombles are a diverse group of anarchists inspired by the Ya Basta! movement who create a large, padded block using protective shields on mass actions in order to repel police attacks.

See also:
Critical Mass, www.critical-mass.org
Reclaim the Streets, www.reclaimthestreets.net
TACT (Temporary Anti-Capitalist Teams), www.temporary.org.uk
For more green groups, see *Local: Anti-privatisation – community – public space*

Trade and debt justice – development

Brazil Network, www.brazilnetwork.org
67 Helix Road, London SW2 2JR
(t) (+44) 020 7732 8810, brazilnet@gn.apc.org
An independent, voluntary organisation based in London existing to publicise social, political, cultural and environmental issues in Brazil.

Jubilee Debt Campaign, www.jubileedebtcampaign.org
PO Box 36620, London SE1 0WJ
(t) (+44) 020 7922 1111 (f) (+44) 020 7922 1122
ashok@jubileedebtcampaign.org.uk
The UK's campaigning successor to the Jubilee 2000 and Drop the Debt campaigns, Jubilee Debt Campaign is a coalition of local groups and national organisations working to change UK government policy and bring maximum pressure on the IMF to end all unpayable poor country debts.

War on Want (WoW), www.waronwant.org
Fenner Brockway House, 37–39 Great Guildford Street, London SE1 OES
(t) (+44) 020 7620 1111 (f) (+44) 020 7261 9291, mailroom@waronwant.org
Long-standing, membership-based organisation campaigning for policy changes in the UK to help eradicate poverty in the developing world. WoW current campaigns include international respect for workers' rights as well the introduction of a Tobin tax on currency speculation.

World Development Movement (WDM), www.wdm.org.uk
25 Beehive Place, London SW9 7QR,
(t) (+44) 020 7737 6215 (f) (+44) 020 7274 8232, wdm@wdm.org.uk
A democratic, membership-based movement with over 100 local groups working
in partnership with other organisations in campaigns against the underlying
causes of world poverty such as unfair trade rules and debt. A leading UK
campaigner against the WTO GATS treaty and a key member of the Our World
is Not for Sale (OWINFS) network.

See also:
Baby Milk Action, www.babymilkaction.org
Cuba Solidarity Campaign, www.cuba-solidarity.org.uk
People & Planet, www.peopleandplanet.org
Trade Justice Movement, www.tradejusticemovement.org

Anti-militarism – peace

Active Resistance to the Roots of War (ARROW)
www.justicenotvengeance.org
c/o NonViolent Resistance Network, 162 Holloway Road, London N7 8DQ
info@justicenotvengeance.org
Non-violent, direct-action affinity group that organises regular vigils and civil
disobedience in opposition to economic sanctions on Iraq, military sales to
Indonesia, National Missile Defence, injustice in Northern Ireland and US–UK
military intervention in the Third World.

Campaign Against the Arms Trade (CAAT), www.caat.org.uk
11 Goodwin St, London N4 3HQ
(t) (+44) 020 7281 0297 (f) (+44) 020 7281 4369
A broad coalition of groups and individuals in the UK working to end the international arms trade. CAAT is a core group of the European Network Against
Arms Trade (www.antenna.nl/enaat), and works with organisations in South
Africa, Canada, Australia and the USA.

Campaign for Nuclear Disarmament (CND), www.cnduk.org
162 Holloway Road, London N7 8DQ
(t) (+44) 020 7700 2393 (f) (+44) 020 7700 2357, enquiries@cnduk.org

Long-standing, campaigning organisation for nuclear disarmament and world peace with a huge network of local organisations and knowledge. CND is today campaigning to scrap Trident, Britain's nuclear submarine system, stop the weaponisation of space and abolish the plutonium trade, as well as being an integral part of the anti-war movement.

Stop the War Coalition, www.stopwar.org.uk
PO Box 3739, London E5 8EJ, office@stopwar.org.uk
A temporary national broad-based coalition (that is increasingly permanent) of over 450 local anti-war coalitions around Britain opposing the recent US–UK-led wars on Afghanistan and Iraq.

Trident Ploughshares (TP), www.tridentploughshares.org
42–46 Bethel Street, Norwich NR2 1NR
(t) (+44) 01259 753815 (f) (+44) 01259 751959, info@tridentploughshares.org
Part of the international nuclear disarmament movement, TP is a national network of activists pledging to disarm the 39 sites in the UK related to the internationally unlawful British Trident nuclear submarine weapons system through non-violent, open, peaceful, safe and fully accountable direct action.

See also:
Campaign Against Sanctions on Iraq, www.casi.org.uk
Campaign for the Accountability of American Bases, www.caab.org.uk
Disobedience, www.disobedience.org.uk
Free Fylingdales Network, www.freefylingdalesnetwork.co.uk
Gloucestershire Weapons Inspectors (GWI), www.gwi.org.uk
Labour Against the War, www.labouragainstthewar.org.uk
Lakenheath Action Group, www.lakenheathaction.org
Media Workers Against War, www.mwaw.org
Neighbourhoods Opposing War, ww.now-peace.org.uk/about.htm
Reclaim the Bases, www.reclaimthebases.org.uk
Voices in the Wilderness UK, www.viwuk.freeserve.co.uk
War Resisters' International. http://wri-irg.org

Asylum – refugees

Barbed Wire Britain (BWB), www.barbedwirebritain.org.uk
A national anti-detention network of local campaigns and national bodies aimed at halting the massive increase in immigration detention in Britain. BWB has so far organised a series of demonstrations at all major places of detention, which are published in a map on its website.

National Coalition of Anti-Deportation Campaigns, www.ncadc.org.uk
National Co-ordinator, 110 Hamstead Road, Birmingham B20 2QS
(t) (+44) 0121 554 6947, ncadc@ncadc.org.uk
A voluntary organisation providing a network for anti-deportation organisations and campaigns to work together mainly to help refused asylum seekers stay in the UK as well as win changes in law and practice which lead to unjust or inhumane deportations.

Palestine Solidarity Campaign, www.palestinecampaign.org
Box BM PSA, London WC1N 3XX, info@palestinecampaign.org
An independent, non-aligned, membership-based organisation aiming to raise awareness and build an effective mass campaign against the Israeli occupation of the Palestinian territories.

See also:
al-Awda – The Palestine Right to Return Coalition, www.al-awda.org.uk
Committee to Defend Asylum Seekers, www.defend-asylum.org

Organised labour – workers' rights

Home Workers Worldwide (HWW), www.homeworkersww.org.uk
30–38 Dock Street, Leeds LS10 1JF
(t) (+44) 0113 217 4037 (f) (+44) 0113 217 4021
A member of Homenet (www.homenetww.org.uk) – the international solidarity network of homebased workers' organisations and supporters – HWW works in collaboration with organisations in the UK and around the world to raise awareness and build and train grassroots organisations of home-based workers.

Institute of Employment Rights (IER), www.ier.org.uk
177 Abbeville Road, London SW4 9RL
Funded by trade unions, individual donations and subscription fees, the IER is an independent organisation providing a wide variety of high-quality publications to stimulate debate and analysis about employment law policies and legal developments in industrial relations.

Labour Behind the Label, www.labourbehindthelabel.org
c/o NEAD, 38 Exchange Street, Norwich NR2 1AX
(t) (+44) 01603 610 993, lbl@gn.apc.org
A UK network of aid, alternative trade, labour and solidarity organisations publicising and campaigning on behalf of garment workers' efforts, at home and abroad, to defend their rights and improve their wages and conditions. The UK platform for the European Clean Clothes Campaign.

No Sweat, www.nosweat.org.uk
PO Box 36707, London SW9 8YA
(t) (+44) 07904 431 959
Inspired by the American anti-sweatshop movement, No Sweat is a broad-based, activist, campaigning organisation in the UK fighting the existence of sweatshops at home and abroad. It has organised major protests, demonstrations and stunts outside (and inside!) Nike and Gap stores.

See also:
Cyber-Picket Line, www.cf.ac.uk/socsi/union
Simon Jones Memorial Campaign, www.simonjones.org.uk
WomenWorkingWorldwide, www.poptel.org.uk/women-ww

Anti-privatisation – community – public space

CASE – Campaign for State Education, www.casenet.org.uk
158 Durham Road, London SW20 0DG
(t/f) (+44) 020 8944 8206, tulloch-case@mcr1.poptel.org.uk
A membership-based national group campaigning for the right of all to the highest quality, fully comprehensive, locally accountable state education, regardless of race, gender, home circumstances, ability or disability.

Centre for Public Services, www.centre.public.org.uk
1 Sidney Street, Sheffield S1 4RG
(t) (+44) 0114 272 6683 (f) (+44) 0114 272 7066, mail@centre-public.org.uk
Independent non-profit research centre committed to public service provision by democratically accountable public bodies, implementing best practice management, employment and equal opportunities policies. Produces publications and briefings, and as well as custom-designed training courses.

Community Matters, www.communitymatters.org.uk
12–20 Baron Street, London N1 9LL
communitymatters@communitymatters.org.uk
The nation-wide federation for community associations and similar organisations, with over 1,000 member organisations. Community Matters promotes and supports action by ordinary people in response to social, educational and recreational needs in their neighbourhoods and communities.

Community Recycling Network, www.crn.org.uk
Trelawny House, Surrey Street, Bristol BS7 9JR
(t) (+44) 0117 942 0142 (f) (+44) 0117 908 0225, info@crn.org.uk
A non-profit organsiation of 300+ members promoting community waste management nationally as an effective way of tackling both Britain's growing waste problem and building the social economy. Superb links to other recycling, environmental and community groups and networks.

Defend Council Housing, www.defendcouncilhousing.org.uk
PO Box 33519, London E8 4XW
(t) (+44) 020 7987 9989, info@defendcouncilhousing.org.uk
A broad-based national campaign supported by a large number of tenants, council workers and unions, community organisations and campaign groups opposing privatisation and defending council housing principles.

MERCi, www.bridge-5.org
Bridge-5 Mill, 22a Beswick Street, Manchester M4 7HS
(t) (+44) 0161 273 1736, merci@bridge-5.org
'Murky' is an independant charity working to make Manchester a greener, safer, healthier and more equitable place to live. It is based in Bridge-5 Mill, redeveloped to be the most environmentally friendly building in Manchester.

Radical Routes, www.radicalroutes.org.uk
(t) (+44) 0113 262 9365, info@radicalroutes.org.uk
A network of independent housing cooperatives providing each other with services and support, and able to raise investment centrally through a national investment scheme. Website has contact details for local cooperatives.

UNISON, www.unison.org.uk
1 Mabledon Place, London WC1H 9AJ
(t) (+44) 0845 355 0845
Britain's biggest trade union representing 1.3 million workers in the public services and essential utilities, Unison is fast becoming an indispensable actor in campaigns against further privatisation, public-private partnerships and GATS. Through membership of its global union federation, Public Services International (www.world-psi.org), Unison is a member of the network OWINFS.

See also:
Aspire, www.a-spire.org.uk
Community Sector Coalition, www.bassac.org.uk/info_csc.htm
Communities Against Toxics, www.communities-against-toxins.org.uk
East Manchester Community Forum, 0161 230 7781
London Action Resource Centre, www.londonarc.org
Social Centres Network, c/o London Action Resource Centre
TELCO, www.telcocitizens.org.uk

Race – gender – sexuality

Anti Nazi League (ANL), www.anl.org.uk
PO Box 2566, London N4 1WJ
(t) (+44) 020 7924 0333 (f) (+44) 020 7924 0313, anl@anl.org.uk
A broad-based organisation that aims to bring together as many people as possible in a united grassroots campaign against the Far Right. Organises the successful and popular Love Music Hate Racism campaign which uses the music scene to create a vibrant counter-culture to racial hatred.

Black Racial Attacks Independent Network (BRAIN), www.nmp.org.uk/brain
Suite 4, 63 Broadway, London E15 4BQ
(t) (+44) 020 8221 2564

A national network of grassroots, independent black voluntary and community groups engaged in activities towards racial justice and the elimination of racism to provide support, information exchange and policy orientation. A member of European Network Against Racism (www.enar-eu.org)

Fawcett Society, www.fawcettsociety.org.uk
1–3 Berry Street, London EC1V 0AA
(t) (+44) 020 7253 2598 (f) (+44) 020 7253 2599, info@fawcettsociety.org.uk
The UK's leading society campaigning for equality between women and men at home, at work and in public life. Fawcett provides analysis, research and a strong lobby for improvements in women's lives.

National Assembly Against Racism (NAAR), www.naar.org.uk
28 Commercial St, London E1 6LS
(t) (+44) 020 7247 9907, info@naar.org.uk
A black community organisations-led coalition uniting representatives from faith-based organisations, trade unions, refugee organisations and youth/student groups in campaigns and educational programmes such as fighting the far right, racial violence and black deaths in custody.

Outrage!, http://outrage.nabumedia.com
PO Box 17816, London SW14 8WT
(t) (+44) 020 8240 0222, outrage@blueyonder.co.uk
The world's longest surviving queer-rights direct-action group, challenging anti-gay discrimination, promoting the public visibility and media debate of queer issues, and offering both legal and personal advice for those suffering discrimination and persecution.

Women's Aid, www.womensaid.org.uk
PO Box 391, Bristol BS99 7WS
(t) (+44) 0117 944 4411 (f) (+44) 0117 924 1703, info@womensaid.org.uk
National charity working to end domestic violence against women and children. It coordinates and supports an England-wide network of over 250 local projects, providing over 400 refuges, helplines, outreach services and advice centres.

See also:
Anti-Fascist Action, www.geocities.com/CapitolHill/Senate/5602
Kick Racism Out of Football, www.kickitout.org

Newham Monitoring Project, www.nmp.org.uk
Searchlight, www.searchlightmagazine.com
Women against Fundamentalism, www.waf.gn.apc.org
Youth Against Racism in Europe, www.yre.org.uk
For more feminist and gender networks, see *Local: Organised labour – workers'
rights; Global: Human and gender rights – resisting oppression; Local and Global:
Trade and debt justice – development* and *Alternative media/analysis – netactivism.*

Democracy – new political parties – the Labour Party left

Campaign for the English Regions (CFER), www.cfer.org.uk
140–150 Pilgrim St, Newcastle upon Tyne NE1 6TF
(t) (+44) 0191 245 0825, info@cfer.org.uk
National organisation campaigning for devolution to the regions of England with
the aim of securing referendums on directly elected and representative regional
governments in England.

Charter 88
18a Victoria Park Square, London E2 9PB
(t) (+44) 020 8880 6088 (f) (+44) 020 8880 6089, info@charter88.org.uk
Independent campaign for a modern and fair democracy advocating dramatic
reform of the UK system of government including: decentralisation of power, a
democratic Westminster Parliament, a Bill of Rights, a Freedom of Information
Act, and proportional voting systems for all levels of government.

Electoral Reform Society, www.electoral-reform.org.uk
6 Chancel St, London SE1 OUU
(t) (+44) 020 7928 1622 (f) (+44) 020 7928 1622, ers@reform.demon.co.uk
A membership organisation campaigning for the strengthening of UK democracy
through changes to the voting system and electoral arrangements that would
create proportional representation through a Single Transferable Vote.

Green Party, www.greenparty.org.uk
London office, 1a Waterlow Road, London N19 5NJ
(t) (+44) 020 7272 4474, (f) (+44) 020 7272 6653, office@greenparty.org.uk
With separate parties for England and Wales, Scotland, Northern Ireland and
Ireland, the Green Party aims to create a just, equitable and sustainable society

through both the electoral system and campaign activism. An open, non-hierarchal, leaderless party in which policy and strategy are formulated by the members.

Labour Campaign for Electoral Reform,
www.electoralreform.connectfree.co.uk
84 Cranbrook Road, Redland, Bristol BS6 7DB
(t) (+44) 0117 942 0141, lcer@electoralreform.org.uk
Following up the Labour Party's 1997 general election commitment to a referendum on the voting system for the House of Commons, the Campaign is a network of over 2000 Labour members and supporters committed to changing the electoral voting system.

Scottish Socialist Party, www.scottishsocialistparty.org
Glasgow office, 73 Robertson St, Glasgow G2 8QD
(t) (+44) 0141 221 7714 (f) (+44) 0141 221 7715, ssp.glasgow@btinternet.com
Scotland's youngest and fastest growing political party, bringing an alliance of socialist platforms with former Labour members and trade unionists to push for an Independent Socialist Scotland as part of a worldwide fight-back against global capitalism. Its weekly paper is the *Scottish Socialist Voice* (www.scottishsocialistvoice.net).

Socialist Alliance (SA), www.socialistalliance.net
10 Cleveland Way, London E1 4TR
(t) (+44) 020 7791 3138, office@socialistalliance.net
Electoral alliance of trade unionists, long-serving Labour Party activists, media workers, well-known campaigners, lawyers and revolutionary parties offering a socialist alternative to New Labour in England. Even at its strength, the SA has proven to be more a consolidating and campaigning network for socialists to join than a serious challenge to the mainstream parties' electoral dominance. Without proportional representation, cracking the problem of electoral representation for the left is proving difficult.

Socialist Campaign Group of Labour MPs, www.poptel.org.uk/scgn
(t) (+44) 020 7622 5734 / 7219 2615 / 07984 401032, campaigngroup@aol.com
An organised network of a small but vociferous number of Labour MPs committed to socialist values and policies, campaigning both within and outside of the Labour Party for a return to its historic roots and internal party democracy. It has its own monthly newspaper *Socialist Campaign Group News* (see web-link).

Tribune, www.tribune.atfreeweb.com
The weekly independent magazine of the Labour left campaigning against the New Labour leadership and Blairite politics.

Alternative media and analysis – netactivism

Campaign for Press and Broadcasting Freedom, www.cpbf.org.uk
2nd Floor, Vi and Garner Smith House, 23 Orford Road, London E17 9NL
(t) (+44) 020 8521 5932, freepress@cpbf.org.uk
A broad-based research and lobbying organisation made up of individuals and affiliated groups working to promote policies for a diverse, democratic and accountable media.

CorporateWatch, www.corporatewatch.org.uk
16b Cherwell Street, Oxford OX4 1BG
(t) (+44) 01865 791 391, mail@corporatewatch.org
A radical research and publishing group investigating corporate structures and the broader system that supports them. The premiere source of information on corporate takeover in Britain, CorporateWatch also runs Grassroots Action on Food and Farming (www.gaff.org.uk). (*See also* Ethical Consumer, www.ethicalconsumer.org; Red Star Research, www.red-star-research.org.uk; The Mcinformation Network, www.mcspotlight.org)

Feminist.Com, www.feminist.com
A grassroots, interactive community by, for and about women, aiming to facilitate information-sharing and encourage mobilisation around political issues.

Indymedia UK, www.indymedia.org.uk
Part of the global network of Indymedias, Indymedia UK (United Kollektives) is a network of individuals, independent and alternative media activists and organisations, offering grassroots, non-corporate, non-commercial coverage of important social and political issues.

Left Direct, www.leftdirect.co.uk
A comprehensive directory of all left, progressive and radical websites in the UK with monthly newsletter and events calendar.

Media Lens, www.medialens.org
A website designed to counter the distorted picture of the world provided by mainstream newspapers and broadcasters of the increasingly centralised, corporate nature of the media which act a de facto propaganda system for corporate and other establishment interests.

New Economics Foundation, www.neweconomics.org
Cinnamon House, 6–8 Cole Street, London SE1 4YH
(t) (+44) 020 7089 2800 (f) (+44) 020 7407 6473, info@neweconomics.org
A research and campaigning body challenging the ideas and structures of the 'old economy' and offering practical and enterprising solutions to the social, environmental and economic challenges facing the local, regional, national and global economies.

Open Democracy, www.opendemocracy.net
23–25 Great Sutton St, London EC1V ODN
(t) (+44) 020 7608 2000 (f) (+44) 020 7608 2666, hello@opendemocracy.net
A channel for knowledge, learning, participation and understanding that is not owned by a media corporation, does not serve a special interest and does not adhere to a single ideological position.

Red Pepper, www.redpepper.org.uk
1b Waterlow Road, London N19 5NJ
(t) (+44) 020 7281 7024 (f) (+44) 020 7263 9345, redpepper@redpepper.org.uk
Independent monthly magazine of the green and radical left, *Red Pepper* provides a monthly round-up of national and international news in addition to commissioned articles from radical thinkers and practitioners on all themes. Online edition contains extra stories, archives and a superb set of links.

SchNEWS, www.schnews.co.uk
PO Box 2600, Brighton BN2 0EF
(t/f) (+44) 01273 685913, schnews@brighton.co.uk
A cult weekly print and online newsletter produced voluntarily by Justice? – Brighton's Direct Action Collective. SchNEWS reports on local and global resistance movements from a green anarchist perspective, features a party and protest calendar and has an estimated readership of 50,000.

Undercurrents, www.undercurrents.org
16b Cherwell Street, Oxford OX4 1BG
(t) (+44) 01865 203661 (f) (+44) 0870 1316103, underc@gn.apc.org
Producer of the award-winning regular 'alternative news video', Undercurrents
has also set up the country's first grassroots protest video archive, supports video
activist training overseas, organises video activist gatherings and helps facilitate
independent grassroots production.

See also:
BeyondTV, www.beyondtv.org
Catalyst, www.catalystforum.org.uk
Conscious Cinema, www.consciouscinema.co.uk
The Corner House, www.thecornerhouse.org.uk
EducationNet, www.educationet.org
The F-Word, www.thefword.org.uk
i-Contact video Network, www.videonetwork.org
Independent Student Media Project, www.ismproject.net
Leeds Underground Film, www.leedsundergroundfilm.org.uk
Lobster: The Journal of Para-Politics, www.lobster-magazine.co.uk
New Left Review, www.newleftreview.net
Print Radio, www.printradio.org.uk
Private Eye, www.private-eye.co.uk
Subvertise, www.subvertise.org
Urban 75, www.urban75.com

THE GLOBAL – INTERNATIONAL NETWORKS

Emancipation – justice – solidarity

Anti-Capitalist Convergence (CLAC), www.tao.ca/~clac
c/o la Libraire Alternative 2035, Boulevard St. Laurent 2nd floor, Montreal, Quebec H2X 2T3, Canada
clac@tao.ca-la CLAC
Recently formed network for Canadian-based anti-capitalist activist groups to come together to militantly oppose the FTAA and actively support local projects and actions. A member of PGA.

Peoples Global Action (PGA), www.agp.org
c/o Canadian Union of Postal Workers (CUPW), 377 Bank Street, Ottawa, Ontario, Canada
A global network of diverse grassroots movements across the world struggling against capitalism and destructive globalisation and for a durable borderless and directly democratic alternative. Key groups in each global region, such as Ya Basta! in Europe and the Brazilian MST, act as information points and convenors for conferences. PGA has helped coordinate the legendary decentralised Global Action Days that have marked WTO Ministerials.

World Social Forum (WSF), www.forumsocialmundial.org.br
Rua General Jardim, 660, 8° andar, sala 81, São Paulo, CEP 01223-010, Brazil
(t/f) (+ 55) 11 3258 8914

A convergence point for groups and movements of global civil society opposed to neo-liberalism and instead engaged in building a planetary society centred on respect for universal human rights, the environment, democracy, social justice, equality and the sovereignty of peoples, to debate ideas, formulate proposals, share experiences and network for effective action. Meeting annually in Porto Alegre, Brazil, since 2001, the WSF has become a world process with the emergence of Regional Social Forums including Asia (www.wsfindia.org), Europe (www.fse-esf.org) and Pan-Amazonia (www. fspanamazonico.org.br).

Ya Basta!, www.yabasta.it
Via Watteau 7, 20125 Milan, Italy
yabasta@sherwood.it
Begun as an Italian solidarity network supporting the Zapatista uprising, it is now an uneven but growing European-wide movement using squatted social centres as places for radical politics and wearing white overalls to symbolise the condition of invisibility of citizens with no rights and power under neo-liberalism.

Trade and debt justice – development

Anti-Privatisation Forum (APF), www.apf.org.za
1 Leyds Street, 3rd floor Cosatu House, Braamfontein, Johannesburg, South Africa
trevor@aidc.org.za
An alliance of two key anti-privatisation struggles in South Africa with affiliates from the unions, communities, students and the left, the APF works to unite workers' struggles for a living wage and jobs with community struggles for housing, water, electricity and fair rates and taxes.

Association for Taxation of Financial Transaction to Aid Citizens (ATTAC)
www.attac.org
9 bis, rue de Valence, F-75005 Paris, France
(t) (+33) 1 4336 2661 (f) (+33) 1 4336 2626, attac@attac.org
The leading international-campaign organisation for the democratic control of financial markets and international financial institutions. A non-hierarchical, pluralist network of relatively autonomous local and national organisations in more than fifty countries, ATTAC produces an excellent weekly e-newsletter.

Corporate Europe Observatory, www.xs4all.nl/~ceo
Paulus Potterstraat 20, 1071 DA Amsterdam, The Netherlands
(t/f) (+31) 20 612 70 23, ceo@corporateeurope.org
A research and campaign group exposing the threats to democracy, equity, social
justice and the environment in the EU posed by corporate power and lobbying.
It publishes a quarterly newsletter, is joint-coordinator of GATSWatch
(www.gatswatch.org) with the TNI and is a member of the OWINFS network.

CorpWatch, www.corpwatch.org
PO Box 29344, San Francisco CA 94129, USA
(t) (+1) 415 561 6568 (f) (+1) 415 561 6493, corpwatch@corpwatch.org
Research and activist network aiming to counter corporate-led globalisation by
disseminating information about the power and activities of corporations and
thereby helping to build a grassroots globalisation of diverse movements for
human rights and dignity, labour rights and environmental justice that enforce
democratic control over corporations. Member of the OWINFS network

Council of the Canadians, www.canadians.org
502–151 Slater Street, Ottawa, K1P 5H3 Ontario, Canada
(t) (+1) 613 233 2773 (f) (+1) 613 233 6776, inquiries@canadians.org
Canada's pre-eminent citizens' watchdog organisation, comprising over 100,000
members, lobbies MPs, conducts research, and runs national campaigns aimed at
safeguarding social programs and the environment, promoting economic justice,
asserting Canadian sovereignty and advancing alternatives to corporate free trade.
A member of the OWINFS network.

Focus on the Global South (Focus), www.focusweb.org
c/o CUSRI, Chulalongkorn University, Bangkok 10330, Thailand
(t) (+66) 2 2187363 65 (f) (+66) 2 2559976, admin@focusweb.org
Independent research and advocacy organisation working on economic, ecolog-
ical, political and cultural developments affecting the Global South and particularly the Asia Pacific region, from a critical Third World/Southern, but
internationalist, perspective. A member of the OWINFS network.

Global Exchange, www.globalexchange.org
2017 Mission Street, Suite 303, San Francisco CA 94110, USA
(t) (+1) 415 255 2341 (f) (+1) 415 255 7498
An international non-profit human rights organisation aimed at forging closer

ties between North Americans and grassroots groups working for democracy and social justice around the world.

Hemispheric Social Alliance/Alianza Sociale Continenta (HSA),
www.asc-hsa.org
sri_cut@uol.com.br
A remarkable coalition of major citizens' networks representing some 50 million people across the entire Americas in a broad-based struggle against the proposed Free Trade Agreement of the Americas (FTAA) and the neo-liberal model of US domination it embodies.

Ibase – Brazilian Institute for Social-Economic Analysis, www.ibase.br
Av. Rio Branco 124, 8° andar, Centro, Rio de Janeiro, CEP 20148-900, Brazil
(t) (+55) 21 2509 0660
Influential research NGO and co-initiator of the World Social Forum process, committed to the defence of human rights, social well-being and the participation of all Brazilians in the construction of a democratic society.

International Gender and Trade Network, www.genderandtrade.net
1225 Otis Street, NE, Washington DC 20017, USA
(t) (+1) 202 635 2757 (f) (+1) 202 832 9494, secretariat@coc.org
Brings together regional networks of women involved in research, advocacy and economic literacy around issues of trade and development with the aim of engaging the global women's movement more effectively in the discourse and negotiations on trade and investment.

Our World is Not for Sale (OWINFS), www.ourworldisnotforsale.org
owinfs@citizen.org
Acts as a vital coordinating and information hub for a grouping of key reform-oriented organisations, activists, progressive trade unions and social movements worldwide fighting against the current model of neo-liberal corporate globalisation embodied in the WTO, and for a sustainable, socially just and accountable multilateral system.

PACS – Policy Alternatives for the Southern Cone,
www.alternex.com.br/~pacs
Rua Joaquim Silva, 56, 8° andar, Centro, Rio de Janeiro, CEP 20241 110, Brazil
(t) (+55) 21 252 0366 (f) (+55) 21 232 6306, pacs@alternex.com.br

An eco-social consultancy and education action centre working in collaboration with the Brazilian social, labour and co-operative movements, and the Workers Party (PT). Its main work is on the 'social economy', and it runs the virtual Workshop on a Socio-Economy of Solidarity.

Public Citizen, www.citizen.org
1600 20th St. NW, Washington DC 20009, USA
(t) (+1) 202 588 1000
US non-profit consumer advocacy organisation fighting for openness and democratic accountability in government, sustainable development and social and economic justice in trade and welfare policies. It runs the important Global Trade Watch, and is a member of the OWINFS network and the national Citizens Trade Campaign (www.citizenstrade.org).

Social Watch, www.socwatch.org.uy
Jackson 1136, Montevideo 11200, Uruguay
(t) (+598) 2 419 61 92 (f) (+598) 2 411 92 22, socwatch@socialwatch.org
An international network of around 300 national citizens' groups checking progress or regression on internationally agreed commitments on poverty eradication and equality.

Southern African People's Solidarity Network,
www.aidc.org.za/sapsn/index.html
P.O. Box 12943, Mowbray 7705, South Africa
(t) (+27) 21 6851565 (f) (+27) 21 6851645, sapsn@aidc.org.za
Brings together the major Southern African NGOs and social movements, such as the African Trade Network (http://twnafrica.org/atn.asp) and the Alternative Information and Development Centre (http://aidc.org.za), to campaign and organise together around the issues of debt, structural adjustment and globalisation.

Third World Network, www.twnside.org.sg
228 Macalister Road, 10400 Penang, Malaysia
(t) (+60) 4 2266728 (f) (+60) 4 2264505, twn@igc.apc.org/twnet@po.jaring.my
An influential, independent non-profit international research and advocacy network of organisations and individuals involved in economic, social and environmental issues relating to development, the Third World and North–South relations.

Transnational Institute, www.tni.org
Paulus Potterstraat 20, 1071 DA Amsterdam, The Netherlands
(t) (+31) 20 662 66 08 (f) (+31) 20 675 71 76, tni@tni.org
An independent global network of scholar-activists embedded in the 'global justice movement' seeking to create international cooperation in analysing and finding possible solutions to common global problems including militarism, UN drug control and alternatives to water and energy privatisation.

World Bank Bonds Boycott, www.worldbankboycott.org
International Coordination, Center for Economic Justice, 733 15th St, NW, Suite 928, Washington DC 20005, USA
(t) (+1) 202 393 6665 (f) (+1) 202 393 1358, bankboycott@econjustice.net
An international grassroots campaign of groups from the 35 Global South countries and the US which builds moral, political, and financial pressure on the World Bank by persuading individual and organisational investors such as trade unions and and universities not to buy World Bank bonds.

See also:
50 Years Is Enough Network, www.50years.org
Alliance for Responsible Trade, www.art-us.org
A SEED – Europe, www.aseed.net
Asian NGO Coalition for Agrarian Reform and Rural Development,
     www.philonline.com.ph/~angoc
Asia-Pacific Research Network, www.aprnet.org
Australian Fair Trade and Investment Network, www.aftinet.org.au
Common Frontiers, www.web.net/comfront
International Forum on Globalization (IFG), www.ifg.org
Institute for Agriculture and Trade Policy, www.iatp.org
Institute for Policy Studies, www.ips-dc.org
Mexican Action Network on Free Trade, www.rmalc.org.mx
Multinational Monitor, www.multinationalmonitor.org
Polaris Institute, www.polarisinstitute.org
Transnationale, www.transnationale.org
Women's International Coalition for Economic Justice, www.wicej.addr.com

Environment – food – water

Greenpeace International, www.greenpeace.org
Keizersgracht 176, 1016 DW Amsterdam, The Netherlands
(t) (+31) 20 523 62 22 (f) (+31) 20 523 62 00,
supporter.services@ams.greenpeace.org
An independent non-profit, global campaigning organisation with 2.65 million
supporters worldwide using non-violent, creative confrontation to expose global
environmental problems and their causes.

Peoples Food Sovereignty Network, www.peoplesfoodsovereignty.org
admin@peoplesfoodsovereignty.org
A loose global coalition of peasant-farmer organisations and NGOs working on
food and agriculture issues that grew out of the OWINFS coalition.

Via Campesina, www.viacampesina.org
ASOCODE (Rafael Alegria), Colonia Alameda, 11 Avenida (Alfonso Guillén
Zelaya), entre 3 y 4 Calles, Casa 2025, Apartado Postal 3628, Tegucigalpa,
M.D.C. – Honduras, C.A.
(t/f) (+504) 2359915, viacam@gbm.hn
A pluralistic, democratic, multicultural movement which coordinates and
develops solidarity amongst small and middle-scale farmers, agricultural workers,
rural women, and indigenous communities from across the world in order to
promote sustainable economic relations of equality and social justice.

See also:
European Farmers Coordination, www.cpefarmers.org
Food First, www.foodfirst.org
Foundation for Science, Technology and Ecology, www.vshiva.net
Friends of the Earth International, www.foei.org
Genetic Resources Action International, www.grain.org
Pesticide Action Network, www.pan-international.org

Organised labour – workers' rights – migration

Brazilian MST, www.mst.org.br
The largest social movement in Latin America, the Brazilian Landless Workers Movement organises hundreds of thousands of landless peasants to occupy and secure land in order to guarantee food security for their families, and set up an alternative socio-economic development model that puts people before profits. A core member of the PGA.

Clean Clothes Campaign (CCC), www.cleanclothes.org
Postbus 11584, 1001 GN Amsterdam, The Netherlands
(t) (+31) 20 412 2785 (f) (+31) 20 412 2786, info@cleanclothes.org
A Dutch-based activist NGO linked to autonomous campaigns in ten Western European countries, which aims to improve working conditions in the garment and sportswear industry through mobilising the purchasing power of consumers.

International Centre for Trade Union Rights, www.ictur.org
UCATT House, 177 Abbeville Road, London SW4 9RL, UK
(t) (+44) 020 7498 4700 (f) (+44) 020 7498 0611, ictur@ictur.org
An organising and campaigning body of trade unionists, labour lawyers and academics worldwide with the fundamental purpose of defending and improving the rights of trade unions and trade unionists throughout the world.

LabourStart, www.labourstart.org
51 Briarfield Avenue, London N3 2LG, UK
(t) (+44) 020 8349 1975, ericlee@labourstart.org
A near-instantaneous real-time online labour news service in 10 languages maintained by a global network of volunteers who constantly upload news stories about trade union and labour struggles they find on the Internet, which are then archived.

Maquila Solidarity Network (MSN), www.maquilasolidarity.org
606 Shaw Street, Toronto, M6G 3L6 Ontario, Canada
(t) (+1) 416 532 8584 (f) (+1) 416 532 7688, info@maquilasolidarity.org
A Canadian network of over 400 individuals and organisations promoting solidarity with groups in Mexico, Central America and Asia, organising in maquiladora factories and export-processing zones to improve conditions and win a living wage.

No Border, www.noborder.org
A European-wide network formed in late 1999 as an information and coordination tool for all groups and grassroots organisations working to improve conditions for migrants and asylum seekers.

StreetNet International, www.streetnet.org.za
PO Box 61139, Bishopsgate, Durban 4008, South Africa
(t) (+27) 31 307 4038 (f) (+27) 31 306 7490, stnet@iafrica.com
An international network comprised of individual vendors, activists, researchers, institutions and other people working to increase the visibility, voice and bargaining power of street vendors throughout the world.

United Students Against Sweatshops,
www.people.fas.harvard.edu/~fragola/usas
888 16th Street NW, Suite 303, Washington DC 20006 202, USA
(f) (+1) 202 347 0708
A US-based international student movement of campuses and individual students fighting for sweatshop-free labour conditions and workers' rights by demanding that their school or university logo is emblazoned on clothing made in decent working conditions.

WIEGO, www.wiego.org
Carr Center for Human Rights, Kennedy School of Government, Harvard University, 79 John F. Kennedy Street, Cambridge MA 02138, USA
(t) (+1) 617 495 7639 (f) (+1) 617 496 2828, wiego@ksg.harvard.edu
WIEGO stands for Women in Informal Employment: Globalizing and Organizing, a worldwide coalition of labour grassroots organisations, research or academic institutions and international development organisations concerned with improving the status of women in the informal sector.

See also:
European Network of Migrants, Refugees and Sans-Papiers,
    http://sanspapier.eu.ouvaton.org
Global Unions, www.global-unions.org
LaborNet, www.labornet.net
International Labour Resource and Information Group,
    http://aidc.org.za/ilrig/index.html
International Restructuring Education Network Europe (IRENE),
    www.mvo-platform.nl/leden/leden_irene.html

Human and gender rights – resisting oppression

Amnesty International (AI), www.amnesty.org
99–119 Rosebery Avenue, London EC1R 4RE, UK
(t) (+44) 020 7814 6200 (f) (+44) 020 7833 1510
The world's largest international voluntary human rights organisation with more than a million members and supporters in over 140 countries and territories. Campaigns to spread awareness and against specific abuses.

Derechos Human Rights, www.derechos.org
An independent, non-profit internet-based international human rights organisa-tion based in USA and Spain working for the respect and promotion of human rights all over the world, with particular focus on Latin America.

International Solidarity Movement (ISM), www.palsolidarity.org
(T) (+(97) 2 2 277 4602, info@palsolidarity.org
A Palestinian-led movement of Palestinian and international activists working to raise awareness of the struggle for Palestinian freedom and an end to Israeli occu-pation. Utilises non-violent, direct-action methids of resistance to confront and challenge illegal Israeli occupation forces and policies.

Sisterhood is Global Institute (SIGI), www.sigi.org
4095 Chemin de la Cote-des-Neiges, Suite 12, Montreal H3H 1W9, Canada
(t) (+1) 514 846 9366 (f) (+1) 514 846 9066, sigi@qc.aibn.com
Seeks to deepen the understanding of women's rights at the local, national, regional and global levels, and to strengthen the capacity of women to exercise these rights. With members in 70 countries, SIGI currently maintains a network of over 1,300 individuals and organisations.

Women's Global Network for Reproductive Rights, www.wgnrr.org
Vrolikstraat 453 – D, 1092 TJ Amsterdam, The Netherlands
(t) (+31) 20 620 96 72, (f) (+31) 20 622 24 50, office@wgnrr.nl
An autonomous network of groups and individuals in 157 countries who aim to achieve and support reproductive rights for women, which include the right of all women to safe, legal abortion.

Women Living Under Muslim Laws (WLUML), www.wluml.org
PO Box 28445, London N19 5NZ, UK
run@gn.apc.org
Formed by an international network of feminists from Muslim countries, WLUML is a network of mutual solidarity and information flow aimed at breaking the isolation of women, Muslim and non-Muslim, whose lives may be affected by Muslim laws in whatever form or context.

Anti-militarism – peace

Food Not Bombs, www.foodnotbombs.net
One of the fastest growing revolutionary movements in the world today, Food Not Bombs is an inclusive, non-hierarchical all-volunteer organisation with hundreds of local groups across the world dedicated to recycling and sharing vegetarian food with hungry people, and protesting against war and poverty.

Global Network Against Weapons and Nuclear Power in Space
www.globenet.free-online.co.uk
PO Box 90083, Gainesville, Florida 32607, USA
(t) (+1) 352 337 9274, globalnet@mindspring.com
A network of over 150 affiliated organisations and key figures from across the world which meets each year in order to bring together key activists to campaign against the militarisation of space and bring the activities of governments to the attention of the global citizenry.

Women in Black (WIB), www.womeninblack.net
A loose network of women world-wide committed to peace and justice and actively opposed to war and other forms of violence, who demonstrate by staging women-only, silent, non-violent vigils in public spaces dressed only in black.

See also:
Iraqi Human Shields, www.humanshields.org
Quakers, www.quakers.org
Women's International League for Peace and Freedom, www.wilpf.org

New parties

Brazilian Workers Party (PT), www.pt.org.br

Formed out of the civil society struggles against the dictatorship in the early 1980s by a rainbow coalition of labour unions, urban and rural social movements, former guerrillas, Marxist intellectuals and Christians close to liberation theology, the PT demonstrates a unique adherence to both representative and participatory democracy, and has gradually risen from winning power in local and municipal goverments to now holding the federal state presidency.

Philippino Citizens Action Party – (Akbayan), www.akbayan.org

An alternative, democratic citizens' political party of labour, peasants, youth, women, gay and lesbians, professionals, overseas Filipino workers and the urban poor that has emerged out of the desire of social movement groups to be part of the formal processes of government.

South Korean Democratic Labour Party (DLP), www.kdlp.org

Founded in 1999 as a parliamentarist wing of the Korean workers movement dedicated to fighting corruption, gangland-style politics and representing the 'marginalised social groups' such as workers, peasants and the poor.

Alternative media and analysis – netactivism

Adbusters, www.adbusters.org

1243 West 7th Avenue, Vancouver, BC V6H 1B7, Canada
(t) (+1) 604 736 9401 (f) (+1) 604 737 6021

A not-for-profit, reader-supported, 85,000-circulation magazine concerned about the erosion of the physical and cultural environments by commercial forces, Adbusters is supported by a global network of diverse individuals aiming to topple existing power structures and forge a major shift in the way we live.

AlterNet.org, www.alternet.org

Online magazine dedicated to strengthening independent and alternative journalism. AlterNet provides a mix of news, opinion and investigative journalism on a range of subjects.

Indymedia, www.indymedia.org
Launched by various alternative media organisations and activists in 1999 to provide grassroots coverage of the WTO protests in Seattle, Indymedia is an incredible global network of collectively run, autonomous Independent Media Centres in 50 countries and all continents using open-publishing.

New Internationalist, www.newint.org
55 Rectory Road, Oxford OX4 1BW, UK
(t) (+44) 01865 728181 (f) (+44) 01865 793152, ni@newint.org
Long-standing cooperative-run magazine reporting issues of world poverty and inequality, and the unjust relationship between the powerful and powerless in both rich and poor nations. Debates and campaigns for the radical changes necessary within and between those nations.

OneWorld.Net, www.oneworld.net
17th Floor, 89 Albert Embankment, London SE1 7TP, UK
(t) (+44) 020 7735 2100 (f) (+44) 020 7840 0798, justice@oneworld.net
A global online media gateway with centres all over the world, OneWorld.Net brings together a network of people and over 260 groups working for human rights and sustainable development from across the globe with the aim of taking these issues to a global audience.

Z Magazine/Znet, www.zmag.org
18 Millfield Street, Woods Hole, MA 02543, USA
(t) (+1) 508 548 9063 (f) (+1) 508 457 0626, zmi@zmag.org
An independent monthly magazine guided by a radical left perspective, dedicated to resisting injustice, defending against repression and creating liberty by assisting activist efforts. Z Magazine runs the ZNet website – an incredible source of alternative information used by over a quarter of a million people a week across the world.

See also:
A-Infos – Weekly International Anarchist Information, www.ainfos.ca
The Electronic Disturbance Theatre (EDT), www.thing.net
Global Internet Liberty Campaign, www.gilc.org
Jay's Leftist & Progressive Internet Links Directory, www.neravt.com/left
Protest.Net, http://protest.net
TruthOut, www.truthout.org

ACKNOWLEDGEMENTS

There are many people in Porto Alegre, East Manchester, Marsh Farm Estate and Newcastle who I want to do a lot more than 'acknowledge'. They have shared their hopes and anxieties, their inside information, their time, their hospitality and in many cases their close friendship. I am hugely grateful. I cannot thank you all and it would be unfair – and maybe embarrassing – to pick on a few! I must thank especially those who read critically my manuscripts as I progressed and gave me vital advice. I just hope that what I have written does justice to what you have all said and done. And I promise to keep in touch and, when it would help, to keep on writing about your/our struggles to create 'another world'.

There are others who have helped by reading drafts of particular chapters, suggesting radical restructuring, providing important information and challenging inadequate arguments. If your best friends are those who tell you the truth, then mine must include: Meg Allen, David Beetham, Roy Bhaskar, my shrewd and patient agent Philippa Brewster, Jim Carey, Dave Carter, Daniel Chavez, Kath Crotty, Mary Doyle, Jane Foot, Richard Hallett, Stuart Hodkinson (who also deserves huge thanks and admiration for producing the amazing resource list, along with Hazel Healy and Leila Deen), Melanie Jarman, Davy Jones, Dot Keet (my tolerant room-mate at many an international event), Marion Kozak, Colin Leys, Jim Mackrell, Su Maddock, Martin McIvor, Judy Rebbick, Corvin Russell, Jane Shallice, Joyce and the late Richard Wainwright – both of whom I have to thank for a lot more than their assiduous and sometimes critical reading of my chapters – Nicholas Watkins and Martin Yarnit.

Three people read the manuscript all the way through and by the end had become a team racing with time to reach the finishing line. The first is Jane

Hindle, Verso's remarkably calm editor, able always to consider the book as a whole as well as pay attention to every detail. Then, working with me in Manchester, Hilary Bichovsky, who untangled many of what she called 'classic Wainwrightisms' – convoluted qualifying phrases which would send you to sleep before you reached a verb. She made it readable, as well as providing constant encouragement and wry wisdom. In the final months Helen Skelton performed similar miracles on convolutions of structure and worked at incredible speed and with extraordinary good humour. Without them I can truthfully say this book would have been absolutely impossible. And without Gavin Everall, Peter Hinton, Fiona Price and Tariq Ali at Verso it would never have been published so speedily and efficiently.

Other sources of support have helped to make this book possible. The innovative politics of the Brazilian Workers Party has been a powerful influence. It was Huw Beynon, then my boss at Manchester University, and Jose Ricardo Ramalho of the Instituto de Filosofia ê Ciencias Sociais (IFICS) who enabled me to carry out research on the development and local initiatives of this party over a period of eight years or so. With the help of the British Council and the Brazilian Conselho Nacional de Pesquisa, they organised a link between their two institutions to carry out comparative research on the labour movements in Brazil and Britain. I was one of those whose work benefited from this link. I owe them a huge debt. The decayed grandeur of the university building at No. 1 Lago Sao Francisco felt like a second academic home, especially with the help and friendship of Bila Sorj, Neide Esterci and Josinaldo de Caxias and Patricia Gouveia. As far as the PT itself is concerned, beyond the many people in Porto Alegre I must thank Ana Maria Stuart (Nani) of the International Secretariat of the PT and Marco Aurelia Garcia, then International Secretary of the PT, for always making me welcome at party events and the party offices in São Paulo and giving me all the information, contacts and translation help that I needed. Marcos Arruda of the TNI and PACS in Rio de Janerio regularly shared with me a philosophical and political compass by which to understand the transforming politics of Brazil.

The Transnational Institute (TNI), that unusual fellowship of committed researchers and writers based in the Paulus Potterstraat opposite the Van Gogh Museum, with its strategic and beautiful director, Fiona Dove, has helped to finance my travel as well as to provide constant intellectual and political sustenance. The International Centre for Labour Studies at Manchester University, and especially Anne Morrow and Gary Daniels, has been a constant source of assistance and stimulus. Carl Purcell, an ICLS graduate, provided vital research help in the first year of the book. The *Guardian*'s Society and Comment sections have helped to provide an outlet and an occasional income in the course of my travels, and I want to thank their most helpful editors, David Brindle, Seamus Milne and Becky Gardiner. Finally a huge thanks to everyone at *Red Pepper*, especially the deputy editor, Dave Castle, who shouldered with unflappable competence far too many responsibilities whenever I bunked off leaving only half-reliable e-mail addresses and mobile numbers through which to coordinate yet another issue in the relentless cycle of a monthly magazine. And board member Fiona Osler, among others, who has kept the magazine more or less on an even financial keel as well as being a regular telephonic companion. Finally, there are several dear friends who have always been willing to be rung up and visited whenever I have arrived at crises or blockages or have just been in need of a reference or an instant comment. I have to thank them enormously and to apologise for moments of obsession. I'm thinking of Joan and John Bohanna, Sue Bowen, Roy Bhaskar, Dave Carter, Derek Clarke and Sheila Rowbotham, Barbara Gunnell, Jenny Hollis, Mary Kaldor, Mike Kustow and Jane Shallice, Nyta Mann, Doreen Massey, Frances and Robin Murray, Leo Panitch and my brother and sister Martin and Tessa Wainwright.

In the course of writing this book, my all-too portable computer was subject to a burglary or attempted burglary at least five times. And I have to say that it was not the book they were after. I must thank my neighbours Jean Adamajtis and Colin Robert for helping me to cope. I also want to thank Veronica Grimshaw, Joyce Kane, Salina Madourie, Jose Antonio Dominguez (Pepe), Andy Shallice, Penny Wainwright, Gordon Walker and Rosie Yates for different kinds of practical help or hospitality.